man no be God

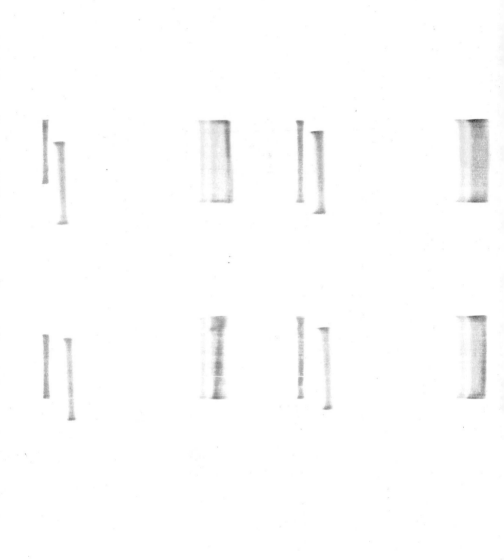

man no be God

Bushdoctor in Cameroon

Dieter Lemke MD

Writers Club Press
San Jose New York Lincoln Shanghai

man no be God
Bushdoctor in Cameroon

Writers Club Press
an imprint of iUniverse.com, Inc.

For information address:
iUniverse.com, Inc.
5220 S 16th, Ste. 200
Lincoln, NE 68512
www.iuniverse.com

ISBN: 0-595-17014-5

Printed in the United States of America

Dedication

For my grandchildren who, someday in the future, may no longer need to ask,

"Opa, why do you have to go to Africa?"

Epigraph

Wanda de fo eni ples

(West African pidgin for: "There is cause for awe and wonder everywhere")

Contents

Acknowledgements

I wish to thank the following people who helped me get this book off the ground: First, my considerable appreciation to Dr. George Dunger and his daughter Daphne (one of my fine colleagues at Banso) for ensuring my historical facts were straight. Our new friend AuKeeRa gave me insight on how Canadians might view what I wrote, and my very good friend and confidant Dr. Jonah Wefuan gave counsel on its potential impact on my Cameroonian friends, patients and colleagues. My thanks to Theo deHoog, who suggested the title and my son Robert for his incisive literary criticism. To my son Markus, who worked tirelessly as my editor—thank you. This actually became a good book!

I am grateful that I could contribute the best years of my life to a worthwhile cause whose success has exceeded my expectations in many ways. Among the most gratifying results is that the medical service of the Cameroon Baptist Convention is now operating and flourishing under highly skilled and capable Cameroonian leadership.

There were also many faithful supporters in our churches in Canada and the United States who were not satisfied with the usual 25-minute reports after years of exciting medical missionary work in Africa. They were the ones who were with me in spirit, praying while I tackled difficult first-time surgery, resting their hand on my shoulder when I was exhausted, lifting my chin when another child died an unnecessary death. Here is the more comprehensive report they have been waiting for.

Lest anyone read and find something with which they do not agree—the blame for that is squarely mine. This story is based on my experience, and I accept full responsibility for it. Names and locations in the chapter on AIDS have been changed, out of respect for the survivors.

Oh, and one more thing. I was a medical missionary. I suppose that needs to be defined, as there seems to be some confusion. I define a missionary as a person who tries to communicate the Greatest Story of God's Love expressed perfectly in Christ, in a cross-cultural setting, i.e. to a foreigner on the foreigner's own turf. The medical missionary does this by spending the majority of his time ministering to the physical needs of people. They may respond to that Christ-ordained activity by becoming followers of His, also.

In the process of communicating Christ's love by the act of healing I learned quickly that people understood me well long before we communicated in words. I began to understand the people I was sent to. I learned to appreciate some of their ways and abhor others. I found them to be human just like me, but also amazingly different, and that is what I wanted to write about. I know there are others who care about fellow human beings across cultural barriers, and wish to learn from them also. Perhaps my story will resonate with them as well.

Dieter Lemke
Edmonton, December 2000

Prologue

It was the fall of 1946. No child went to school in our area of recently conquered Germany. Nazi schoolbooks were unusable, alternatives unavailable. Even writing material was hard to find. Nevertheless, some concerned parents managed to restart the local Middle School in Twistringen, a small town near Bremen. Entrance examinations were held. My mother was certain that I would pass the competitive examinations, although I had missed most of grade four in the turmoil of war and flight from our home in East Germany. I was a refugee and survivor. I had just come through my first culture shock at age ten.

My Father was still "missing in action", so mother made the decisions for me. But I protested her plans; I did not want higher education. My life was filled with soccer and imaginative boyhood exploits. Mother sent me for the examinations. I passed in all other subjects, but received an "F" in mathematics. She was incredulous. A mistake had clearly been made! I was allowed to sit for a supplementary exam—same result. I had simply never been taught some of the material expected. Mom was tenacious. She took me to the principal's home where I had to endure her pathetic pleading on my behalf. She won, of course. I was squeezed into a class of 65 students who were already well into their studies. My very first class was an English lesson. So I was forced to learn a foreign language, an absolutely essential basis for my University entrance in Edmonton a dozen years later. A providential God and a caring mother had their own agendas.

I had never been interested in medicine nor in sick folk. Hospitals smelled bad, people died there, and those places had a depressing, prison-like atmosphere. Doctors did not usually attend my own few serious illnesses. I remember (or do I?) a severe concussion at seventeen when I did not even get a skull Xray. Another time a constrictive throat infection kept me off food and drink for days, fighting for breath and life, but I had only the ministrations of my dear mother, because there was no doctor and no medicine. Mother treated most of our illnesses. When I suffered from a painful infection of the thumbnail-bed she sent me to the pasture to collect fresh cow-dung, which she applied as a poultice to my thumb.

When all her children came down with a peculiar body rash she was certain that an application of urine would help us (we begged to, at least, be allowed to use our very own issue). No wonder we tried to conceal our injuries and fevers, with but little success. The flu induced a particularly trying form of mother's "cure". Wrapped naked in scratchy woollen blankets we had to "sweat it out" for hours.

Small wonder I was never interested in the practise of modern medicine till much later in life. But the extremes of my childhood and the faith of my family taught me to pray. My trust in God began to grow.

My impassioned interest in motorised machinery led me to believe that I should become a mechanic. The persistent blockage of this legitimate aspiration appears as divine intervention to me, in retrospect.

I graduated from middle school at age 17, with honours in mathematics, chemistry and religion. My father had returned from prison camp, and painstakingly rebuilt his business. But always having the very best in mind for his five children, he willingly sold his store, and bravely joined the post-war wave of immigrants to Canada. A second painful culture shock was apparently needed to prepare me for my future calling. I faced a hostile climate, hard physical labour and isolated incidents of hatred and abuse during the first few months in Canada. For an immigrant there were few job opportunities in Edmonton's winter of 1952. I made the most of them and worked in a foundry, laundry and maintenance. Through correspondence courses I became a power engineer.

I thoroughly enjoyed being part of a lively youth group in our German immigrant church. Youth bible studies and inspirational books by Oswald B. Smith, and Dr. Paul White's "Jungle Doctor" series opened my eyes to the need for cross-cultural missions. I was repeatedly challenged to follow God's plan for my life by godly youth leaders, pastors and visiting missionaries. Young people around me dared to follow the Christ in personal obedience to biblical truth. I finally surrendered my personal ambitions to Him when I was twenty-two with only a grade ten education, a power-plant engineer's ticket and a maintenance man's job (The job title was "Chief Engineer", but the pay was a maintenance man's).

I cannot identify a specific call to a particular mission field, apart from a deep and driving inner conviction that I needed to grasp the opportunities I saw opening before me. These were clarified even further by the exciting Youth Bible studies and my own avid reading. I became keenly aware of the boundless opportunities for service in Africa. I had reservations—most missionaries I had heard were gifted public speakers, a frightening prospect for me! But not all missionaries were speakers—some spent their lives selflessly devoted to easing pain and saving lives. Could God possibly be pointing me towards medical service? How could I know if I was even a suitable candidate? Would I be able to enter and complete the rigorous study of medicine? I became determined to explore and follow God's plan for my life, whatever the cost.

I had met missionary/anthropologist Dr. Paul Gebauer and his brother Pastor Gerhard in the fifties and sixties. Their clear vision and articulation of God's work in Cameroon and Canada had impressed and inspired me. I liked their style of leadership as we had similar cultural backgrounds. I also liked their thorough research; Gerhard's in theology and Paul's in mission/anthropology. They built solid bases for their followers. Gerhard was a great expositor of the Scriptures and established a vibrant immigrant church in Vancouver. Paul had become the first Field Secretary of the newly established Cameroon Baptist Mission in the nineteen-thirties. And now there are tens of thousands of native Christians who do not hesitate to express their culture in the young and mushrooming church and nation of Cameroon, because Dr. Gebauer and his fellow missionaries laid a solid foundation for that expression. After he had retired, Dr. Gebauer accompanied me on a clinic trip over unforgettable roads to Mbem in the seventies. It was his last visit to Cameroon. His work in leadership of the Cameroon Baptist Mission had earned him "the Order of the British Empire" personally awarded by young Queen Elizabeth II on her visit to Cameroon in 1960. It was this old man who urged me: "write that down!" whenever I told him about a recent experience. He knew what he was talking about-much earlier, before my missionary career, someone going through Dr. Gebauer's personal papers in a dusty attic found a treasure trove of circular letters which he had written monthly both to other missionaries and the organisation that sent him. His observations, and indeed orders to others serving with him, contained some marvellously pithy statements that encapsulate the missionary experience very well. "Do not criticise the work of missionaries who served before you, You will have ample opportunity to make your own mistakes". "Read your Baptist Herald—and burn it!" he admonished. The reasoning was that this monthly publication was meant for missionaries, not opportunistic Africans who could scan the pages for addresses in North America-to whom they could then send plaintive and inventive letters with bold requests for financial aid. "No missionary worth his salt will fail to rise before the sun—lest his credibility among the natives be totally destroyed", he remonstrated. This was the same man who, after being plagued with an audience of fifty people attending his weekly bath, finally emerged from the tub, paraded once around the room stark naked, and got back in the water. "I only showed them what they had come to see", he later said. "After that they left me alone". I also witnessed a lengthy church service in Canada in which he was featured as the exciting speaker. The preceding special numbers and announcements took an inordinately long time. Finally came Dr. Gebauer's opportunity to speak. Everyone sat up as he began: "You have left me five minutes of my allotted time to give my missionary report, so—five minutes of it you will get" He spoke for five minutes and sat down, leaving us very hungry for more.

Somehow I mustered my Dad's impulsive optimism (which I had dismissed as unrealistic in the past), and my Mom's brashness as I approached the University of Alberta's admissions department. A psychologist gave me a thorough going-over. I recall a three hour drilling with multiple tests which gave some very revealing and eagerly awaited answers: Yes, I could expect to complete a course in medicine, if I worked hard. My English was marginal, of course. And yes, I had some aptitude for the field; but my major interests lay in Music and Engineering. That surprised me, but I was very encouraged by the assessment.

During the interview I was also advised to stay away from driving a bus, from work in a funeral home and from any form of salesmanship, as I would do poorly in those fields. Those jobs are apparently not suitable for high-risk takers like me. I distinctly remember the lady's smile as I thanked her for confirming God's plan for my life.

I never intended to practise medicine in Canada at all. Medical school was to prepare me to serve God and the sick in Africa. Looking back, it still amazes me that this, my stated objective was accepted by the admission interviewers at the University of Alberta Medical School. (Were there two ways to qualify for graduation? I heard it rumored that certain European medical schools awarded two tiers of diplomas: 1."Pass" and 2."Fit for colonial service"). I was overjoyed when I was accepted into medical school after only two years of required premedical courses. Now I quickly found out that I was to receive a first class medical education at the University of Alberta. I was actually on my way to realising my dream. With my goal and purpose firmly in mind, the study of medicine now became quite fascinating. I listened intently whenever tropical diseases were discussed. Infectious diseases, in particular, had my full attention. During my third year of medicine, shortly after marrying Marlis Semler, we applied to the Missions Board of our denomination. North American Baptists had medical work in Cameroon and Nigeria. The Director's reply was terse and brief: "We do not have need for your services now, nor in the near future, but will keep your application on file."

This was not what I had expected. How could eight years of training not get me to a place of service? In correspondence with a doctor working in Cameroon I was advised to take up further training. I could choose any speciality while waiting for an opening in one of the mission hospitals. I decided that general surgery would be most useful, especially if I was to work alone. So I enrolled in a four-year course of postgraduate studies to follow my internship at the Royal Alexandra Hospital in Edmonton.

Those were formative and mind-stretching years, and the long wait to get to the mission field became a real test of my faith. The need to permanently assimilate huge amounts of knowledge without a chance to think through implied truth did not seem to make me wiser, just "top-heavy". My responsibilities in hospital training left little time for family and church. On-call duty, particularly, was very difficult for me. Sleep deprivation reached an all time high. My young wife was most supportive through the long months of internship.

Halfway through my surgery-residency, after 10 long years of preparation for missionary service, the call finally came. There was an urgent need for a doctor in Cameroon. Could we be ready to leave by July 1967, barely months away? For me there was no question, I was ready. My dear wife Marlis, however, had some very legitimate reservations. She had made her own commitment to serve God in Foreign Missions at age 15. Now a mature young mother of three boys aged one, three and four, she was very much in charge of a busy little household, living on a small hospital stipend in a basement suite off 95th street. During recovery from minor surgery Marlis recommitted herself to unconditional service to God, but she also prayed about two specific concerns. She was her mother's only daughter and theirs was a close-knit family. The very afternoon of Marlis' prayer her mother visited and spontaneously expressed her sacrificial willingness to release her daughter's family to four years of painful separation. But how would God solve the problem of homesickness? It was my young wife's earnest request that the Almighty would spare her this expected misery. It amazes us to this day how God honored her sell-out to Him by granting her lasting freedom from homesickness.

I deeply appreciated Marlis' decision. She gave up the hope for a comfortable life with a well-earning husband's salary. She could have reasonably expected a stable and secure lifestyle in Canada. Instead, she chose to go along to the wilds of Africa strictly on her husband's merits, something few modern women would even consider. She became a beautiful servant to scores of leprosy patients who praise her for teaching them handcrafts and a sense of self-worth. She created embroidery designs that became intricately ornate tablecloths under crippled, insensitive leprosy fingers. She became the honored mother of five men whom she taught the three R's. She grew into her varied roles as mission station hostess, wife and mother. She saved our family thousands of dollars by cutting our hair, sewing much of our clothing and looking after our physical needs. Besides home schooling our boys through grade three or four, Marlis enjoyed gardening, introducing and nurturing plants and flowers wherever she was planted. Her photographs adorned hundreds of hospital greeting cards. They also provided effective visual communication tools to enhance our reports to supporting churches when we would return for year-long furloughs in Canada.

The two youngest of our five sons were born in Cameroon. I took risks in delivering them myself. All have benefited greatly from growing up in a fascinating cross-cultural setting. The hardships they endured have made them into good men.

Our departure date approached rapidly. Our apparent ignorance and naiveté may have raised eyebrows, but we trusted God for our welfare. Even contrary counsel by some seasoned and respected elders could not dissuade us now.

Four 200 litre barrels of personal belongings were shipped by ocean vessel, according to suggested equipment lists provided by our mission headquarters. We did not really need to take camp beds, toilet paper and

Sauerkraut, but learned to appreciate the small electric generator, the meat grinder, the children's shoes and our classical record collection. None of those items were available in the remote areas of Cameroon at the time. I felt a bit guilty about taking the music, yet later found it a source of great comfort to our family. Marlis took charge of her first of many transoceanic shipping exercises. It took some mental gymnastics to anticipate the needs in clothing and shoe sizes for the next four years, and the next and the next. She has become an expert in packing.

Now that we were ready, the Forces of Darkness were also on alert. Our journey from Edmonton to Mbingo Baptist Hospital (MBH) gave us at least three reminders that we were about serious business: We stopped over in Detroit at the North American Baptist Triennial Conference for our commissioning. Our little family took the opportunity to walk the streets of the busy city. Robert rode on dad's shoulders, Markus held mom's hand, but three year old Thomas, in his usual quickness, stepped off the curb into 100km/h traffic. I was barely able to grasp his collar and haul him back from certain injury or death. God's mighty hand was protecting us.

Our Jet touched down in Cameroon's port city Douala before sunrise. The moment the cabin doors opened we were greeted by the unfamiliar sounds and smells of tropical Africa. A chorus of tree frogs and crickets filled the heavy humid air. I was gripped by an overwhelming feeling of gratitude to God. We were finally in our country of service. It had really come true. God had granted it in His mercy. We were in high spirits in spite of jet lag and input-overload.

Unfortunately, there was no one to meet us at the airport. It was at this early point that we were introduced to a philosophy that was to become a constant and familiar companion, known by all who have lived in this part of the world as "WAWA—West Africa Wins Again". We spoke little French, had no local currency, no milk for the baby and no instructions on how to proceed. A small airline that was to ferry us to our next stop had decided to suspend operations that very day. In fact, the flight we missed was the airline's last. WAWA.

The children fell asleep on the wooden benches in the airport and we waited and prayed. There was little else to do. Our prayer was answered when we were rescued 5 hours later by the Mission Field Secretary Rev. Fred Folkerts, who had been patiently waiting at Tiko airstrip, our intended final landing place. When we did not appear he was able to secure the service of a small plantation aircraft to ferry us across the swampy jungle to West Cameroon. There we had the pleasant surprise of meeting my younger brother Bernard who had begun serving in Cameroon the year before in the areas of pastoral education and building projects. He introduced us to the venerable Land Rover-our trustworthy mode of transport for the first of many memorable inland trips. Somehow our Field Secretary always ended up with the oldest and most abused of these vehicles. Perhaps that is why the rear differential suddenly locked up both rear wheels while the car sped along the narrow road to the grassland plateau. I shouted to the children to "hang on" as we spun out of control towards a steep embankment, coming to rest on its edge. God was in control all the way, as He chose to show us once more.

We made it to Mbingo on the third day after arrival. The fitting conclusion to our inland journey was a three-hour grind, in four-wheel drive, over 35 km of a muddy mountain track that now takes 35 minutes on the newly paved road.

Were we discouraged? Not at all! The adversities seemed to confirm that we were at our destination: "in the hollow of His hand".

Enemy Number One

The steady stream of outpatients had slowed to a trickle. The consulting room door flew open. A breathless woman rushed towards me with a limp infant draped over her outstretched arms. The mother's pleading eyes met mine as she released the gasping child into my arms. The tiny lips were pale, the body blazing with fever, the eyes rolling back in the lolling little head. The spleen was 4 times normal size. No words were spoken as I turned to rush to the treatment room with the mother and the *turntalk* (interpreter) close behind me. Someone ran for the lab-man for "stat" blood-work, I put the oxygen mask over the tiny face, gently propped the baby's head and back on pillows to ease its breathing and ordered the mother to sit on the nearby dental chair. I prepared to drain blood from the mother's arm into a transfusion bottle, just as the laboratory assistant arrived to collect blood samples from the baby's heel and the mother's forearm for a cross-match. I was hoping the mother's blood would be compatible.

There was no need for a local anesthetic as I proceeded with a cutdown on the child's ankle vein. The child did not react to the scalpel's sharp cut. In another minute we knew that mother and child had the same blood group, so I began transfusion as soon as we had collected 250 cc of her blood. Within half an hour the grunting baby's lips were noticeably pinker and it began to move its flaccid limbs. The cross-match was completed and proved compatible, the malaria smear was highly positive. Intravenous quinine was given in a slow drip. By the next day the child was playful and free of fever.

I don't know why this particular incident remains vivid in my mind. Perhaps it was the speedy and spectacular recovery from the very edge of

1

death? Or the risky transfusion before the blood was even fully matched? Or was it the mother's intense interest and quiet gratitude? Certainly, there were patients who survived with Hb values even lower than the 1.8 mg/dl (10% of normal), but this was a typical example of the devastation malaria is causing in Africa.

Folklore has it that Sierra Leone declared the mosquito its national bird—it kept the white man away. But how the black man suffers! In low-lying areas nearly all children have chronic anemia caused by the relentless destruction of their red blood cells by the parasite. Their distended bellies carry huge spleens and enlarged livers until they either die or else develop some degree of immunity, at least to the local strains of the parasite. Travel to an area only 50 km from home may expose them to a different strain resistant to their immune system, and they get the dreaded fevers again. As many as 50% of children under five may succumb to the repeated attacks.

It was my routine during village visits to estimate spleen size in all the children that came close enough for me to catch them, so as to get a good idea about the prevalence of malaria. And my routine question for the mothers was: "How many children have you borne, and how many are alive?" It was not unusual to have only two of five or even one of nine children survive.

Although it is more than 30 years ago, my first encounters with the deadly malaria still haunt me as if they happened last week.

An eight-year-old boy walked 2 km to the hospital with his mother. He had fever and headache, like so many others that day. He had neither neck stiffness nor serious anemia. A blood test would be an un-necessary expense. He left the outpatient department of Mbingo Baptist Hospital (MBH) with a handful of Chloroquin and Aspirin. The next day my *turntalk* shocked me with the news that the boy had died on the path back to his home.

A few days later a five-year-old arrived unconscious. He had had fever for several days. His body was hot, his extremities cold. The spleen was large, the heart was pounding. The parasites had destroyed most of his red blood cells. It was easy to make the diagnosis. He was dying from malaria. I started the quinine via intravenous drip and remained by the critically ill child. Fifteen minutes later he had a cardiac arrest and could not be revived. I was deeply shaken. I was not used to seeing patients die under my very eyes while giving them my very best care. I was learning about my biggest clinical enemy.

Malaria always ranked first or second in our annual mortality reports.

A 20 year old arrived with fever, headache, joint and abdominal pain. He had a huge tender spleen. He told me that he was the last survivor of his mother's eight children. I suspected that the family had sickle cell disease, but this young man also had malaria. We began intravenous treatment with quinine while I was making rounds on the other patients in the ward. Suddenly the young man let out a scream of pain and terror. He became restless, irrational, and finally, very still.

The grieving family granted me an autopsy, a rare permission. The man had only a thin rim of a large spleen, which had ruptured, spilling massive amounts of old and fresh blood free into his abdomen.

We were never without malaria patients at Banso Baptist Hospital (BBH). Every admitted patient was treated for malaria in addition to his or her main complaint. The treatment scheme was simple enough in the sixties and seventies. Chloroquin was usually effective, well tolerated and safe in the correct dosage. Intravenous quinine was reserved for complicated cases. The most critical aspect of malaria treatment was its prompt initiation upon mere suspicion. One could not wait for the scientific laboratory confirmation! A positive history, physical examination and suspicion were sufficient grounds to begin treatment.

Inadequate or late treatment could lead to increasing anemia and heart failure, or the two rarer complications, "cerebral malaria" and "blackwater fever". Any severe attack of malaria can suddenly render a patient irrational, and progress rapidly to frank stupor when the overwhelming mass of parasites and broken red cells clog the tiny blood vessels in the brain. This is but one way that malaria kills, but it is certainly most catastrophic and spectacular. At the beginning of the rains we always had at least one cerebral malaria case on the wards. One day I counted seven such patients in our 120-bed hospital. There are few diseases that can turn a healthy, vigorous youth into a groaning febrile irrational fighter within a few hours, and kill him in a day. I lost too many of these battles. On the other hand I was surprised how completely most of these patients could recover with prompt anti-malaria treatment after even several days of coma. It was the unpredictability of the outcome that raised everyone's anxiety level and frustrated me to no end.

I searched the meagre literature on the subject of cerebral malaria. I tried a variety of conventional and unconventional methods of treatment. The results did not change. Once the parasite load exceeded a certain concentration in the patient's blood it was invariably fatal.

"How can I save more of my cerebral malaria patients?" was my burning question when I returned to Canada after my first four-year stint in Cameroon.

I questioned colleagues and searched the literature at the University of Alberta medical library. I returned to Cameroon without answers.

Only recently did I read of an unconscious Canadian tourist returning to Toronto who survived a severe cerebral malaria attack with a high parasite load by receiving a complete exchange transfusion. That kind of treatment is simply out of the question for the developing world!

I remember being fascinated by each of the seven cases of "blackwater fever" I treated over the years. This rare and rapidly fatal complication of malaria happens when massive red blood cell destruction causes the kidneys to excrete hemoglobin. The urine assumes an eerie black color heralding impending death from anemia within hours. Six of my seven patients survived with aggressive treatment.

Blackwater fever was a common cause of death among missionaries to West Africa before the twenties and thirties when the use of quinine was pioneered. Carl Jacob Bender, one of the first North American Baptists working in Cameroon died in the year of my birth of this dreaded complication while in the prime of his life. He lies buried at the entrance to old Soppo church in the shadow of the Mt. Cameroon volcano.

In the decades since Rev. Bender's death very few missionaries have died from malaria, since better and better anti-malaria drugs became available as preventive medications. But the tide has turned again as more and more incidents of drug resistance occur around the world. Malaria prophylaxis for expatriates travelling to endemic areas today is no simple matter. I am familiar with ten different drugs that can be used alone or in combination. None is invariably effective. Most are toxic, all have side effects and may even kill the patient.

Having personally treated somewhere between fifty and a hundred thousand patients for malaria I should be thoroughly familiar with the disease and all its nuances. But I missed the diagnosis at least once, with serious personal consequences. Our five month old son Russel ran a low grade fever and voided pink-colored urine 6 weeks after returning to Canada from Cameroon and while still on malaria prophylaxis. A weekend visit to a University Emergency Department did not reveal the diagnosis. We returned home and watched our baby become more and more lethargic and pale. His blood level dropped to 30%, before my wife and I decided to treat him for malaria, without having any laboratory confirmation. He perked up within hours and recovered rapidly. My son's diagnosis was confirmed the following Monday by the pediatrician. It was then that we recalled the night in Kribi seaside rest house, where we had spent a brief family holiday on the white Atlantic beach. The resident staff had assured us that there were no mosquitoes in the rest house when we asked about a net for the baby crib. My gullibility was inexcusable as our baby received hundreds of mosquito bites during the night. We had stopped counting after we saw 90 bites on one arm alone. The infestation with falciparum malaria parasites had smouldered in his little body for two months, only to erupt seriously when we were home in Canada.

The World Health Organisation has dropped its plan to eradicate malaria in the world. It now aims for "control", and even that battle is being lost rapidly with only a few new medications under development and the parasites developing resistance to most old and new drugs. Decades of research have not yielded an effective vaccine as yet. Already, a million African children die each year from malaria, and it is far more difficult and expensive to treat malaria today than in the seventies. 1.)

When I arrived on the high grassland plateau of West Cameroon I saw malaria only among people who ventured into the valleys. But in recent years mosquitoes have reached higher and higher altitudes so that even living 2000 m above sea level no longer guarantees escape from the malaria-carrying mosquito. And since people living at these altitudes have no acquired immunity from childhood exposure, they tend to get more lethal attacks.

According to current Canadian medical literature several people die every year in North American hospitals because of a delay in malaria treatment. A Toronto woman was infected, without having left Canada or having received any injection or transfusion. (Possibly by a mosquito travelling on an aircraft?) We may need to revise our teaching and certainly need to increase our vigilance in this day of rapid international travel. In 1998 over 1.3 million Canadians travelled to the tropics.

Every few years I get excited about a new promising mode of treatment for malaria appearing in medical journals, only to be disappointed again and again. My newest hope is for gene-splicing researchers to come up with an effective vaccine soon. I eagerly wait for that day.

Crossing Cultures

One bright Sunday morning I drove the hospital Land Rover on a newly hand-dug path clinging to the mountainside into Mbesenaku village. The road was hacked out of the side of a deep gorge of volcanic terrain, dropping away 500 metres on the right. Mbesenaku was rife with dark-leafed kola nut trees, ancient and majestic. While unsophisticated, the village had an air of mystery about it—its inaccessibility seemed to preserve a timeless wisdom and way of life. I manoeuvred the Land Rover over a small trickle on the road—one, which a scarce two seasons later was to be the scene of a terrible tragedy. The local government authority requested a post mortem examination when during one of those torrential tropical downpours, the trickle grew instantly to a huge wall of water, cascading down the mountainside like an avalanche and sweeping five unsuspecting women, gingerly stepping over the quiet brook, to their death hundreds of meters below. My job was to perform autopsies—but there where no bodies, none were ever found.

As the vehicle entered the village, a swarm of boys gathered quickly to look at the belching beast. I explained the function of the vehicle's various parts to the admiring audience. When I asked if I should start the monster's engine they agreed enthusiastically, only to scatter in all directions when they got a whiff of the exhaust. "It stinks!" they proclaimed disgustedly, as they held their noses and ran. I was a little disappointed with their harsh judgement of our Land Rover, generally acknowledged as the greatest all-around technological advance into the African bush.

There were many occasions when I had the privilege of carrying patients on their very first trip in a motor vehicle, to a house with long rows of glass windows, with curiously soft beds and clean sheets where they underwent painless surgery to repair their hernias. I was also the reluctant loadmaster who determined the cargo limits for each passenger. One patient carer assured me that he would not be responsible for overloading the precious Land Rover as he would solve the weight problem by putting the extra bundle on his head while sitting in the vehicle!

On a warm evening in Koffa village I received an education in local ingenuity and commerce. The little village impressed me so much that upon my return I urged my wife to also visit this enthralling place. The main industry of Koffa village revolved around the palm tree—both for the oil and the collection of the sweet sap that was fermented to make the universally popular mimbo-for which Koffa was justifiably famous as any French vineyard in Bordeaux. One of the young men in the village took time to educate me in the intricacies of both these highly developed industries. First, though everyone in the village knew which trees belonged to which households, the villagers had never planted any of the trees. These were established by God-primarily through the use of a little bird thought responsible for spreading the seeds. This bird was scrupulously avoided while hunting-its job was much more important than gracing the family cooking pot. (All other small birds were fair game, caught using a variety of snares, some with horsehair loops, others using sticky lime on twigs.) My guide then illustrated in detail how the fruit of the palms was collected and processed. Mimbo involved the interesting challenge of collecting as much sap as possible without endangering the life of the tree. It all depended on the placement of the spigot near the crown of the tree-how deeply it was inserted and exactly where. Unfermented, this sap made a sweet and refreshing beverage—which presented a strong invitation to the swarms of forest bees.

A cleverly designed stopper fashioned from a particular species of moss was molded around the spigot, sealing off the curved neck of the calabash suspended below it to collect the sap. Every morning the adult males of the village would locate their trees in the primeval forest-how they partitioned them was a mystery to me-and climb up to a hundred trees each, collecting the liquid for fermenting—an easy process, since leaving the sap in the sun in bottles previously used for the same purpose guaranteed an alcoholic beverage within hours. Gazing up at the branch-less trees, most over eight meters high, I had to ask how that was possible. My guide showed me an ingenious climbing belt fashioned exclusively out of a single rib of the palm-frond, curved into a belt. This device was swung around the tree, locked in a second with a simple lever and providing a safe means for scampering up the trunk. I removed my shoes and was up and down the tree in no time. As I was unlocking the belt, my guide casually mentioned that everyone in Koffa knew well enough not to drink fermented mimbo before the morning climb. I appreciated the consequences. I was later to meet several patients with serious fractures of pelvis or spine resulting from falls off the palm tree.

The other lucrative source of income for the Koffa people was derived from processed palm oil that came from the same tree. Harvesting the palm kernels required another ascent to the crown of the tree, where the fifty-pound clusters of the prickly fruit were gingerly hacked off to fall to the ground below. The cluster contained hundreds of chestnut sized yellow and orange husks laden with the waxy oil, around an edible white core-that could either be eaten raw or processed into another oil-though much less desirable and more difficult to process. The kernels were washed and placed into a giant five-meter long hollowed out tree-trunk—like a giant mortar with many pestles, located in the center of the village for communal use. Smashing the husks from the kernels must have been every bit as festive an occasion as trampling grapes for wine, with the village joining in. The oil/fibrous mass was then boiled down thoroughly in massive clay pots and bottled for sale. I noted the complete absence of modern implements of technology in the processing. These remote villagers demonstrated remarkable ingenuity and self-sufficiency. Palm oil is an irreplaceable staple in the Cameroonian diet-guaranteeing the livelihood of this remote village.

As evening fell I joined a bunch of kids swimming in the local stream. Looking up we saw a jetliner flying its route ten kilometers above the Dark

Continent. I asked the children about their impressions of modern civilisation. They showed a curious mixture of admiration, naiveté and curiosity in their answers. How could a small object so high up in the sky make so much noise and carry three hundred people. *"White man is just too wondaful".* The local mud-brick school had a 100% pass rate in their graduating class of grade seven students, yet it was meaningless to ask them: "what would you like to be, when you grow up"? There would be but few choices. Decisions about their future were not left to them even if their family could somehow find the money for secondary education. Their clan would decide their entire future, from choice of marriage partner to choice of career. And they would be expected to latch on to any opportunity that would come their way, regardless of their personal likes or aptitudes. If graduation led to a job, they would be expected to contribute heavily to the education of their brothers, cousins, nephews and nieces.

These children had never seen a white child, a TV or movie, a submarine or aircraft, except the one flying overhead at the moment. Most of them had never even seen a car or a bicycle. Yet they would eagerly embrace the scraps of modern conveniences: the battery operated radio, the aluminum pots, the tins and bottles and plastic containers that found their way into the bush, and especially the chance to get an education and venture out into the exciting modern world.

As we ambled back to our sleeping hut we came upon an ancient stone circle. The site of animal sacrifices? Fertility rites? It had fallen into disuse. The paths were overgrown, the upright basalt columns covered with moss. We talked into the night about the beliefs and fears, the hopes and disappointments of crossing cultures.

However deep in the "bush" people may live, to them it is the centre of the universe, and they could just be right.

Each of the eight villages that I visited on this exploratory trek had something to teach me that contrasted sharply with my own world. Was my own world-view really superior?

Kwaja was one of three villages that used to practise the difficult skill of iron-ore smelting and the manufacture of implements. Who knows how many centuries this art had been practised before the arrival of "civilisation"? Only one of the three hamlets still produces excellently smithed iron tools, but the smelting process has long been made obsolete by the more easily accessible, better quality steel from vehicles that are left to rust by the roadsides of modern Cameroon. But I will remember Kwaja, since this is the origin of the "marriage shovel" that adorned my private little home museum. My friend Enoch had paid forty of them as the dowry for his stately bride only 40 years ago. I found the shield-shaped half-meter long rusty iron by the roadside, of no practical use or value today.

People of ancient cultures and their ways intrigue me. I must know what is behind a cultural expression. How else can I understand my patient?

The fact that the DNA of a Tibetan and a Fulani may be more similar to each other than that of any two Dutch neighbours speaks volumes to me as a member of the human race.

We are created equal, yet profoundly unique, we share more commonality than appears on the surface and yet, each individual is of great value to God. We are "fearfully and wonderfully made", as King David proclaimed. And we ought to learn from each other and from our Maker.

My continuing study of, and involvement with, the "crown of creation" leads me to seek and worship the Creator. By failing to acknowledge God and refusing his gifts we diminish ourselves and live without the vertical dimension.

The Africans I met have a deep appreciation for the spiritual aspects of life. Their culture revolves around the spirit world and their need to interact with it daily.

The missionary is a cultural change agent. His mere presence, like that of the explorer and the tourist, the Peace Corps Volunteer and even the anthropologist, encourages change. Not to mention the fact that the change-agent himself undergoes change.

But the missionary is accused of wilfully setting out to change a culture. As if it was all that easy to change "unsophisticated" natives! I will make no apology for trying to teach people a better way of life and health. No culture can be shielded from all outside influence. And who determines what is harmful?

The vaunted ideal of the "Noble Savage" is a myth. It soon became painfully evident to me, contrary to what some anthropological study would indicate, that the overwhelming motivation among "primitive" people is fear. Fear that is countered by elaborate rituals codes and taboos. With death and disease so prominent and capricious, it is necessary to appease the spirits, to do things in the right way and so gain a measure of peace, even joviality in the face of the overwhelming and unknown dangers.

For several years I was puzzled by the behaviour of certain people around me. Driving a Land Rover through the primeval mountain forest on terrible roads took skill and concentration. Often I would chance upon a toothless, pipe-smoking old mother returning from a hard day's labour on her farm. Without warning, the meekly plodding senior would jump, as though galvanised by some sudden internal burst of electricity, directly in front of the Landrover and dart to the other side of the road, scaring and enraging me at the same time. This happened repeatedly, each time the pedestrian escaping death in the nick of time.

This whole scene made no sense, till someone kindly enlightened me: The more narrowly I missed killing the suddenly spry septuagenarian, the more surely I would hit the spirit who followed and haunted her. No wonder the mirth and cackle that came from the toothless tiller who had outwitted the spirit.

When I returned to Cameroon in 1994 after an eight-year absence, I was greeted enthusiastically by my former co-workers. In typical fashion, I was not only welcomed elaborately but was also given some important instructions: "doctor, do not tell our patients that they will die". A negative prognosis from a prominent authority is interpreted as a curse—almost as if I sentenced my incurable patients to death. Apparently I had left the lingering impression that I had immense powers, both for good as well as evil! In this setting scrupulous candor was a misplaced virtue.

I was also warned early never to shake a finger in someone's face, nor to even point a finger at someone. It could too easily be misinterpreted as a curse. The power of a curse has undeniable consequences.

Once I asked a hundred senior high-school students: "How many of you believe that you would get seriously sick if someone cursed you". Practically all raised their hands.

The changing of the seasons in Cameroon is accompanied by violent winds and mighty thunderstorms that echo magnificently along the valleys of the high grasslands. When lightning flashes far and near at the rate of more than once a second, it is little wonder that several people get struck every year, and that there are strong beliefs attached to this phenomenon. The human psyche strives for explanation, reason and logic. We abhor random "acts of god". Many would seek protection and insurance and others will make a business of forecasts.

Practically every Cameroonian I met believes that certain native practitioners can *send tunder* (invoke lightning to strike an enemy). The doubt is not about the ability, but whether the person requesting the awesome power to be released does so with a proper attitude: i.e. a pure motive and total lack of personal guilt. For if there is even a shadow of unjust intent the lightning cannot be prevented from turning around and striking the one who invoked it.

Two men hovered in a small hut near Banso market, waiting for a heavy storm to pass. Lightning struck and both fell to the ground, paralysed from the waist down. They were carried to men's ward where I met them moments later. They smelled singed, but were obviously relieved to have so narrowly escaped death.

I could see no burn marks on their skin, but sadly they showed me the money from their pockets. The larger paper nominations, which had been wrapped around the thick 100-franc coins, were shredded to bits while the coins showed "spot welding" marks left by the high voltage current. Not only had their enemy tried to kill them, but he had also taken most of their money!

One man regained feeling and strength in his legs by evening time, while the other was able to wobble home the next day. He worked as a cook for one of our missionaries, and did not waste any time to ask for a leave to his home village to consult the *ngambe man*, an expert in the art of spider divination. This authority in village social dynamics was consulted frequently in all manner of disputes for which he employed a pet tarantula that lived in a cavity near his home. Bits of bone, twigs and stones would be arranged under half a calabash together with morsels of food for the wise (hungry?) hairy spider. The *ngambe man* would give his decision according to the rearranged objects under the gourd (and his intimate knowledge of who held a grudge against whom?).

A couple of weeks later the cook returned with the news that the sender of the lightning had been located and had admitted to the deed. A palaver had ensued, reconciliation had occurred and a feast had sealed the matter.

Another lightning strike had a more tragic ending: A 6-year-old boy had been struck and killed while walking on the open road. The *ngambe man* had pointed to the grandfather as the person responsible for the death. The entire family of this rather well to do old man had packed up and left him in his compound surrounded by his sheep and coffee plants. He became increasingly depressed and lonely as the weeks wore on and everyone shunned him. One evening, as he was boiling his 3 Irish potatoes he was overwhelmed by his utter hopelessness. The police and I came on the scene the next day. The fire under the pot had quenched, the water evaporated, the potatoes were charred and cold. The door was ajar, a half-length of native hemp rope lay across the doorjamb of his hut, pointing to the nearest young avocado tree. And there he had ended his misery.

*   *   *

The traditional week in the grasslands of Cameroon has 8 days. The market day is considered the highlight of the week. People will wear their best, take their produce to market and do a whole lot of greeting and socialising. The sale of produce is not the most important aspect of marketing; the complex game of bargaining, and the opportunity to exchange news is. Once I recognised the significance of the African market, I could get into the festive spirit of it a lot better. Rather than despairing over the heavy workload at the hospital on market days, we all tried hard to finish the work so we could catch at least the tail end of the market scene. I could usually find an excuse to be where the action was. There were bargains to be had. I picked a perfectly serviceable pair of "Birkenstocks" out of a pile of European cast-off shoes. One could hardly go wrong for 8 dollars! With great delight I spotted the first mangoes of the season, "*number one's*" (so-called because of their complete lack of stringy pulp and sweet butter-smooth texture). I purchased six for the outrageous price of 50 cents. Since I lacked my wife's marketing skills I had obviously paid too much, but the *buy-um sell-um* (middleman) threw in a small *wata pruf* (plastic bag) so I could transport my treasure home on the motorbike. Some good quality wild Oku honey (if one ignored the dead bees, wax and debris that came with it) was available in either small glass jars or 20 litre kerosene tins, at a bargain price of 32 dollars. It was a tempting offer that I opted to decline for that day.

I always liked to check over the native doctor's medicines, the blacksmith's wares, and the drug peddler's booths. Today I could buy at least five brands of Acetaminophen, as well as Chloroquin in inadequate doses and Tetracycline, Ampicillin and Chloramphenicol antibiotics in amounts too small to do any good and very apt to lead to drug resistance. Ruefully, I remembered my past requests to local Government authorities to put a stop to this illegal business. It had been futile. I only hoped that these "antibiotics" were "made in Nigeria", the capsules could then in fact be harmless as they might just be filled with useless Cassava flour. Not many customers trusted the market medicine dealers.

A drug was only as good as the person giving it. That was driven home to me one busy morning as I hurried through my outpatient consultations. A young mother presented her infant with scabies. The diagnosis was obvious. I wrote the shorthand prescription to be filled at the hospital dispensary and handed it to the mother. She did not get up. "Is there a problem?" I asked. "You have not touched my child" the mother replied haughtily. She judged my touch to be absolutely essential to the healing process. I was embarrassed and resolved to always "get in touch" with my patients.

While my wife drove a hard bargain over the latest African cotton prints I could meet my soccer friends at the butcher's slate and check out some prices at the motorcycle parts store. Sauntering along in the hustle I was constantly interrupted by smiling people greeting me or offering me their goods. Good-natured bantering and practical jokes would enliven the scene. Market day was great!

Nevertheless, there were still many ways in which we Westerners repeatedly ran afoul of local customs. Chancing upon a serious medication error by a nurse I was apt to ask loud questions in an irritated voice and in the presence of other personnel. This was totally unacceptable in West African culture. To raise one's voice in anger seemed to be as crass a sin as adultery. But to call someone a fool or to merely label an action "foolish" was the worst insult of all, and practically unforgivable.

For several years I would cause a stir when blowing my nose in public. It finally dawned on me that this might be a cultural affront when people in church kept looking at me over their shoulders to see who the perpetrator was. In Africa the snot is not kept lovingly in a cloth and returned to one's pocket!

Swearing and the use of "strong language" were simply unknown. Our operating room staff was stunned and deeply embarrassed when a visiting physician indulged in a blast of profanity over a minor matter.

A quick opening of tight lips and a single rapid, short indrawing of air between the teeth indicates scathing disgust.

No one ever shouts across an open area to get a friend's attention, as this is uncouth.

Lately a curious hissing sound (a sharp "ksssss") emitted between tongue and teeth is used to get someone's attention, and it is amazingly effective.

To make someone lose face without giving reasonable chance for rebuttal is a common cross-cultural no-no. It is very difficult for a Cameroonian to say the words: "I am sorry, I made a mistake". (It ain't easy for most of us, either.) But people do have a way of admitting a mistake that is foreign to Westerners: they will give such a transparently silly excuse that will immediately be recognised as an oblique admission of guilt.

Our cook accidentally dropped the charcoal iron and it broke on the concrete floor. His response to my wife's question was "the wind blew it off the ironing board".

Strongly held Western cultural beliefs and practices, ranging from exercise for its own sake, or vegetarianism, all the way to New Age philosophy and radical feminism were periodically brought to Banso by their proponents, and undoubtedly appeared even more strange to the local inhabitant than the habits of the missionary of 100 years ago. Why would you foolishly refuse any food set before you? And if you are lucky to get a bit of meat once a week, why not enjoy it? And why would a dignified doctor want to put on shorts (the attire of a servant) and run to no-where and back? Everyone else knows exactly where he or she is going. Why didn't he figure out where he was going before he started running, like any normal person would?

What do you mean—"the earth is my mother?" and "the animals are our brothers?" You can't be serious!

But the strangest new puzzle for the Cameroonian male must surely be the fight for Women's Rights. I was witness to a graduation address by a prominent Cameroon politician who reiterated in her speech the feminist rhetoric of a recent Women's World Congress. It was a humiliating scene as the mixed audience disdainfully drowned out the speaker by producing a continuing buzz of small talk, an unusually impolite gesture I had never before experienced in Africa.

Many a western female medical student was unaware of the stir she caused among the virile young males that swarmed about her. Western body language and dress needed tactful advice from resident missionaries. Slacks and shorts were typical dress for Cameroonian prostitutes, at least until Western TV and videos hit the country. The increasingly popular hugging now prevalent in North America is distinctly foreign to traditional native culture, certainly between male/female unmarried youth. Young girls in Kom would avoid eye contact and cover their mouths while speaking to adult males. Not to do so would mean a strong "come on" in the social order.

The Kumbo Black Stars football club was largely made up of non-Nso people. There were two or three Nigerian traders as well as several professionals and civil servants from other tribes posted to local government offices. I was formally invited to join this team as soon as I arrived at Banso. Players half my age soon tackled me as hard as one of their own, but polite reserve and respect prevented them from telling me the truth about my "odd body odor". It took them years to work up the courage. Physicians generally learn to adapt to offensive human odors without losing a keen diagnostic curiosity about them. But I had to tell my friends that they smelled strange to me too!

Another thing I learned playing soccer: Cameroonians love to win a football match, but to win an argument presents an even greater challenge. The referee is the most important person on the field and not even a little pick-up game is possible without the man with the whistle. When a controversial decision is handed down the teams become wildly gesticulating verbal combatants. It would never come to blows, nor would the decibels rise significantly. The skill to be sharpened was confined to verbal acrobatics.

I soon learned that it was better to go home after five minutes of it, for the game would never start up again. The sun would go down with the arguments still going strong, and I would feel cheated out of a great game of soccer by the cultural demonstration. But that was just the way it was, and there was always another day for football!

Many of these games were interrupted by emergencies at the hospital 800 meters away. I did more than one C-section in my soccer cleats. Some patients may even have died because I was playing soccer. But I needed a physical outlet for my strain, and my wife jested that it was better to kick the ball than to take it out on her.

"I didn't see you at the football game" I said to my tailor friend Sulemanu when I met him in his market stall. *Wok done distop* (my work interfered) was his pithy answer. Even routine, ordinary day to day work has a "disturbing" quality to it. It prevents me from carrying out more important things like social interaction with friends.

There is no word for "please" in the local languages. "You should give me" is the closest approximation to this Western nicety. The "thank you's" however, are plentiful and sincere. It is difficult to out-give a native of the grasslands.

One of my plastic surgery triumphs, a 10 year old boy, whose cleft lip I had just repaired, returned 3 weeks later with his father. He clutched a giant rooster in his arms and gave me a huge smile. I was taken aback by the fresh blood in his mouth and the missing front tooth. "Oh that's nothing", he had fallen onto some rocks on the steep stony path to the hospital this morning, and knocked out the tooth, that was all. But here was his offering of gratitude for making him look normal.

It was impossible for me to decline the offering of his feathered gift. A poor African had out-given me again.

Hospitality is written large in the culture. One does not wait for an invitation to visit. It will never come. One simply announces one's coming: "I have come to visit you".

To have a stranger as a guest of the compound is considered a high honor. Many times I was put to shame when poor people would quickly slaughter their very last fowl and invariably prepare a meal when I honored them with an unannounced visit to their humble hut. It would take a while to prepare the meal, of course. And I could hear the family catch the chicken, imagine its slaughter, *hear de scent* of its burning feathers, wait for the gutting, hear the snapping sounds as its long bones were broken for a better taste of the marrow, smell the pungent palm-oil soup and finally be served the delicious meal.

I would first be offered a dishpan with cold water to wash my right hand, which was to be my only cutlery. A towel might be offered, but rarely any soap because "it would spoil the taste of the food". Grapefruit-sized balls of fufu, the customary firm corn-meal mush, would be placed on a banana leaf, dishpan-cover or tin plate, the hostess would dish out the salted palm-oil soup and her choice of meat for the guest. The "big man" at any meal would be expected to partake of the *particulars* i.e. the gizzard (often this included heart, liver and assorted minor organs). I would be eating with anyone in my company or, sometimes, the head of the house, in silence. The family would eat later and be happy with the leftovers.

A choice of soft drinks, beer or "*shweet mimbo*" (unfermented palm-sap) may be offered with the meal in richer homes, a glass of water (of doubtful purity) in others. Banana or fresh pineapple might be offered as dessert, but "who wants to spoil the delicious belching of fufu", an obliga-tory sign of gratitude expected of the visitor?

Customs have changed a bit. A few invitations to supper have trickled in, a few meals have been enjoyed in the presence of a host couple or even a whole family, and conversation may ensue. But it is certainly not traditional.

In my job as medical missionary I saw myself thrust into several roles I did not enjoy. I was expected to act as administrator and disciplinarian, employer and treasurer. But there were other roles I grew into with per-sonal rewards—bedside teacher and chief of hospital maintenance, enthu-siastic clinic team leader and village soccer player. I adopted a lot of Cameroon culture and in turn gave back a bit of my own. I could not help but model the Christian work ethic in its compassion and integrity. My western time consciousness and knack for improvising seemed to rub off on some of my African co-workers. My wife and I enjoyed enthusiastic affirmation of the Christian love marriage we modelled and taught. Friends who have observed me in both Canada and Cameroon assure me that I am a different person in Africa. It flatters me that my body language and mannerism blends in with the natives, though I regret that I will never fully understand them.

Adaptability is a prime requisite for missionaries. Adjustments to people, situations and adversity were not confined to the first few weeks after our arrival but would have to become habitual.

We had to adjust to our co-workers. It seems a miracle to this day how we were able to work closely with a large variety of people in stressful situations and not only get the job done, but always continue to remain on speaking terms. I do not take the credit, but praise God's grace for this gift. It was helpful that mission policy provided separate, if simple, living quarters for their missionaries.

I adjusted to the new workload by largely ignoring what I disliked and speeding up the things that were already going well. The change from medical school and postgraduate training to this kind of frantic practise was one momentous surprise to me.

On arriving at "New Hope Settlement", home to 350 leprosy patients, and the 70 bed Mbingo Baptist Hospital I was told that there would be a turnover of eleven days from the departing doctor.

New languages, money, culture, disease pattern, co-workers, treatment schemes and techniques needed to be learned. The learning curve was so steep that I do not even recall this my third episode of culture shock. God had provided two such major episodes in my past and I, in turn, had consciously prepared for this new challenge for 10 long years. So now was the time to face up to it.

The first shock to my western-trained mind was the need to make difficult diagnoses simply on the basis of physical signs and the few plausible symptoms I could coax out of my patients. Worse, to then go ahead and treat patients without scientific confirmation of such empirical diagnoses made me cringe. It struck me as a highly unscientific and inferior way to practise the High Art of Medicine. Only gradually did I find out that all the doctors in the Third World were forced to work in that way, and it really was acceptable under the circumstances.

Not long after arriving at Mbingo I had an experience that should have warned me about the things I would be up against in the next few years.

A young teacher presented in the evening with abdominal pain. I did not yet know that teachers were particularly innovative in regaling me with elaborate pathological presentations. He convinced me after a thorough examination that we were dealing with acute appendicitis. I did not yet know that this diagnosis was extremely uncommon in Cameroon. I confidently decided to operate. After all, I had done this surgery a few times in my training.

The theatre staff was called, I carried the Land Rover battery to the generator house to produce light for the operating theatre, but the temperamental generator would not start. I had never really learned its peculiarities in the short turnover. Well, we would operate by the light of a Coleman kerosene pressure lamp, which would give us a fair bit of heat in addition to the desired light. Unfortunately we also needed to use open drop ether for the anesthetic. Ether is highly volatile and flammable, but not very explosive unless mixed with oxygen, which we did not have. Geraldine Glasenapp (Gigi), the missionary nurse who administered the ether could not stand the sight of blood, so she hid behind the patient's head screen and inhaled a fair bit of ether herself.

We were ready to begin. Scrubbed, gowned and gloved we proceeded with the surgery. I found the appendix at about the same time as the theatre came alive with large numbers of lovesick termites fluttering all over the operating room. They entered in ever increasing numbers through the generous cracks around the door, intent on reaching the brilliant light over the O.R. table. Singed by the hot lamp they began to fall onto our sterile field. Someone suggested a mosquito net. It was rigged with difficulty and I was able to continue after removing one or two of the winged ants from the wound. The hissing lamp had to be included under the net, of course, where it warmed our hot heads. We were bathed in perspiration by the time the surgery was done. The patient recovered quickly, but his appendix was entirely normal. That did not stop my patient from the belief that I had cured him.

I learned a lot of things that evening, but not how to eat live termites. My kids tell me, "You have to bite them before they bite you!"

Gigi who gave the anesthetic that evening made a most significant contribution to my own evolving life-plan. In her usual confrontational style she asked one day; "Just what are we doing here and what are we trying to accomplish?" I did not realise that she was not really talking to anyone in particular, but I couldn't wait to get home and write out a plan of action with the over-arching goal of "Working ourselves out of a job". That was to be my guiding long-term objective. It helped to get this in focus early in my career.

After a year at Mbingo we were transferred to the 120 bed Banso Baptist Hospital (BBH) four hours away. Here I faced new challenges with the additional work of a large maternity ward, the supervision of a maintenance department, the 85-student Nursing/midwifery School and its dormitory building project. Most weekends were scheduled for visits to outlying clinics. The first of these clinics was included in the three-week turnover from Rev. Dr. Peter Fehr, the lone doctor working in this busy 120-bed hospital. He also acted as "field missionary" for fifty-some churches that had sprung up in the area as a result of eighteen years of medical missionary activity. I would, of course, be expected to take over that aspect of the work to the best of my ability.

The Land Rover was packed and ready at 6:30, a half-hour after sunrise. The trip was both exhilarating and hair-raising. Through primeval mountain forest the steep and winding road had turned into a slick and rocky obstacle course. It hugged the steep mountainsides, crossed raging streams and finally descended into a narrow valley.

Jickijem clinic had only been opened a year earlier. But it was very well attended. I could hardly believe what I saw! It seemed there were at least 400 people awaiting our arrival. My colleague gave me the option of either consulting the 180 patients or else pulling decayed teeth. I opted for the latter. My dental skills were far from slick and had only recently been acquired through trial and error. The patients lined up confidently, taking their turn to sit on a wooden stool on the elevated veranda of the maternity building and, one by one, submitting to my local anesthetic injections.

There were a total of seventeen candidates, several of them with more than one badly decayed tooth. While the anesthetic began to take effect I realised that my extraction technique was about to be scrutinised by an audience of about 200 mothers with babies waiting for DPT inoculations. I became an integral part of a dramatic and bloody tableau, as with every extraction, each candidate solemnly and accurately spat great gobs of blood, scattering the onlookers, who dutifully regrouped to sympathetically observe the next extraction. Not all my anesthetics were successful on first try but I did improve my technique this day, simply by virtue of repetition.

I learned that the people of the Oku tribe have teeth with very long roots! Retrieving a broken root takes great skill and a good assortment of instruments. My patients showed wonderful patience with me that day.

Medical school had been a constant overwhelming barrage of information with little "doing" of any apparent value to the patient. Now my medical practise was all: doing, serving, and giving at a mind numbing pace without a chance to 'fill up at the pump'.

I knew in theory that 'people work only as hard as they want to', but I often felt obliged to cut my personal needs to the minimum.

I gave up shaving every other day to save a few minutes. I rarely spent more than ten minutes at the noon meal. There seemed to be little time for reading medical journals, studying up for surgeries I had never done or seen before, preparing for weekly bible study and administrative meetings, or even personal devotions. This kind of work pressure sometimes continued for months. Even after BBH became a two-doctor hospital; if a colleague became ill, needed time off to recuperate or went on a journey for a day or a week, the workload was shifted onto the person left behind.

In 1979-80 I was the only doctor/administrator in the 160-bed Banso Baptist Hospital for a period of 8 months. That year was most stressful and challenging. Uninterrupted on-call duty with weekend clinics to visit, meetings to attend, an average of 3 major and 4 minor surgeries per day, and the usual teaching load, all brought me close to total exhaustion. Brief spells of relief from visiting doctors helped only a bit.

I had delegated accounting and payroll duty rather quickly after my arrival at BBH. I felt unqualified to carry the key to the hospital safe. Hospital maintenance was more to my liking.

When it came to the hospital budget preparation, I realised that there would be few questions as long as there was money left over at the end of the year. I could even carry out a small building project or buy a badly needed vehicle or generator as long as there was no deficit. So I made sure our income exceeded our expenses.

My brief reports to government, home church and mission authorities became briefer. Since procrastination always made things worse for me, I did unpleasant bookwork and drug orders promptly. Meetings were not my forte, so I tried to avoid them as much as possible. Fortunately there were others who could tolerate them better, making up for my deficiencies.

To the credit of our mission administrators, I never had occasion to question their sincerity, and there were adequate avenues for complaints. I did not agree with all decisions that were made, but I gained great respect for all of my fellow missionaries, even those with irritating little quirks in their personalities, as they so lovingly tolerated mine.

Once I travelled to Douala with a briefcase bulging with shopping money. I was purchasing hospital and building supplies. Banking was cumbersome, checks not accepted. The French shop-owners would not take anything but cash. While browsing through a store I was bumped by another customer and minutes later I found that an expert pickpocket had relieved me of the shopping money.

The loss was equal to several months of my salary. My fellow missionaries took up a collection that made up for two thirds of the loss. I was overwhelmed, especially since they were as poor as I, and I could not even thank them personally, as the gifts were made anonymously. What an honor for me to work alongside people like these.

It seemed as if I was always in a hurry. That did not particularly worry me, as it suited my personal style, but one can cut corners only so far before bumping into them. There had certainly been enough warnings in my pre-medical days in the form of accidents and mishaps to remind me of that painful fact, but when it came to dealing with patients, I needed to slow myself down just enough to think procedures through, remember the pitfalls, and follow landmarks. Interruptions were almost welcomed as new challenges to be overcome, sort of quick fixes towards another record to be set.

Obviously that mindset could lead to disaster on occasion.

Tamfu Joseph, the nurse, called from men's ward. A pastor had just brought his seven-year-old daughter because she had suffered a fracture of her right elbow. The frightened child was in pain, but trusting. She let me examine her deformed limb with but a whimper. This needed correction under general anesthesia. I checked the pulse at the wrist, as this type of fracture could have injured the main artery to the forearm. The pulse was strong. I told Joe to heat water and prepare the cast material while I gently picked up the child and placed her on the rickety operating table in the outpatient department. The father reassured the child and remained standing by her side. Restraints were not needed. This would be a very brief anesthetic, it would take but a minute to reduce the fracture, check the alignment and pulse, and apply the cast while the child would be coming out of the anesthetic. (I was working without X-rays, of course). I reached for the open drop ether mask and the two glass bottles with the powerful anesthetics. We used a chloroform/ether mixture for quick induction and would switch to pure ether as soon as the child was asleep. The child struggled only briefly, as the father convinced her to take deep breaths of the irritating vapour. My mind flashed back to my son Thomas' fracture of the forearm that I had to treat similarly just weeks prior to this event. Unpleasant fears had to be suppressed on that occasion. I had to anesthetise my own child since there was no colleague to take over the task. Thankfully, all went well that day.

Not this time! It seemed not even a minute went by and the little child was deeply asleep. So deep, in fact, that I became alarmed. She had stopped breathing! Was there a heartbeat? Joe listened. "No heartbeat doctor". I grabbed for the stethoscope from the nurse's neck. He was right. No heartbeat! I felt my face flush. I looked at the father, who watched silently, trustingly. "You better go outside and pray". He obeyed. "Joe, do mouth-to-mouth". I started gentle, rhythmic cardiac massage on the small pliable chest. Joe's breaths inflated the lungs with reassuring regularity. I kept up the compressions. What had gone wrong? The girl had very little fat, so the ether would saturate her minimal fat stores quickly before getting to her brain in rich quantity. But it was only a minute! And what about the pre-medication? A quick dose of atropine would have protected the heart against dangerous reflexes when assaulted with the noxious fumes that irritated her trachea. We did pray before the procedure, didn't we? "Stop. Is there a pulse…No,….keep going." Joe continued his measured breaths into the small mouth and nose. Again I listened with the stethoscope. There it was: a definite, still irregular thump… thump inside that chest. "Thank you Lord". I stopped compressing the chest. The pulse at the wrist appeared. The chest began to heave with occasional gasps. Joe kept up his breathing. The lips became pink. We called the father back into the room. Calmly he reported that he had prayed. We did not explain much. *God e de!* (God is in control)

The cast formed a rapidly hardening support for the properly corrected and aligned elbow. Another check of the pulse at the wrist. It was strong. A sling was applied. Joe carried the sleeping child to the ward for recovery.

This had been close. I would never, ever again neglect to give atropine, no matter how brief the ether anesthesia required! A little girl almost paid with her life for my calculated risk taking.

Every anesthesia is risky, of course, and ether has long been outlawed in Canada because of the many dangers associated with its use, (chloroform has not been used for decades because of its proven liver toxicity). We needed to find better alternatives in future.

The night calls presented another challenge. Rare was the night without interrupted sleep. Most of the problems could be handled over the phone, once I installed three ancient hand-crank phones donated by a friend from a Chicago church. But there were the complicated deliveries and the serious surgical and medical emergencies I could not manage without leaving the warm bed, getting dressed by the light of the flashlight, walking down the 80-some steps to the hospital and dealing with the life-threatening problem. One to three hours later I could possibly try to get some more sleep. Unless the 6 o'clock sunrise was near, in which case I usually continued with inpatient visits, a quick breakfast, staff devotions, more rounds, surgery, outpatients and emergencies.

I think the ideal doctor should be able to fall asleep anytime, anywhere, if possible even in advance. I plainly couldn't, often lying wide-eyed after a difficult procedure, unable to calm down from the excitement, reliving the drama of a life-saving procedure instead of catching up on rejuvenating sleep.

West African culture places a high value on mimicry and imitation. Learning is primarily done by meticulous copy of the master's work, whether that be in oration or the carving of a mask. The master carver will teach his *"learner boy dem"* to copy his own creations to the "t" until they get it right. Originality is largely discouraged.

In the Third World as elsewhere "knowledge is power" and can be sold at a high price.

Apprentices pay the master who teaches them. The rather mundane task of repairing flat tires is taught to an "apprentice" over the span of two years or more, before the new craftsman can set up his own roadside business. His equipment will consist of a small box of patching and vulcanising material, a number of cut-up old tires and tubes and, most importantly, an "engine" i.e. an ancient gasoline plant of indeterminate origin with a belt-driven compressor of some sort. Old automotive air-conditioner pumps will usually do the trick.

Once I got used to the West African way of learning and teaching I was determined to enter the fray. With the vast knowledge I had acquired over 23 years of schooling and life-in-general it was obvious to me that I was teaching all the time, whether I liked it or not. But I found that I rather liked it. It also fit my goal of working myself out of a job.

I made teaching in the school for nurses and midwives a priority for myself. It was refreshing to teach students who were eager to learn and the 100% pass rate of several classes delighted me. People with foresight and wisdom had established the School of Nursing and Midwifery at BBH. It has grown into an establishment that now trains health personnel in eight different categories, from dental assistants to ward-aids. From the very beginning we strove for close co-operation and sought approval from Government licensing authorities in training staff for all the Protestant Health Facilities in the English speaking Provinces of Cameroon. My own contribution to formal health education was not entirely motivated by selflessness.

Many times I would be called after clinic hours to see a patient whom the nurse thought critically ill. A number of these patients were in acute psychosis, a diagnosis the nurse could simply not make because of lack of training. Psychiatry was not on the Government proscribed teaching syllabus.

When a new government decree postponed examinations and graduation of one of our best groups of students by 6 months, it almost resulted in a revolt among the affected students. We were barely able to calm the waters by assuring the nursing students that they would be the best-trained class we had ever taught. I volunteered to teach Psychiatry and was pleasantly surprised that the students not only showed great interest in the subject, but the entire class performed well in their examinations. Very soon thereafter my night calls for psychiatric emergencies decreased markedly.

*　　　　　*　　　　　*

When Yaounde medical school opened in the early seventies I wondered if our hospitals would be considered for rotating internships of their final year students. On my next trip to the Capital I sought out Dr. Anomah Ngu the Vice-Chancellor of the University. I found him at his home. He was a well-known anglophone surgeon respected for his cancer research well beyond the West Coast of Africa. I received a warm welcome and the assurance that he was planning exactly what I had come to propose to him. Our agreement led to many years of fruitful co-operation with the bilingual Yaounde University Medical School. It also raised the distinct possibility that some of these young doctors would one day be employed in our hospitals. I saw a pattern evolve in my mind that pointed straight towards the goal I had set during that first year at Mbingo: to work myself out of a job.

The medical students eventually arrived. But they brought with them a long list of skills they were to acquire during their four-month internship at BBH, from spinal taps to Caesarean sections, from hospital administration to public health projects. I undertook this task with enthusiasm and optimism. Other physicians followed in the same spirit. Several of these students graduated with distinction. Many outstanding students remember their tough training time at BBH with fondness. Some began to work in our hospitals as valued colleagues.

Another highly rewarding interaction occurred with short-term student interns and residents from western universities who applied to our hospitals for 2 to 3 month electives. Medical schools in Canada, the U.S., Germany, Switzerland and even Australia somehow obtained our address and eagerly continue sending us their students to this day.

Who would have dreamed that we would be teaching medical students from Harvard, Heidelberg, Tulane and Edmonton, and among them, atheists, agnostics, Mormons, Jews as well as Christians-in our Christian "bush-hospitals" one day. Many of these students continue to correspond with us and several have set their course into cross-cultural and Third World medical practise.

My wife and I also adapted and taught courses in Personal Development, Christian Marriage, Child Rearing, Christian Living and AIDS Prevention. My all-time favourite lecture, however, was: "How to use the telephones", because it saved me valuable minutes of sleep, and ultimately my marriage, as I no longer needed to yell into the receiver: "turn the phone around!" "No", "The hand-piece"," the handle", "*dat ting fo yu hand, torn um*".

I had to make adjustments away from work as well. Our food was a mixture of African and Western meals. Once I was properly hungry the local meals began to taste better and better. Though certain staples reminded me of papier-mache and other unmentionable substances, I was grateful to my mother for having taught me to eat what was set before me. Having gone through months of real hunger in 1945 helped as well.

The climate at BBH was moderate at 1800-m elevation. The seasons became a little unpleasant for only a few weeks with very heavy rains in July/August and extreme drought in January/February. The nights always cooled off to 12-17 degrees Centigrade which helped us to obtain refreshing sleep.

Housing was adequate with concrete floors, covered verandas and zinc roofs. No lullaby can compete with soft rain on a tin roof. Kerosene refrigeration (when it worked) facilitated a single market-shopping day per week. Running water from gravity fed springs was adequate for ten months of the year. I took the children to the spring catchments in the overgrown hollow above the hospital for the monthly measurement of our water supply. It became a ritual only occasionally interrupted by an attack of "*drivers*" (army ants). These wicked little soldiers of the forest floor had an uncanny ability to attack anyone resting near their warpath with lightning speed and well co-ordinated effort. How they could crawl up to my belt-line without my becoming aware of them, how they found all of us at the same time and how they knew to all begin biting simultaneously, was a real mystery. But bite they did. We literally had to "unscrew" their fangs out of our skin. We would lose all inhibitions, rip off our clothing and dance about. To help the screaming children first or attend to my own multifocal points of need was tough to decide.

African experts told us how these aggressive little beasts could strip a horse to its bones by going first for the eyes of the unsuspecting animal. We suffered an attack on our rabbit hutch one evening, when the caged animals attracted our attention with an unholy ruckus. Several animals could not be saved.

So we always gave driver ants a wide berth whenever they invaded our home from time to time. It was best to leave the place to them for a few hours till they cleared out all vermin on their way through. At least our cockroach plague would be solved for a while.

Year-round gardening was a special pleasure for us Canadians. With a little effort and liberal application of manure we harvested a large bowl of strawberries daily. Other missionary tended roses, raised poultry and rabbits, built small biogas collectors and operated ham radio stations as hobbies.

Our children grew up in this setting and naturally adopted its culture to a much greater degree than we. They experienced considerable culture shock when re-entering Canadian society.

Bernard's grade three teacher complained about his stubborn refusal to answer questions in class. We could not believe our ears, as our little Bernie was a most compliant and obedient child.

Then we understood. He answered "Yes" like an African, by quietly raising his eyebrows. A modulated grunt meant "No".

The teacher began to adapt.

The boys had to learn that it was O K to drink water from the tap in Canada, and not O K to void by the side of the road in public view.

Robert, age four, was unable to hide his amazement about "another two-storey house", and the elevators and escalators were a new-found toy on his re-entry into "civilisation". Three year old Russel exuberantly announced: "Airstrip!" when he first saw real paved highways in Nigeria, but we had to hush him quickly when he spotted the national flag and loudly announced: "windsock!"

Our salary was sufficient for the necessities of family life, food, clothing and the children's boarding school fees. It was not quite sufficient for operating a personal car in the manner of the North American norm.

I suspect that the major budget item for most missionaries was help for the many who came begging at their doors. Compared with the general population, our affluence was striking: some of us even had small pieces of rugs on the concrete floors of our homes, which our visitors studiously avoided to step on. But somehow it did not seem right to me, to be the envy of those we came to serve.

We were pleasantly surprised in 1986, after a six year absence from Cameroon, that now we found a small but significant middle class of professionals, craftsmen, traders and farmers. Missionaries were no longer alone in the middle class.

That said, it should be stated that one could not become a missionary without having sound financial management skills. Nor could one embark on a missionary career while still paying off student-loans.

Ninety percent of western missionary aspirants fail to make it to the field for lack of financial support. Our parents' and family's blessing and support were a great source of joy for us during our long years of absence from them. Their letters, parcels, prayers and gifts are all recorded in heaven, I am convinced.

Ever since my early childhood people at work have fascinated me, whether they were skilled craftsmen or ingenious improvisers. There is ample opportunity in Cameroon for watching carvers and brassworkers, tailors and cobblers, welders and upholsterers, because they all work out in the open. People will also try a wide variety of temporary or custom designed solutions for tough problems: A wheel falls off the taxi? Borrow a nut from each of the other three wheels and carry on. Leaking petrol-tank? *Gom-um widde shoup* (fix it with soap). Lacking sophisticated electronic measuring devices? Try a bulb and a wire and some ingenious testing procedure. Battery not holding the charge? Try replacing the acid and slow-charge it. Broken mainspring on the Land Rover? Use a few lengths of the ubiquitous 2-cm wide tire-tube straps and wrap them around the entire bundle of leaf springs. It has to be tight, but it'll get you home.

Peugeot 404 station wagons were the 'cat's meow' before the Corollas arrived in the eighties. A good imported second-hand 404 would fetch top dollar among the taxi operators. It had to be modified, of course, because it would be expected to carry more than double its suggested maximum weight. The standard front brake pads had to go. They would hardly last a month, so they were replaced with discs carved out of Mercedes truck brake shoes glued together for extra thickness. Seat-springs were reinforced with wooden planks directly under the thin upholstery. A three-quarter inch pipe was welded into the center of the passenger compartment to hold up the roof, as it had to support a large roof rack for all the bundles, goats and chickens of the 9 to 12 passengers. Rear springs were replaced with Land Rover issues. Several thick rubber blocks (carved from truck tires) were inserted between the front coil springs for extra clearance of the deeply rutted roads.

It was against the law to carry more than one person in the front seat beside the driver, unless one could find a uniformed person needing a ride in the general direction of one's destination. And with a Gendarme, policeman or soldier sitting in front, the driver now found himself above the law, i.e. halfway out the window. There could now be as many as five people sharing the front seat.

Strolling through the market I chanced upon a 16-year old barefoot youth sitting on a low stool surrounded by a number of broken cast aluminum pots. I know how difficult it is to weld aluminum. This boy's only regular equipment was an oxygen tank and welding torch. The acetylene tank was homemade and periodically charged by quickly throwing a piece of carbide into it and locking the ingenious opening. The boy's welding skill held me spellbound. He had no safety equipment whatsoever, not even goggles to protect his eyes. But he was an expert aluminum welder.

Medical Practise too can cover a wide spectrum of sophistication. I have dispensed medicine out of a single box while on a weeklong exploratory trek in a remote area of the Northwest Province. I have also established a well-functioning ophthalmology/eye surgery department with very limited resources in staff, money and equipment. I was continuously on the lookout to improve our service at BBH. The watchwords were always: is it cost-effective? Can the poorest people afford it? Should we be the ones to provide this service? And last, but not least: is there reasonable hope that a new service will not be dependent on the innovator alone? Too often a brilliant idea blooms only as long as the facilitator sticks around. The disappointment of a discontinued service is bitter medicine for the people left behind. *De ting done spoil* (it fell apart) is heard all too frequently in West Africa. It can refer to an abused bicycle or a new political movement. Things just keep spoiling.

The commonest reasons for failures in the provision of specific continuing medical services are 1.Mechanical breakdown of sophisticated equipment that no one knows how to repair, and 2.Unreliable supply of essentials. Lack of money is rarely the root cause of trouble, nor is lack of personnel the most pressing need in our hospitals any longer. Of course, it is always "impossible to replace" a Mother Theresa or a Dr. Helen Marie Schmidt or even a Davido (our invaluable hospital maintenance man). What is noteworthy in this regard is Christ's only specific prayer directive to his followers: "Pray therefore the Lord of the harvest to send workers into the field which is white, ready for harvest"…, a prayer I do not recall hearing in church very often, nowadays.

I do not wish to take all the credit for the many workable solutions that were found for the vexing problems that confronted us, but they need to be documented. This is where I could make a significant contribution to

BBH. Not all the problems were of equal urgency or significance, of course. And most solutions were simple adaptations of other's ingenious ideas, some just trials of something we had heard about.

People without exposure to even the simplest machines, nuts and bolts early in life often have no idea about their correct use. We had an inordinate number of ruined water faucets on the hospital compound from over-tightening, as people simply didn't have an idea on how tight was tight enough. In dry season this led to a significant water shortage. Solution: we trimmed off most of the brass handles, so that it became mechanically impossible to over-tighten the taps with the human hand. No more ruined water-taps, fewer leaky faucets.

Our children's ward was a clean and neat area during the daytime. Sick children rested outside on the grass, on benches or sleeping mats surrounded by family and visitors. Nurses called patients and carers into the ward to give medication and injections. The feeding, bathing and socialising happened out in the sunlight. At night, however, it was almost impossible to get to the nurses' desk or attend to a seriously ill child. By the light of dimmed kerosene lanterns I had to step over and around sleeping carers who had settled on their 5-mm thin woven grass mats on the concrete floor beside and under the children's beds. Most of the sick children slept on the floor with their mothers. Nearly every bed was empty! It was easy to see the problem. Imported children's beds were ignoring readily observable social and cultural norms. It took a few months to replace the pediatric beds with locally made adult beds and mattresses, so that mother and child could sleep together in familiar comfort and security. I was able to reach the nurses' desk without stepping on any toes.

We charged for medical care according to the seriousness of illnesses treated. Regardless of our costs, Aspirin treated minor illnesses and was therefore sold inexpensively. An operation treated a serious or potentially lethal condition and would cost the patient considerably more. Those who could not pay would often abscond without paying their bills. A variety of measures were tried to reduce the number of non-paying patients. We had significant success with the following measures: as soon as a patient indi-cated difficulties with payment of a hospital bill, a simple job would be offered to one of his relatives. This took considerable time and ingenuity of the "headman" and administrative staff, but proved particularly useful during times of construction. Extra manual labor was always welcome because machinery was largely non-existent. The felling and splitting of rapidly growing eucalyptus trees for firewood was an ever-present need. Grass cutting, roadwork, gardening and preparation of bandages and applicators were other chores available. Alternately, relatives or friends on the hospital payroll were allowed to co-sign for debts. And finally, African staff was put in charge of bill collection. They obviously knew how to recognise truly destitute patients. Absconding became rarer. Missionaries had one less worry.

With only a single generator and insufficient funds hospital electricity supply was restricted to four hours after sundown. We designed a new operating room with large windows and experimented with a skylight. This gave adequate illumination for daytime surgeries. As an alternative we used an automotive battery and a 12 to 110 Volt inverter, which gave adequate light via a 150-Watt bulb in an old-fashioned OR lamp equipped with six satellite mirrors. For eye surgery a smaller operating room lamp could be fed off the battery for several hours.

A patient had been hit in the eye and had suffered a blow-out fracture of the orbital floor, trapping his inferior rectus muscle, so that the eye could not look up. I had once seen an ophthalmologist insert a Teflon plate below the eye to close such a bony defect. I had no Teflon, but from organic chemistry lessons I remembered the structure of polyethylene as being highly inert. So I asked my wife for a new lid of her Tupperware containers and fashioned a suitable piece of it for the orbital floor of my patient. He had a good result.

Many of our ectopic pregnancy patients came so late, that more blood seemed to be free in their abdominal cavity than in their circulatory sys-tem. It was logical to put it back where it came from. With scoops and kidney-basins, simple gauze filters and the ordinary blood administration/filter sets we could auto-transfuse many a patient back to health in minutes, long before this method became revived with modern "cell-savers" in North-American hospitals. Only once did I hear of a problem. If the blood remained in the abdomen too long and became partially hemolysed, it could lead to renal shutdown. I was consulted on such a case when there had been no urine output for two days. With judicious intravenous fluid maintenance and prayer the young patient fortunately decided to resume her kidney function in about a week. She had a complete recovery.

In the maternity we would often see jaundice of the new-born which, in the vast majority of cases, is treated simply by exposure to ultraviolet light. Ordinary 2-foot fluorescent tubes mounted close to the baby's exposed skin, while protecting the eyes, worked very well. This was appropriate technology: inexpensive, available, replaceable, teachable, and unsophisticated—unlike the following problem in obstetrics: Someone sent us 4 fetal monitors which sat in storage for a long time while I pondered their use. There was little of the special recording paper that would be required by the meter, should we ever want to use the machines. Several other vital parts were missing, as happens so often with donated equipment from overseas. I was relieved when a visiting volunteer, an obstetrician giving valuable refresher courses to our midwives, declared the fetal monitors to be "inappropriate technology" for our institutions.

Several significant advances evolved in the treatment of dehydration at BBH. When I arrived in Cameroon the relatively minor skill of intravenous (IV) fluid administration was still restricted to the four missionary nurses and the doctor. The average annual IV consumption was a scarce 100-200 litres for the 120-bed hospital. The mainstay of postoperative fluid therapy was "rectal feeds". I scoured medical texts to find that this was indeed an effective, if somewhat unconventional, way of maintaining hydration in conscious and co-operative patients who could not eat or drink. Salt and glucose could also be absorbed in this way. As we modernised, more and more African staff was trained to start intravenous lines.

I even tried filtered rainwater in early efforts to make our own IV solutions when our supplies ran out. Our present Central Pharmacy staff with its modern 50 litre/hr distillation unit and on-site IV manufacture will react with horror to these revelations, but they can't argue that it didn't save lives!

Children and babies were largely dependent on oral re-hydration, a slow and precarious business until the World Health Organisation provided excellent guidelines for feeding mild to moderately dehydrated children. Various techniques were tried and perfected, such as slow naso-gastric drips, while the mother continued breast-feeding. We also tried intra-peritoneal and bone marrow infusions for tiny infants with collapsed veins. For the seriously dehydrated children we reserved the cut-downs that our skilled African staff could do in a matter of two or three minutes. There has been remarkable progress from relatively common deaths due to diarrheas, dysentries and dehydration to their virtual elimination.

From the excellent quarterly British journal "Tropical Doctor" I gleaned many a suggestion not found in standard medical textbooks.

When a new-born or very young infant is accidentally dropped on a hard floor, it may result in a depressed "ping-pong fracture" of the skull. (This, of course, never happened in our hospital!) I used to elevate these fractures surgically by open reduction, until I learned to use the small metal cup of the vacuum extractor from maternity applied directly to the scalp. It gave a characteristic "pop" sound, which could usually be clearly heard even over the cries of the infant. This resulted in a highly satisfying instantaneous and lasting success in the few cases I tried to treat in this way. Consulting my neuro-surgery-resident friends years later, this method of treating ping-pong fractures did not raise any objections.

It was inevitable that BBH would receive its share of patients with serious head injuries. One hazy day in dry season Cameroonian President Ahmadou Ahidjo came to visit Banso. Elaborate preparations had taken several days. Innocent looking rocks by the wayside were painted with whitewash to give the town a festive atmosphere. Trees could hide murderous assassins, so the evergreens were trimmed liberally, often leaving only the very topmost branches.

The large military helicopter landed on a soccer field one km from BBH. There was much excitement and commotion. My wife was asked to lend cutlery and dishes for the president's luncheon to which we were both invited. As we left the crowded football field a Land Rover filled with youths was heading down the road just in front of our vehicle when a 13-year-old boy suddenly fell off the vehicle, and onto the road headfirst. He was immediately gathered up unconscious and taken to our hospital. The father gave permission for the drilling of pressure-reducing burr holes when I suspected a blood clot between skull and brain. I found two of the needed drills, rusty and dusty, in our garage. Engine oil and vigorous cleaning produced a workable tool. It was sterilised while we prepared the seriously injured boy for surgery. The ingenious one-inch conical core-drill functions much like a carpenter's tool that is used to install door-locks, and is eminently safe for the novice surgeon. I removed two plugs of bone from the boy's skull, relieved the pressure, evacuated some clot with great care and a bit of anxiety and returned the patient to his bed. But by now it was too late to meet President Ahidjo at the luncheon, though I confess that I had a greater feeling of satisfaction from being in surgery than I would have had being present at such a politically correct event.

It took a week or two before the patient was able to take food, but he did not fully wake up for six weeks. He made giant strides after that and was left with but a slight limp, a weak right hand and a crooked smile. His father was effusive in his praise of God and BBH. Being himself an edu-cated man he assured me in a future meeting that his boy would certainly follow the high calling of medical service to mankind.

Fortunately I only had to use this procedure a few times as I am defi-nitely out of my area of expertise when it comes to working inside some-one's head. Our survival rate of patients with burr holes was about 50%, among them one of the chief's sons. He was one of two motorcyclists involved in a head-on collision as they were preoccupied with dodging a thousand potholes on the road to the market. There were no helmet laws at the time. The Prince sustained significant brain injury but was able to learn and practise tailoring after his recovery.

Since there was no seat belt law either, we saw the terrible head and facial injuries in Cameroon that we used to see in North American emergency departments in the early sixties.

A motor vehicle accident had caused a "facial smash" of the leForte type 3 variety. My expertise in plastic surgery is limited. It seemed to me that I needed a "sky hook". So I fashioned a skull cap out of plaster, incorporated a stiff coat hanger with hooks in front of the face and connected the stainless steel K wire from the cheekbones to the hooks with rubber bands. The jaws were wired together for 3 weeks. The patient did well and looked normal to me after the swelling subsided. I did, however, have the advantage of not having known him before the accident.

Our hospital was in need of simple reliable suction machines for many of our surgical post-operative patients. Some ancient hand-pumped vacuum tanks were in use on the wards before the days of 24-hour electricity. But for the OR these were too inefficient and too labor intensive. International Planned Parenthood Association (IPPA) is an organisation dedicated to reducing the number of unwanted babies in the world. They offered us help in the area of birth control by supplying free intrauterine devices (IUDs), birth control pills and even a powerful suction machine for therapeutic abortions. I availed myself freely of their offer, informing them about the laws of the country at the time. Under Cameroon law public birth control information was prohibited whereas information and supplies could be given in private doctor-patient consultation. The law presented a dilemma in our teaching of nurses and midwives while Ahidjo was president. Abortion was and remains illegal and punishable by law. The powerful IPPA suction machine has been performing excellently reliable work for general surgery in our operating room for many years. I did not mislead the donors, yet the suction/abortion machine has never been used for its intended purpose.

A grateful patient who had been treated in a small central Alberta town wanted to donate a significant modern piece of equipment to the institution where she had received such excellent care. The patient decided to donate a brand new blood-gas analyser, even though the hospital already had a ten-year old unit. The used machine became available for donation to a worthy cause. A friendly sales manager took me for an hour's ride to the country hospital and we viewed the machine. I was on the lookout, as usual, for ways to improve our hospital service and diagnostic capabilities, especially since going back and forth annually as a Volunteer. The rapidly available test results of arterial blood gas analysis that I had used extensively in emergency medical practise had impressed me as being a major advance in the care of critically ill patients. We certainly had enough of those at BBH! And now this machine was free for the asking.

The machine was lovely. It was not too bulky. It could be carried on the aircraft and could accompany me on my next trip. It was functioning well and showed no sign of ageing. Its market value was certainly in the thousands of dollars. The transport would probably cost me fewer than one thousand. However...daily manometer readings had to be obtained from the local weather office. (Was there one in Cameroon?) Four or more reagents had to be replenished regularly and stored within painfully precise parameters. Standardisation procedures took an hour a day (more for novices). Every single test required a special disposable heparinised syringe. They would not be cheap, and how could we ensure a regular supply?

I had to decline the wonderful offer, painful as it was, but I could not involve myself in more experiments with "inappropriate technology". It would have been nice. Once in a while I still dream about that machine and the fabulous help it was to me in so many tough situations in the emergency department in Canada.

Then I remembered the pulse oximeter, an electronic gadget with non-invasive readings of arterial oxygen tension taken from a finger or toe with a soft clamp (batteries included). It does about half of what the gas analyser can do and it does it instantly and painlessly. The pulse oximeter is of great help in monitoring patients under general anaesthesia and it helps to sort out the real sick kiddies with asthma, croup and pneumonia. We secured two for each hospital. If only we could have one or two more of them, it would truly advance our diagnostic capabilities.

I never did find out who paid for the pulse oximeters. But God knows, and He will reward the donors. This does not absolve us from writing "Thank you letters" whenever possible and I wrote many of them in my years of acting as medical officer in charge.

Very early in my years in Africa I saw the need for oxygen for many critically ill patients. I found suitable reducer valves in the hospital stores and modified the North American connectors to fit the local threads. Oxygen bottles could be ordered from the fellow who supplied the welders in town.

The very first day I had assembled the apparatus the need for it arose rather acutely: A British subject of East Indian heritage was visiting our station from her teaching position 35-km upland. She was a tall young lass in her twenties. She had collapsed in a bathroom from where she was rescued by tiny nurse Daphne Dunger who climbed through a narrow window to rescue her in the nick of time. I arrived on the run and saw the telltale cherry red lips of carbon monoxide poisoning in the deeply unconscious teacher. A poorly vented water heater had been the cause. We needed oxygen badly! I sprinted to the workshop where Davido and I had just rigged up the 80-kg oxygen bottle. I managed to load it onto my shoulder and lug it to the rest house at the other end of the compound, where I arrived in need of oxygen myself. Even with high flow oxygen the lady drifted in and out of consciousness for more than an hour. But her recovery was complete. God's timing was perfect once again.

Many patients have since been saved with welder's oxygen, but with rising prices new sources of oxygen have had to be found.

Someone shipped us surplus oxygen concentrators from North America that can deliver up to 5 litres/minute of 90% oxygen. This is a perfect invention for the Third World: simple in concept and design, easily maintained, effective for the majority of needs, low in initial and ongoing costs. A small electric motor drives a compressor and uses 2 nitrogen-absorbing canisters alternately. We installed two of the units in our "Pediatric ICU". Someone raised the legitimate question how we knew whether these machines were actually producing oxygen. When the first anesthesiologist-volunteer arrived at BBH, I posed the question to her and the ingenious experiment she conducted left us gaping for its simplicity.

Knowing that oxygen is heavier than air, she filled one of two large glass bottles with the product of the oxygen concentrator. She then placed candles in each of the 2 bottles and covered them simultaneously. Measuring the time it took for the candles to extinguish she could easily calculate the percentage of oxygen produced.

Our hospital was very fortunate indeed to be able to supply linens, mattresses, pillows and gowns for our patients. In many government hospitals the patient's relatives had to bring these things, or do without them. The supply of our linens has been the wonderful contribution of hundreds of ladies in mission societies of North American churches. Our problem was, how to keep these linens clean, a task of significant difficulty, when we had many patients who had never even seen a western bed, mattress or pillow. Some had walked barefoot all their lives. Some needed detailed instructions on the use of toilets and showers. And a few vain older folk used black shoe polish to keep their youthful hairdo appropriately coloured.

The hospital laundry was run with surplus domestic Maytag washers driven by gasoline engines. The laundry water was heated in old 200-liter steel drums perched over a wood fire. I saw a neat design for a hot water heater at Mbingo Baptist Hospital and designed our own 8-cubic meter model that was still working with minor maintenance twenty years later. It was fully automatic, with a float valve keeping the water level topped up. The entire tank was elevated to produce sufficient water pressure for the laundry machines. The tank was enclosed in burned brick and covered with an insulated weatherproof cover. Burned brick was also used to build a firebox under the tank and a chimney with an adjustable flue damper.

Several galvanised water pipes were suspended in the roof of the firebox that set up an automatic convection current through the tank. The nightwatch maintained a wood fire for only 8 to 10 hours of a 24-hour day. Even when industrial washers replaced the small domestic machines and electricity finally reached us in 1979 the heater continued to provide adequate amounts of hot water for the needs of the hospital laundry.

Male circumcision was practised at birth in our area. (Clitoridectomy is still widely practised elsewhere in Africa, but I was fortunate to never have seen any of its unfortunate victims.) I was not convinced of the need for male circumcisions either, but when I witnessed two deaths and several severely anemic babies because of the native doctor's work, I became an enthusiastic proponent of the procedure in our hospitals and maternity centres. It was a simple case of "If you can't beat them, join them". Others before me had devised a quick and simple method using ordinary surgical instruments and cautery with a heated 5-inch carpenter's nail. My own "refinement" of the procedure was to increase the speed to less than 2 minutes per baby and to teach it to nursing assistants.

All through medical school and post graduate training I was alert to simple effective cures for the common afflictions of man: operations I would be able to utilise, instruments I might need, procedures with which I needed to become familiar.

Sometimes I was met with strange stares when I expressed the desire to learn something outside of my narrowly defined field of general surgery. Only after much pleading was I allowed to perform a single C-section before leaving for Africa where I had to do several hundred. Other physicians however, particularly in anaesthesiology and urology went out of their way to discuss potential future problems with me and show me ways I might try to overcome them. I gathered bits and pieces of surplus equipment and assembled the first intubation anaesthesia apparatus to be used at MBH and BBH. I could not fathom doing thyroidectomies only centimeters away from an open drop ether mask without intubating the patient. Later we purchased a simple "EMO" air-over-ether anesthesia machine that did not require a source of pressurised Oxygen or air. Someone in England specifically designed the EMO for use in the Third World. But the induction with ether alone was too slow for my liking, so I modified the machine by attaching a surplus Penthrane dispenser in which I used a few millilitres of the very expensive Halothane for faster induction.

It took a great adjustment for me to realise that I needed to be my own anaesthetist while doing surgery. This was only partially resolved by depending heavily on expatriate teaching nurses who had largely learned anesthetic and monitoring skills on the job and by teaching a few African nurses the basics of anaesthesia. The ultimate responsibility for the patient during surgery was still the surgeon's, not the anaesthetist's, as it is in North America.

Still later we began using the veterinary anesthetic Ketamine. This drug is approved for humans in Canada and the US but not in parts of Europe. Even in North America it is not in wide use because of some of its peculiar characteristics. Ketamine causes increased muscle tone and a rise in blood pressure, intra-ocular and intra-cranial pressures as well as some movement of the anesthetised patient that can be disconcerting to the uninitiated surgeon. The main argument against its use in North America is the occasional episode of hallucinations of the awakening patient, (which is easily managed with sedatives). On the other hand Ketamine has many desirable attributes. It preserves the swallowing reflex, has very low toxicity and overdosing is never a problem. We have had an incredible safety record with the use of Ketamine and have learned to live with its shortcomings, primarily because of its relative safety and low cost. Many an anesthetic cost less than a dollar.

We also made extensive use of the spinal anesthetic. I estimate that I have done over six thousand spinal punctures. This is not nearly as remarkable as the fact that the neighbouring hospital had an African nurse trained in Italy who did hundreds of epidural anesthetics which are superior to spinals but much more difficult technically. They also cost much more.

One of my most appreciated teachers was a urologist who practised at the Royal Alexandra Hospital in Edmonton. He went out of his way to discuss some of the problems I would encounter in Africa and even coached me through an older and simpler operation than the modern trans-urethral resection of the prostate. Dr. Fred Marshall (and a few like him) did not seem to mind teaching me without any benefit to himself. Eventually, however, I largely abandoned this operation as the blood loss could be considerable and I did not like the potential mortality rate. In my search for a non-surgical solution for the prostate problems of old men I heard a novel idea in Kenya from another medical missionary. A sclerosing solution containing tannic acid and formaldehyde could repeatedly be injected directly into the prostate in very small doses. It was to scar and shrink the obstructing organ until voiding would become easy again. I tried this method with some success but abandoned it when we finally enjoyed the volunteer services of a small series of urologists who began teaching more modern approaches to the age-old problem of old age men.

Change and upgrades are a constant—maybe more so in a mission hospital, where even the smallest of innovation made such a big difference. When I left, plenty of challenges remained—and any innovative technician, physician or teacher who likes a knotty problem would thrive in finding ingenious solutions to problems which the hospital encounters daily. For example....the BBH pediatric intensive care unit(ICU) was basically a "hole in the wall" where children were isolated from the large public ward. Its equipment consisted of three hard wooden treatment platforms ("beds"?), welder's oxygen, suction apparatus, an old incubator, an "Ambu" respiratory resuscitation bag, IVs and medications. There was close proximity to the nursing desk and its excellent nursing staff, but we had to rely heavily on the relatives for constant observation of the critically ill children. The ICU also served as the only Xray storage and view box room for the children's ward. All this happened in a space of 2 by 3 meters.

The standard joke was, when the patient awakens from his unconscious state enough to be able to say, "I see you" (ICU), he or she is ready for transfer to the general ward.

All manner of specialists in areas such as anaesthesia, intensive care, computer and instrument technology, public health and many others who have a gift for improvisation could make a significant contribution in the battle to improve care and reduce costs. (Age is no barrier, as I remember a 68 year old Volunteer who repaired and devised more hospital apparatus than anyone before or since). The BBH pediatric ICU would be a great place to start the next visionary innovator on the road to deeply satisfying service to those loveable sick little children at BBH.

*   *   *

The medical care of my fellow missionaries was probably my most miserable personal hang-up. I developed an elaborate system of excuses to the point of rudeness in order to escape having to do annual physical examinations and other consultations of missionaries. My favourite excuse was, "I was called to serve Africans, they are my first priority".

In hindsight I realise that my unreasonable stance needed an attitude adjustment. My problem reached its pinnacle one particularly busy day when a fellow missionary consulted me for an ingrown toenail, while a hundred African patients waited outside my consulting room. "Take a Chloroquin tablet, 250 mg, and chew it slowly", was my facetious advice. "And that will cure it?" asked the astonished Reverend. (Chloroquin is exceedingly bitter). What's worse, he seemed to take me seriously.

I did not fully appreciate that my care could save valuable mission dollars and safeguard our greatest resource on the field—dedicated people. This was driven home to me particularly painfully with the illness of my valued friend and co-worker, Dr. Les Chaffee. Les and Edna Chaffee were the first medical missionary couple to serve Cameroon Baptist Mission at the opening of the fledgling BBH in 1949. After twelve years of pioneer service they had returned to the US when their children needed tertiary education. Nine years later the Chaffees returned for a further term of service as Les approached retirement age. I enjoyed eight months of working next to a saint. His prayers, his humility, his insights, his joy linger in my memory. Finally I had someone nearby who could give me much needed advice and wise counsel. It seemed that Les had seen it all and done it all with far less resources than I now had at my disposal. To me he was the epitome of the pioneer, (the secret dream of most of us missionaries).

Having a second male on station was great. Les sang a wonderful bass and we formed a well-blended mixed quartet with two nursing school tutors.

I automatically think of Les whenever someone quotes the verse of James' letter to the early church: "The prayer of a righteous man is powerful and effective". (James 5.V 16.)

His prayers definitely had a powerful effect on us.

Our two oldest sons, age ten and nine, were facing their first term at the boarding school in Nigeria. We thought it advisable to travel to the school and hostel as a family to introduce Markus and Thomas to their new environment and so try to ease the pain of separation we all dreaded. We planned to travel overland to the closest airstrip in Nigeria, book a flight on a twin engine Piper aircraft operated by the Christian Reformed Church's flying service and make this trip into a great family event.

Our VW jeep was packed and ready for the difficult journey to Warwar Hospital in Nigeria, the first stop on the two-day journey to the boarding school in Jos. Two young short-term missionaries and I had taken that eventful trip on motorbikes the year before. We had been asked to reassemble a small Diesel generator that had been disassembled and head-loaded across the Cameroon-Nigerian border from Mbem to Warwar, our two established mission stations on each side of the border. Incredibly steep mountain ranges and deep ravines had to be traversed on that trip. Several small rivers needed to be crossed, and they became formidable obstacles when heavy rains could swell them to raging torrents of muddy water. All manner of transport over this picturesque terrain had been attempted before our time, from horseback to Dodge "Powerwagon". But the surest way was still on foot, which my brother once managed in 12 hours by utilizing the many narrow footpath "*cut-shorts*" across the never ending hills and valleys. I developed a standard word-game with my guides and uninitiated travelers whenever we trekked in unfamiliar territory. "How far to the next village" I would ask. The guide's "One small water to cross" I would translate into "Three big rivers" for my fellow travelers, and "one small hill" usually meant "at least two big mountains". For the most accurate assessment I adopted a particularly shrewd method of getting the information I so desperately wanted. "When you stand on top of that mountain just ahead of us, can you see our destination from there?" Pressing the guide in this manner, I would usually be able to deduce whether we would still be trekking before darkness fell.

Native carriers were still employed in our era for the usual 28kg head-loads, with negotiable prices for overweight loads. The 50-kg flywheel of the generator had been the most difficult head-load. Its carrier slipped and fell only once during the arduous all-day trek.

There was only one thing missing for our elaborately planned 700km journey to Jos. We had sent our passports by special runner to the Nigerian Embassy in Cameroon, 500 km in the opposite direction, for the necessary visas.

The fellow was now three days late and we were getting antsy. The plane had been booked for Monday morning. The missionaries in Warwar were expecting us Sunday night, at the latest. The runner had plenty of time to get back from Buea by the middle of the week, but Wednesday, Thursday and Friday went by without a sign of our runner. Daily we packed and unpacked the vehicle. On Saturday our prayers took on an urgent tone.

Still no sign of the runner with the documents. Sunday morning the mammy-wagons (ancient Mercedes trucks converted for passenger service forming the backbone of the Cameroon transport system of the sixties) rolled into town for market day, but none of them brought our anxiously awaited runner with the passports. It was now a question of hours. Our motorcycle trip had taken twelve hours from Banso to Warwar, (flat tires and waist high river-fordings included). We were now deeply disappointed to see our elaborate plans collapsing. Taxis stopped coming. We needed help! Comfort! Advice!

"Let's go see Les", said my wife. Dr. Chaffee would know what to do. Up we trudged to his house with our four boys. There we spread our anxiety and dismay before our wise missionary friend. He suggested that we pray together. Well, what did he think we had been doing all these last few days and hours? "We will just pray specifically, that the messenger will arrive in time". We agreed, silenced and close to tears. Les offered a short, earnest prayer on our behalf. We turned to walk back to our home when someone spotted the messenger running up the steps to the missionary homes. We were simply floored, overcome with emotion and relief, grateful to God and deeply stirred about His divine approval for our mission. The runner's taxi had been held up in a mud-hole in the middle of the coastal jungle (Never mind that it was dry season!) where he and others had spent the night sleeping under the trees.

Our own journey could finally begin. It did not take even ten minutes to repack the "Kuebelwagen" and leave BBH in a cloud of dust. In an hour we descended into hot Mbaw plain and the family agreed to drive with the convertible top folded down. The four boys stood on the rear seat and held onto the roll bar I had welded into the vehicle. They had a great view on the entire journey. We even tried driving with the windshield folded down, but that's when mother objected. The hot wind threatened to dislodge her contact lenses. In another hour we began the arduous climb out of the plain onto the Mambilla plateau. Shallow rocky streambeds had to be navigated cautiously, steep tight curves strained the low first gear, boulders and elephant grass narrowed the path. Inch by inch the jeep climbed over innumerable rocks and washed out gullies.

A long-limbed red patas monkey scampered into the trees. Brilliant red and green foliage luxuriated in moist hollows.

Customs and immigration posts delayed us only briefly and we had a memorable shady picnic stop near the first Nigerian village. Marlis had planned it well—home baked bread, hamburgers and guava jam. She even spread a tablecloth on the red earth. We rolled onto Warwar Hospital compound as the sun was setting over the brown Mambilla hills. Less than 7 hours for the arduous journey of 160 km! The missionaries met us coming out of their weekly meeting where they had just finished praying for our timely arrival. A decision had been made to cross the river with the last ferry of the day, and to cancel our flight early the next morning. We had arrived not five minutes too early.

We could only thank God again for His perfect timing. It assured us greatly that we did not need to worry about our family's needs when we were about His business. The separation anxiety for our small family was blanketed in a precarious but very real peace.

But there was more adventure awaiting us on this trip. The 9 km long descent from the Mambilla plateau into the hot plain below was interrupted by a refreshing dip in a delightful roadside pool fed by a clear mountain stream. In Serte we met pilot Gord Buys with his twin engine Piper and were thrilled by the effortless 2 hour flight to Jos, the northern Nigerian city where our sons would soon attend the famous Hillcrest school for missionary children. Our two oldest met their house-parents, toured the school and tried to warm to the idea of many months away from home.

Our return flight was delayed by a day due to poor visibility. The harmattan, a layer of fine dust originates in the Sahara and blankets the entire West Coast of Africa for half of the year. Its yellowish-brown haze may turn the sun into a dull red light that dampens the spirit and dries the skin. The fine dust can reach more than 2000 meters into the sky and vary in intensity with prevailing winds, but it never really disappears until the monsoon winds bring the rains in April.

On the day of our planned return trip we heard of a Sudan United Mission pilot who had to land on the narrow highway because he could not find the Kano airport in the thick harmattan haze. The following day our own pilot arrived with bandaged hands. The extremely dry air had created such static that a spark had caused a small fire during the refueling of our aircraft. We wondered what would be next on this eventful trip. The harmattan seemed light enough when we departed from Jos, but it became thicker and thicker as we approached the Mambilla plateau. Serte airstrip is surrounded by hills, so the pilot dared not dive into the thick haze. He elected to make a tight turn and descend to about 100 meters above the ground where he found a road that led to the alternate landing site, Takum. Following this bush-road's many curves soon led to universal motion sickness of all the passengers and we were relieved to get onto the ground safely.

Several hours later veteran pilot Ray Browneye decided to "give it a try" and we received a lesson in bush piloting in Africa. With visibility no better than 500 meters this man seemed to know the terrain like the back of his hand. Uncannily he seemed to lift and twist that aircraft between a maze of hills that passed near our wing tips "close enough to touch" and delivered us safely to Serte after an exciting 20-minute flight. Another lesson about trusting God and the skill of devoted men.

A few weeks later Les became ill with influenza. He had to sit down while attempting to "make rounds" in children's ward. I was not even aware of his condition until he developed viral pneumonia and myocarditis with cardiogenic shock. I consulted the Dutch doctor at the neighbouring Catholic hospital and we considered evacuation. But all our efforts failed to stabilise him sufficiently for that option.

I was deeply shaken by his virulent brief illness and death.

The Nso people showed their love and respect for the *doctor wid de woman hand* (left-handed doctor) by attending his burial at the front of the hospital. They came in the thousands. Traditional masked jujus were sent from surrounding tribes to dance about the grave in honor of the first doctor of BBH.

Then I was the only doctor again and I missed my old friend terribly.

The solo practise of medicine has its dangers and follies, as I was painfully aware from my first two years of missionary medicine. Nor are the follies restricted to practising in "the bush". On the one hand there is the temptation to develop a "messiah complex", when the doctor practising in isolation becomes a little god, retaining outdated or even harmful treatments and unscientific procedures in ignorance. On the other hand he may persist with ineffective treatment out of feelings of pity for desperate patients, laziness, or even greed. In addition, he may not welcome the transparency and accountability that a second opinion will afford, even when it could greatly improve his effectiveness. I longed for the comfort of another physician's opinion and critique of my practise.

Even under the intense demand which a mere 25 doctors for a million West Cameroon inhabitants created, this need for professional interaction stimulated us to form a very rudimentary Provincial Doctors' Association. During one of our rare meetings a colleague presented a series of "100 successful appendectomies for intractable abdominal pain" from his busy practise. Unfortunately, none of our gentle reminders that the literature acknowledged the rarity of appendicitis in West Africans, nor meek questioning about pathological confirmation of his diagnoses (there was none) would persuade the surgeon that he stood alone in his beliefs that he had found a unique new way to treat chronic abdominal pain. Sometimes, even willing professional interaction doesn't cure the problems which solo practice can produce.

Appendicitis seems to be a disease associated with a Western diet. In eleven years of practise I diagnosed only about five cases, all ruptured because of late presentation. Only in my twelfth year of African experience did I find the first un-ruptured "hot" appendix at the time of surgery. With the volume of an estimated three hundred thousand consultations I should have seen at least five hundred cases by that time, had I been in

North America. The incidence in West Africa is now on the rise, but still only about one case per month is seen at BBH.

As for patient care, I now needed to make some changes. Once there were more than 120 outpatients to see in a day, I knew I would miss important diagnoses. I was simply unable to treat every patient with the same attention. So I made a special effort to be on the lookout for the sickest patients and treat those with my utmost care and speed. I would even find time to read up on puzzling cases in the evening, if they seemed to be curable and we had the appropriate medication in our stores or sample boxes. If, however, someone did not appear seriously ill, I decided it would not matter much whether I gave them malaria treatment, worm medicine or Vitamins. So I gave all three in a "shotgun approach". But I never wanted to miss someone really sick and in need of care that I could reasonably give.

I made complete inpatient rounds on adult wards only twice a week, thrice on children's ward. In addition, I would visit very sick patients as often as needed. The support of keen and knowledgeable nurses and midwives now became most important. I soon found that there are some people who seem naturally gifted for nursing, and others can't learn it in a lifetime. It had little to do with intelligence or education, and certainly not skin colour. It was more a question of observation and common sense, compassion and judgement.

I wish every doctor could have the fortune to work with at least a few of these "natural nurses" in his or her lifetime. I get a distinctly warm fuzzy feeling when I think of them even now: Rose and Trudy, Baba and Deb and Jody, Julie "the general" and several more!

I have great admiration for single missionaries. There are a disproportionate number of lovely saints among them. At both Hospitals I worked primarily, often exclusively, with these deliberate celibates.

I have been able to do my job only because I could lean heavily on my spouse. She shared some of the heartbreak and despair, the utter misery of failure, and the times of longing for our young children in far away boarding school.

I would have broken under the load had not my wife been at my side, listening without reproof, suffering with me, encouraging, caring and praying.

I was not cut out to remain single. Yet many of the Singles I worked with went through similar circumstances as I, and their personalities did not get warped, their spirits had secret sources of strength. They not only functioned well but even thrived.

A young woman patient arrived the moment I climbed behind the wheel to leave for a clinic. I examined her quickly, determined she likely had an ectopic pregnancy but her general condition was excellent. I decided she could wait for my return in the late afternoon. I gave orders and left the hospital without a doctor. I felt uneasy all day, my thoughts returning to the patient I had left in the care of the nurses. My first question on my return was about her. She was alive, but barely. We rushed her to surgery, but it was too late. She died while we lifted her onto the operating table. I had erred. There was no one to blame but me. Ardice Ziolkowski had gone through deep personal grief when her fiancé died shortly before her wedding. It was then, that she had become a compassionate missionary nurse. Ardice was present throughout my involvement with this patient. She comforted the family. She comforted me. I do not remember her words. Perhaps she mentioned the many patients we had helped that day. But it was her positive strong attitude of trust and reliance on God that helped me in my misery. That was Ardice, always positive, unshakeable in her trust in God. And the others demonstrated their unique God-given attributes in similar ways.

One day a missionary wife needed round the clock intensive care. Mrs. Esther Wanyu, the midwife in charge, had just completed a tough day shift in maternity. That did not stop her from volunteering, insistently, to remain with the critically ill patient for another 16 hours. I felt humbled to work with these saints, both black and white.

In surgery I realised that we had to streamline our work to maximise efficiency. We used two surgery tables side by side, so I could switch back and forth between patients, while delegating parts of the procedure to my nurse-assistants. Certain basic principles had to be closely adhered to. Wound infections had to have causes and would be rigorously pursued for possible breaks in technique. From the excellent medical mission book "Another Hand on Mine" I learned that Dr. Becker in the Congo had done up to 30 major operations in one day. If he had done surgical scrubs according to North American standards he would have had raw hands from over two hours of daily scrubbing. So I decided to schedule all longer, intra-abdominal cases early in the morning and scrub properly only for the first case, then only wash hands instead of formal scrubbing between all following cases. This worked well. Our low infection rates were remarkably similar to North American ones, often better. If an elective surgical wound became infected and responded well to first line antibiotics the infecting organism was not likely from hospital sources, I reasoned, so our technique was not to be blamed. If it was resistant to most of our antibiotics the bug was acquired in hospital and a complete review of our technique and procedures was in order.

Visitors to BBH would often comment about the hospital's distinct odor. We used a dilute Lysol solution to clean floors, beds and equipment. The mildly unpleasant smell reminded us about the importance of cleanliness, at least. Dr.Lister would have been proud of us.

*   *   *

We arrived in Cameroon only seven years after the British Colonial Government had left the country. Much of the administrative structure, the laws and customs still had a fair bit of colonial flavour. It seemed that Cameroonians had inherited some of the worst of each of their former master's bureaucracies. The German's tedious attention to minutiae, the French tendency to enact numerous laws, but leaving them open to negotiation, and the British "office piling system" created a virtual nightmare when dealing with officialdom. With only 25 physicians (8 of us Canadians at one time!) for the million inhabitants in West Cameroon there were a few medical tasks left undone. Bui Division (the administrative county in which BBH was located) had no government physician, so the mission doctor had to be conscripted as the local medical examiner/coroner, whenever the need arose.

I was given little detail and no training for my duties, but was willing to give it a good try. The duties ran the gamut—The police brought a seat cushion stuffed with marijuana for positive identification. I had to give medico-legal opinion regarding injuries sustained in domestic squabbles. A new law involved me in the State's effort to control prostitution with a number of semi-voluntary physical examinations. I decided to be guided by Canadian medical ethics in some of these delicate matters.

The National Government came out with new decrees rather frequently. Some of them were difficult to follow in our remote area. One year I was asked to certify hundreds of market peddlers as "safe food handlers". I had to decide for myself what the spirit of the law intended. Obviously I could not do a thousand chest X-rays to weed out a handful of tuberculosis carriers. Nor could I see stretching our laboratory resources with hundreds of low-yield tests that would cost the poor food handlers unaffordable amounts of money. The diseases most to be feared were probably typhoid fever and active hepatitis "A", for which I had no tests. Several types of dysentery were also endemic.

I simply decided to make this a miniature public health education exercise by asking first for an inexpensive, but quite reliable stool examination. If we discovered any parasite at all, the food handler was given a stern lecture about proper hand washing. I offered treatment and a chance to return in a week. Anyone with dirty hands or fingernails was also denied the highly desirable certificate. Then I asked the food handlers about their particular brand of business and their utensil cleaning routines.

My efforts seemed to bear fruit as I began to see large numbers of people with meticulously manicured hands in the following weeks.

It was in these varied interactions with a wide spectrum of the population that I learned a bit about the land and it's people; what made people laugh, cry, despair, or rejoice.

It came as a shock to me that the Nso tribe (Banso and its environs) had quite a number of suicides. The word for suicide was in fact identical to "hanging". Depression or psychosis was often the underlying cause of these tragedies. I also learned that people would threaten suicide to impress someone. One of the hundreds of job applicants tried to evoke my pity in that way: "I will commit suicide if you won't give me a job!"

It was my duty to accompany the police to the sites and verify the causes of death whenever a suicide occurred in Bui division with its 120,000 people. One Christmas season I had twelve such deaths to verify.

My expert opinion was also required in all sudden unexplained and accidental deaths. Premeditated murder seemed to be rare except for cases of suspected poisoning, which could, of course, not be properly investigated for lack of any semblance of a "crime lab". There were a few "crimes of passion", when a Fulani might be outnumbered and draw his foot long knife rather quickly.

One such victim of a Fulani-knife arrived hours after a violent land-dispute with most of his small bowel lying in a heap outside his abdomen, where someone had wrapped it in a soiled piece of cotton print. The stab wound near his umbilicus measured hardly 4 cm in length but the pain had literally made the patient "push out his guts". Fortunately the knife had not punctured the intestines nor its rich blood supply so that he had survived the two hour long jolting ride on the back of a crowded public transport truck. It took a relatively minor surgical intervention to enlarge the stab wound and stuff the bowel back into the abdomen, though the cleansing job took some effort. Of course the patient did splendidly well.

Occasionally I really had to think hard and try to reconstruct the scene before I could reasonably dismiss violent intent as a cause of death.

A man was found dead in a shallow river with his ancient muzzleloader near by. He had been on a hunt with two youths and his gun had been discharged from close range into his frontal mid-chest. The boys had been apprehended but were of no help, as they claimed to have been far ahead on the path. I could not imagine how the man could have accidentally fired a gun with such a long barrel at himself, until I asked in what manner people would carry a gun when crossing a river.

It immediately solved my puzzle, as I was shown how to grasp the barrel in both hands, with the stock high up above the head, in order to keep the powder dry. That is how the hunter had stumbled over the numerous rocks in the river bed, pitched the gun forward in the fall and shot himself in the chest as it fired when the stock hit the rocks in the river. Case solved.

Another time the police Land Rover took us to the very edge of Nso territory into a large mosquito infested plain. It was very hot and the roads extremely rough, rocky and steep. A body had been found in the river near Mbaw-nso and I had to determine the cause of death. I remember few of the details, except that I had to use my well-proven mouth-breathing technique to avoid being overcome with nausea, self-pity and related emotions, especially since I was not being paid for this service to mankind. This time I could not reach a satisfactory explanation for the death, but the police officers suggested that we had expended sufficient effort and they were anxious to return home. With the task completed I waded through a small stream, after stupidly removing my footwear. A sharp pain in the sole of my foot brought me to my senses, but it was too late. I never found out what stung me, but within an hour I was shaking with rapidly rising fever while the lymph nodes in my groin began to swell painfully. We needed three long hours to return to BBH and I wasted no time yelling for a Penicillin injection as soon as I hit the hospital compound. Thankfully, it was rapidly effective in overcoming the dangerous obscure infection.

I still have (somewhere) a reminder of that trip: Two dried python skins, each over four meters in length, which a hunter sold me for three dollars each. He was busy selling large chunks of snake-meat for four bucks a piece upon my arrival in the local market.

A travelling trader later offered to take the skins to a traditional tanner in North Cameroon and I eventually brought them home to Canada without any customs problems. Canadian laws have since changed, and the mere possession of such articles is now retroactively illegal. People in the enlightened West apparently believe that the snake was killed so the hide could be sold to a tourist. I believe it was killed because it is a dangerous animal, and its meat provided income for the hunter. But who am I to argue.

Trouble is, I don't even remember where that skin is now. If I do remember someday, I will just have to destroy it, or else go to jail. I don't yet know which I would prefer.

In all seriousness, the natives I knew would kill any edible wild animal that crossed their path. In fact, the customary walking stick was most often a spear. Yet the melodious hunting song of the Mbaw hunters is heard but rarely any more. As the population grows, wild animals are crowded out.

When I saw elephant tusks that served as footrests for local chiefs and leopard skins that adorned their thrones I gathered that all these magnificent animals used to be part of the scene. However, I have never seen lion, elephant or gazelle except in the wildlife parks of Cameroon, Nigeria and Kenya. I would still see the occasional baboon, red patas, common green and rare colobus monkey when driving to remote clinics in the mountainous grasslands. Once I narrowly missed a cobra slithering across the road while travelling in the hot plain on my motorcycle. Another time I killed a deadly green mamba snake caught in the entrance to our living room. But to see wild Elephant, Gorilla and Chimpanzee one would have to live in the southern half of Cameroon were the equatorial rain forest is still thick and sparsely populated.

One of my interesting assignments as a coroner was the exhumation of a sub-Chief to determine the cause of death, three months after his burial. It was obviously going to be near impossible to make a diagnosis.

But the task turned out to be less arduous than expected.

First I enquired how traditional doctors performed post mortems in order to take my clues from them. I was shown a certain type of cutlass with curved edges that was historically used exclusively for that purpose. I would be expected to open the heart to confirm (or rule out) native poison as the cause of death. Next I armed myself with a special pair of very thick black rubber gloves and a few basic tools of the trade. Curiously, just then I remembered having been warned against this kind of work by that psychologist back at the U of A when I was just embarking on my career in missionary medicine. Somehow I must have changed during my long training, for I had very few inhibitions at this point. Besides it would have done no good to refuse a judge's order in such a grave case.

The excavation had been done by the time we arrived. I learned about the proper burial of a *big man* on that day. The corpse had been buried in a side chamber to the main cavity of the grave, placed in a semi-sitting position, with a slender hollow bamboo leading from his mouth to the surface of the grave which was located in the centre of the compound. Regular offerings of *mimbo* (alcoholic sap of the palm tree) to his spirit had to be poured down that bamboo pipe during the annual death celebration.

There was no odor whatsoever. It was easy to locate the heart and upon opening it, to declare that the cause of death was "indeed natural".

A young epileptic girl "went missing". She had last been seen going to the family farm to do weeding. She was known to have had frequent major convulsive attacks but had never been on effective epilepsy medications. Almost two weeks had elapsed before the police was called regarding a suspicious finding. I was summoned to examine the evidence. We clambered up the steep slopes of a Wainama hillside and were led to a human skull and a single long bone lying between the ridges of a neatly worked farm. Yes, the remains could have belonged to a fourteen-year-old girl, and the time of death could have been roughly a week or two ago, since the skull still contained some decaying matter. There were tooth-marks on the bones, but how could I be sure the bones were those of the missing girl? Not until I met the smiling mother greeting me in the village: there was an uncanny resemblance in the faultless set of teeth to those I had stared at moments earlier. Not only was the alignment similar, but the front teeth had been filed in the same characteristic fashion.

I was the fastest 100m runner in my grade ten class. I also did well in long jump and high jump, but at this point I employed the very best of my athletic abilities, (according to my dear wife) that of "jumping to conclusions".

The bones were those of a young female. I concluded that the girl had had an epileptic attack while alone at the farm. She probably obstructed her breathing during the seizure and died. There were plenty of hungry wild animals that had left little to be examined by me. The police and the villagers seemed satisfied with my pronouncement.

A college student had returned to his mother's village for the holidays. It was rainy season and the slippery footpaths between the compounds were nearly obscured with vegetation. The boy got up very early one morning to make his way to the quarry. He carried a heavy solid iron bar to loosen basalt stones for building purposes. He had found some newsprint to wrap around the centre of the cold bar where it touched his neck and shoulders. His hands and forearms were lazily draped over the bar as he walked along a slight incline between the coffee bushes and avocado pear trees.

That is where we found him, face down, dead, but not yet cold.

Did he have any enemies, any seizure disorder, any reason at all to suddenly pass from life to death in an instant?

The police officer interrogated the villagers at a distance while I got down to work. I examined his plastic shoes. There was a bit of dirt scuffed up at the front of one shoe and a scratch-mark on the footpath just under his outstretched legs. He had slipped and fallen. The bar lay across his back at the level of his shoulder blades. The paper wrapped about its center was a Catholic publication with the title: "Meeting Christ" (a coincidence?).

I examined the ground next to the body and found the indentations the iron bar had made in the soft earth. I dropped the bar a few times and found that it had fallen from less than a half meter of height. Then I turned my attention to the corpse. There was absolutely no sign of injury on the body, no swelling, bruising, abrasion or fracture. This was puzzling.

I stood and pondered and came to the following conclusion: He had slipped and pitched forward, unable to break his fall sufficiently as his hands were steadying the bar across his shoulders. As his upper torso hit the ground and bounced back up, the heavy iron bar was still accelerating on its way down. It hit him in a vulnerable spot of the neck just below the skull. The reason there was no swelling or bruising at all, was because his circulation had stopped instantly. Tissues without circulation do not show signs of inflammation.

I rested my case while the policeman continued his investigation.

The family would not let the matter end there. A reason for this death had to be found. Someone, a spirit or, more likely, a living person, had caused this tragic calamity. The *ngambe man* would be consulted. An animal had to be sacrificed, a culprit would be named and asked to confess and make restitution.

My cultural ignorance must have been perplexing or annoying to my patients and their families many a time, but nowhere did it become more obvious to me than in the area of death and dying. These common encounters provided me with valuable insights and learning opportunities.

Mammy Theresa had lost all fingers and toes to leprosy. She planted her corn on hands and knees storing the kernels in her mouth and spitting them into the holes that her finger-less little paddle-hands had dug in the soil. When she was admitted yet once more to the leprosy ward at Mbingo she decided it was time to die. She had no serious illness, she simply said: *na today, me, I go die.* She remained cheerful till evening, when she turned her head to the wall, gave up the ghost and left us awed. A person's will to live is essential to the healing process—in this case I witnessed a person's willpower achieve the opposite.

I had to determine yet another cause of death in the company of the police when we came upon a corpse hanging from a tree. The sun was setting, and I was eager to get the body down, examine it and sign the required forms in duplicate. I was allowed to examine the body suspended from a branch about 3 meters above the ground. But when I requested a knife to cut the crude native rope I was told to wait. I began to argue that I had no time to waste on the dead, when I was so badly needed back at the hospital where I looked after the sick, yet very much alive. I was told that only a brother could cut down the body, and that *odder man go follo e fo back* (there would soon be another suicide if this procedure wasn't done right). I did not want that to happen so I gave them another 10 minutes. It stretched to 15, 20, then 30 minutes and it was definitely too dark now to do any examination in detail.

Finally an old man appeared, dressed in rags, and now I became the witness, even an integral participant in a proper ritual for this occasion. The grim old man scurried about, murmuring to himself (or the spirits?), spraying each of us and the body with a switch dipped in a calabash full of a broth-like substance that he had obviously mixed up while we had waited impatiently. He plucked a hand-full of grass and placed it between the first and second toes of the corpse, he blew a whistle facing away from the body, shouted over his shoulder, found a raw egg in his woven bag and threw it against the man's chest. The egg broke and its contents dripped into the scanty clothing covering the lower torso. Another vigorous spraying of all the bystanders with the switch freshly dipped in the broth and we were ready to proceed. A brother appeared. He climbed the low tree with agility and determination and used a traditional double-edged knife to saw at the rope while we eased the stiff corpse to the ground.

I had the choice of two causes of death, as long as I could be sure that no one else had strung up this fellow. Even though there was no suicide note, I was assured that the man had a history of being *off senses* in the past. So it was either a broken neck, or more likely, because of the low height and slender branch, self-inflicted suffocation. This is what I chose to write in my report.

The *cry die* (*pidgin* for "die cry") is an all encompassing term for a variety of events. It can be a feast in memory of an important family member who died last year, a cultural gathering to annually commemorate a former Chief, or it can be the immediate loud expression of sorrow that accompanied each and every death. It was the latter that caused me the most grief. First, it often awoke me in the night, as the mourners would make sure that their way home would lead past my house so I would be able to share their grief. Secondly, though often melodious and varied, the sound would make me painfully aware that I was part of the problem. (Interestingly, when our cook heard us play a record of a famous operatic tenor's aria, he asked respectfully if that was a *white man cry die*. My wife told him it was not a die-aria.)

Thirdly, the die cry in the night was sure to rouse my curiosity as to which of my many patients had just left for the better land. A curiosity that could be satisfied in two ways:

a) By a messenger from the hospital with a note from the nurse on duty informing me of the death. (Many a time resolutions had been passed **not** to wake the doctor **after** the fact, but before!) Or b) by reading the report of the night duty nurse before my morning rounds. Though this was the preferred method, the die cry nevertheless prevented me from going back to sleep on many occasions. Finally, the wailing announced to anyone in earshot that we had failed yet again. Even in a fatalistic society I could do without such immediate, shocking publicity.

A six year old contracted measles. Since his father was a wealthy Divisional Officer the wife transferred the child to our hospital when complications arose. In spite of our best efforts the child died the night after admission. The mother had excellent lungs and I was well aware of the death long before the *watch night* arrived with the demand for immediate

Land Rover transport of the corpse to the home village two hours away. The hospital driver was not available. I was in my first year of ignorance of the local customs and felt obliged to drive the family home. I felt my absence from the one-doctor hospital would also be less crucial during the night and payment of the large transport bill would not be a problem. The wailing and howling was very loud indeed and became unbearable in the confines of the Land Rover as we left the hospital grounds. To my surprise it soon decreased and stopped altogether when we were on the road between villages, only to rise again whenever we met anyone on the road. The wail rose to a truly magnificent crescendo when we neared the home village of the bereaved family. I gathered then, that the wail serves as an announcement as much as an expression of grief. Quite therapeutic too, according to modern psychology, but quite distressing to me, the foreigner.

With the traditional burial of all family members in their family compound it caused considerable inconvenience when patients died in hospital. The urgency to carry the corpse home rose with the status of the deceased. Very few patients were ever abandoned by the relatives and would then have to be buried by hospital employees. Some very poor families could not afford the expensive transport of the deceased and his mourning relatives, so the chief granted us land for a hospital cemetery. The absence of funeral homes and morgues, the hot tropical sun and the greed of taxi drivers made matters even more urgent. Many a family would place the body of the departed in a sitting position between them in the rear seat of a Corolla taxi for a long and jarring ride to the home village for burial. Fresh leafy branches stuck into the taxi's grill would indicate the presence of a corpse among the passengers. *Die-man de pass,* the children would whisper to each other as the vehicle raced by.

There is growing pressure to provide a refrigerated mortuary at the hospital, such as is available in the Provincial Capital. When my friend Enoch Jingwi died recently his sons were summoned from England and the United States. The body had to be kept at the refrigerated morgue for a few days to wait for the sons' arrival. *Dem been put um fo flask* (they put him in a thermos) was the important message passed on among the thousands of mourners for the former laboratory assistant, later mayor of two remote villages.

The cost of dying in Cameroon is often greater than several years of wages of the dearly departed. There may be a large hospital bill and the transport to the village, but the major expense is an elaborate feast that exceeds any other celebration in scope. For if the die cry is not appropriately celebrated, the spirit of the departed will bring no end of grief to the family members responsible. The ancestors demand respect and sacrifices. They will exact their dues from the most vulnerable of the clan. A child will soon fall ill, or even die.

African Society is child-centred. A child is of immense value and cannot be entrusted to the care of only two biological parents. The entire clan claims ownership and responsibility for its upbringing and protection. Everyone has **many** "fathers and mothers".

The acceptance of children born to unwed mothers varies widely from tribe to tribe. In some areas it is considered desirable to prove a girl's fertility before her marriage will be arranged. Her bride price will be higher if she has borne a child. The father of this first child will never be the one to marry the girl, the baby will remain with the girl's father and carry his name.

In other areas there is no bride price, and marriage is consummated and dissolved rather easily.

In case of infertility divorce is almost automatic and vigorously encouraged by the relatives. Infertility is invariably considered to be the wife's fault.

Our patients were fond of supplying the doctor with their complaints in written form. One of the letters in my collection taught me just how strong the desire for a child is in African society.

The letter read thus:

"Complaint.

1.At first menstruation was after 26 days

2.Later it changed to after 21 days

3.The menstrual period is extraordinary and lasts for 5 days

4.At moment the menstrual period is painful and there is stomach-ache.

5.It is now one and one-half months since marriage but no pregnancy."

I had the distinct impression that it mattered not so much who the child's father was, as the fact that a precious child was produced. With the historically high infant mortality rate one can understand the desire for many children in an agricultural society where both old age security and status are directly proportional to the size of one's family.

Amshatu was a pleasant young Hausa woman with a history of a previous C-section now presenting with twins. She delivered the twins without a problem, but had a severe postpartem hemorrhage, which I treated with a manual removal of the placenta and a pitocin drip (a pituitary hormone that contracts the muscle of the uterus). When she bled again she had to have an emergency hysterectomy (removal of the uterus), at which time I found a retained piece of placenta in the old scar. She had a very stormy post operative course, with protracted vomiting, failure to produce breast milk, transfusions and finally a collection of pus under her diaphragm, which had to be drained surgically. Her discharge from the hospital was a relief for me, but for years thereafter Amshatu would plead in a most irrational fashion, that she needed to get pregnant again. Or, if that was not possible, could I at least help her to menstruate again. She blamed me for her subsequent infertility, although she had cost me more than my share of anxiety and grief.

I was asked to examine a baby in maternity. It was entirely normal. Surprising, as it had just been found crying from the depths of a pit-latrine (out-house), retrieved from among human excrement, brought to the hospital, thoroughly and lovingly cleaned and fed. And now an enraged village population joined the hunt for the suspected young mother. She would surely be brought to justice. The baby would go to the grandfather who had very nearly been deprived of another precious child. I never heard about the outcome of this episode.

Once in a while a young girl would try to obtain an abortion or even resort to infanticide. Most often the stated reason was that a very expensive secondary education had been jeopardised by the untimely pregnancy. Abortions were practised by unscrupulous medical personnel (medical students, professors, nurses, pharmacists and native "doctors") and though against the law, I never heard of a prosecution. I was witness to more than a few horrendous deaths from septicemic shock following criminal abortion attempts. What surprised me, however, were the several married ladies who begged me to perform the illegal abortion procedure when they were still nursing a child who was "not yet walking". The almost universal historical method of birth control across large sections of West Africa is maternal abstinence. I never met a stronger taboo in all my years of work with thousands of women. Child spacing had to be at least two years apart, in some tribes close to three years.

A little personal episode illustrated the pervasive power of this moral convention. Whenever our young family would stop at the roadside for a greeting, people's attention would immediately settle upon our two oldest children, born only 13 months apart. "Are they twins?" was the guaranteed first question. When informed of the ages, the disapproval was clearly written on the face of the questioning native. "Ignorant, undisciplined white man, can't even control himself to ensure the survival of his child".

I was quietly minding my business in the consulting room with three or four patients lined up on a bench for greater efficiency, when suddenly the door burst open and an angry gendarme in uniform dragged a crying, protesting young woman into the room. Disregarding everyone present he pointed at her and shouted: "she has committed adultery! Examine her! She is pregnant!" I was taken aback by the violent accusation. Only gradually was I able to piece together the story: This was his wife. They had a small child. The child was not yet crawling. It had fallen ill. He, the husband, had definitely not slept with his wife since the child's birth. Therefore someone else must have, contributing the "sperm that turn the mother's milk sour", making the baby ill. Even when I confirmed the wife's non-pregnant state by examination, the husband would not stop his raging. "Every man knows that women can't be trusted". But what made him so furious was not so much her supposed marital infidelity as the fact that she had caused the child's illness.

Now I had to swallow hard. This was no ordinary marriage spat. I was being introduced to significant family and marriage dynamics that would be absolutely essential to my understanding of this strange culture I was now part of. Marriage existed primarily for the production of children. There seemed to be very little intimacy and sharing of hopes and fears between a couple. The marriage partner was not the trusted confidant with whom to share one's dreams and secrets, and certainly not one's finances!

The very strong taboo regarding sexual abstinence between husband and wife led not only to perfectly spaced children in a family, which was clearly beneficial for maternal and child health, but was also the main historical reason for polygamy, prostitution and poor marriages. I sharply disagreed with our spinster-matron that this custom of abstinence was worthy of support. I believed that I had biblical back up for my view, and in the age of AIDS and sexually transmitted diseases this taboo achieves the exact opposite of it's intended purpose. It kills parents rather than preserving healthy infants. For, though a mother will usually obey this taboo for fear of failing to raise a healthy baby, many fathers do not feel bound by this restraint. I have, in fact been told by more than one woman, that she would rather send her husband to a prostitute, than to risk the health of her baby by breaking age-old rules of marriage relations. Even women educated overseas have admitted to me that their conscience does not allow them to break this taboo.

A fine young teacher from a neighbouring tribe taught in the local primary school and became interested in one of his class seven students. She was a well-developed sixteen-year-old princess, daughter of the powerful old ruler of Nso. Obviously this created a problem. True, there would be no need to pay a dowry, as princesses were above this sort of thing, but the chief's children could never marry someone from another tribe. It just wasn't done. Elopement was a possibility, but the teacher was an upright Christian man and would not consider such a move.

In considering his very limited options his thoughts turned to me, the local representative of his employer, "the mission".

Under cover of darkness he came to my house and revealed his bold request. Would I be so kind as to take a *dash* (gift) to the Fon and plead on his behalf for the hand of the princess? This was an unusual role for me, for which I had neither natural talent nor inclination. But I liked the man. He was humble, yet forthright and obviously suffering from love-sickness, something I had been afflicted with myself, a scant few years before.

I would give it a try. The old Fon received my request, my gift of a blanket, and me, with surprising acquiescence. Of course they could marry, there would not be a problem at all. I was almost disappointed that I did not need to develop my carefully thought out proposal. The next day, however, I had an unexpected visitor. The princess's mother asked to see me urgently on the veranda of my home. I was unprepared for the torrent of angry words the *wintoh* (chief's wife) poured out over me. Fortunately I did not understand most of her long speech, but I got a good feel for the emotions behind the words. Who did I think I was, to dare interfere with the customs and taboos of the tribe, to propose a foreigner for her lovely twin daughter?

This was not the last time I had to endure this prominent but unso-phisticated farm woman's wrath. O well, there was nothing I could do now, and besides, I did have the Fon on my side!

The marriage was consummated and soon the young princess was heavy with child. She was all of a meter and a half tall though otherwise not limited in any dimension. Several episodes of threatened miscarriage and ante-partum hemorrhage seemed to prove the old woman's ominous warnings, that the spirits could not possibly bless this union. The pregnancy prevailed. The princess became very large indeed. But her delivery was routine. A boy and a girl came forth and received the triumphant names of Victor and Victorine. Each was over 3000 grams in weight and they quickly added more. Plainly this was proof that I was involved in a just cause. The *wintoh* now became my somewhat pesky confidante and "friend", for to deliver twins was a blessing. Had not she herself delivered twins and had not both of her twin daughters delivered twins in turn?

The Cameroonian mother carries the child on her back every waking moment until it is ready to move on it's own. (Perhaps, the straddle explains the total absence of congenital hip dislocations that we occasionally see in the West?)

The infant sleeps with the mother, has its needs met instantly and is never slapped or even reprimanded. Somehow it signals its need for excretion by subtle body movement that the mother learns to interpret instinctively. I have rarely seen a baby soil a mother's back, even though diapers were unknown in those days. This physical closeness between mother and child creates an unparalleled bond of security and forms the basis for strong personalities and a universal scarcity of those severe developmental personality disorders that are rooted in a traumatic early childhood. Thumb sucking, sleep-disorders, childhood neuroses and autism were practically unknown in my practise. There was little shyness or lack of self-confidence either.

The bombshell exploded, however, with the arrival of the next baby. "Number One" now had to be relegated to an older sibling's back where he got a very different quality of attention. This considerable trauma could not destroy the earlier groundwork for personality development, but more often led to malnutrition, bed-wetting, a heavy worm load, neglected hygiene and inadequate clothing. A strong self-image and survival instinct led the child to find its place in the family hierarchy, and may explain the nonchalant attitude of adults towards the petty theft that young children frequently engage in.

Overall, I became convinced that this Western man could learn a thing or two from Africans about the care of babies and infants.

Making rounds on children's ward was actually a pleasure. With children being so very secure in the love and care of their parents, they were very trusting even of the pale stranger. I could often examine whole rows of children without having even one of them cry. This was wonderful. I wanted to learn all I could about child rearing that produced such contented children.

Child discipline is everyone's business. John our yardman told me the following story: "There was a village disciplinarian in my home village Taku. He was a single elderly man who lived alone but was always well informed about matters of concern to the community. Young boys in the village who might be up to some mischief especially respected him. This man would casually show up at a family evening meal and quietly become a participant. The boy with the bad conscience would grow increasingly restless till, suddenly, the visitor would jump up, seize the boy and 'lay on a good lickin'.

The parents would watch dispassionately and might not even ask about the reason for the beating. Whether it involved stealing from the neighbour's fruit-trees or accidental damage to property during a particularly rambunctious prank, the parents would usually mete out no further punishment. The matter was settled!" Child rearing is an art that needs the wisdom of many minds.

My wife and I decided early to disregard the absolute taboo against married folks being seen together in public. We even sat together in church. But we drew the line at handholding in public as the implied message was simply too strong: we were heading straight for the bedroom!

Two young male friends commonly hold hands while walking together. They are simply good friends. Homosexuality is virtually unknown.

It was around this time that the enormity of my task as a Christian missionary began to dawn on me. Was I really convinced that Christian love marriage and family life was superior to the local contracts between clans for the primary purpose of creating offspring for the extended family? Was the whole elaborate culture built around the survival and well being of the child not actually superior to my own? I had only to think of Canadian day-care and the children abandoned to it, and the comparison silenced me.

I was also surprised at times with the evidence of an inherent traditional moral code that was remarkably similar to the Christian ethic. I can remember the righteous indignation of a father who brought his trembling daughter after she had been raped. *Ye be de spoia my pekin* (he ruined my child) he repeated over and over. There was no question of the loving relationship this father had with his child, and it mattered all the world to him how she was going to be treated by men.

At Nso, the mother of the groom would vigorously wave a fluttering white rooster among the wedding procession if, and only if, the bride was known to be a virgin. And I witnessed this ritual with my own eyes.

The biblical picture of marriage and family life that I tried to model and propose had to divest itself radically and totally of all its Western cultural trappings. Was I willing to give up my culture and teach only the essence of Christianity? Then "why not polygamy" indeed. The practise of polygamy ("polygyny" more accurately) is legal in Cameroon. I estimate that close to half of the children in the fifties and sixties came from polygamous unions.

When I felt compelled to search for scriptural guidance I could not find a Biblical basis for outlawing the practise of polygamy. There were only subtle warnings of its consequences, and Jesus' teaching of a better way: "In the beginning it was not so" (when asked to give his judgement regarding marriage and divorce). I was convinced that nature also had something to teach us in this regard.

Around the age of twenty the slight numerical preponderance of males over females at birth has disappeared and the ratio is exactly 50/50! I was amazed to learn how many West Africans tried to justify their strong cultural preference for polygamy by the erroneous belief that there are more girls born then boys. I decided on a little experiment. I asked people from the entire spectrum of the "age of reason" to give me their best estimate of the percentage of boys and girls born in their society and the world at large. The almost universal answer was "two to one in favour of girls". I found the exception to be almost exclusively among young married females, both educated and from humble background; they had it closest to the correct answer at 50% each.

The Minister of Health came for an inspection tour of BBH. I answered all his questions to the best of my ability, but during our walk through maternity I dared to ask him my standard "research" question. He protested, citing his lack of training in the medical sciences. I persisted and he gave the classic cultural answer: "two girls to one boy." I confronted him with the evidence of our maternity birth records. He did not appear convinced or even interested. Customs and culture derive from psychosocial needs, emotional assertions and strongly held beliefs that are not easily shaken by facts.

So I prepared a lecture, contrasting polygamy with Christian love marriage. I was proud of its logic and persuasive power. I contrasted the master/multiple servant role of the polygamous union with the mystical union of two equals becoming One in a Christian marriage, where there is unlimited, lifelong sharing of finances, fears, hopes and goals (A revolutionary idea in traditional marriages in West Africa). I exposed polygamy as selfish and unnatural, as it is numerically illogical and unfair.

Many young Cameroonian Christians are desperately looking for models to follow as well as like-minded prospective partners to put these new ideas to the test. But as Africans became aware of the preponderance of divorce and remarriage in Western society, I could also hear the cutting criticism: "You whites simply have polygamy in succession!"

Polygamy certainly dealt with the destitution of widows and orphans, they were taken care of. Perhaps the stabilising influence of a large extended family may just be what the newly married western couple so often misses.

Polygamy remains a legal option in Cameroon. Our Missionary Treasurer married an African lady. The civil registrar asked if the marriage was to be registered as monogamous or polygamous. The surprised/amused missionary chose the monogamous option!

Most Cameroonian young people now enter marriage with the idea that it will be lifelong, productive of children, mutually satisfying and monogamous. But when the marriage is barren, when social standing rises and wealth is accumulated, people are tempted to fall back into old patterns of behaviour. Especially when traditional honors and titles come his way, many an ageing head of the house will feel the pressure from his relatives and friends to enhance his stature and enlarge his family by adding a younger wife. His first wife may even initiate such a move, or at least acquiesce silently. Will she not welcome the help in farm and household?

*   *   *

Through my daily practise I gradually learned to get a pretty good idea of people's ages, but the fact remained that practically no one kept track of his or her age in Cameroon until quite recently. Only with the arrival of such modern inventions as birth certificates can anyone be sure of his age, but even so, the date on the document does not have any real significance for anyone. It may just be a starting point for a good argument.

Westerners are very time-conscious while Africans are event-oriented. Most people I met could not tell me their birth date, let alone celebrate that day, but things are changing. The first birthday is becoming a major social event among educated young families. Many adult guests come to celebrate with cake and candle, alcohol and fancy dress, but usually without presents. All further birthdays are ignored.

The traditional world-view needed radical adjustment with new government decrees setting age limits for admission to schools and insisting on birth certificates for many applications. It was difficult, for example, to qualify youths for the "Under 16 World Soccer Championship" when nominal age was deemed negotiable in Cameroon.

A father brought his daughter, a shy budding village beauty, for consultation. "How old is she?" I asked. "Four" was his straight-faced answer. I guessed fourteen or fifteen. He simply had no clue.

The authorities decided that a valid "age declaration" could only come from a recognised authority on the subject—the doctor. My consulting room was subsequently favored with thousands of youths, eight or ten at a time, crowding in to get the all-important document that was to ease their entry into a world of opportunity. I took a quick look for third molars, peeked inside the shorts to assess maturity and questioned the children about *"follow back dem"* (younger siblings). Historical events surrounding the time of birth, and a shrewd estimate of possible benefits to the subject led me to issue a signed and stamped certificate with the estimated "birthday".

I gently encouraged each applicant to pick his or her own birthday: *"dem born you for which day?"* *"De first of January, Sah"* answered one after the other, with confidence. "You can't all be born the same day!" I remonstrated in mock despair. "And when were you born" I challenged the next fellow. *"De second of January, Sah".* He shrewdly replied.

He got his certificate.

When old Chief Mbinglo died, the newspapers claimed he was 128 years old. My own estimate was closer to 80, but who wants to argue his age, power or importance. Even the number of his wives was not up for discussion. All that mattered was that there were "many".

There was great disappointment with the published presidential election results in our division. Only 99% had voted for the great leader, while our neighbouring division had managed 126%!

One needs to interpret all statistics cautiously.

The naming of new-borns is a special event in many societies. The desire for uniqueness, the parent's high hopes for that small bundle of the combined gene pool and a good measure of pride often produce curious results.

Cameroonians usually went by their family names first, mentioning their given names second. This was especially true of those in authority over others—you simply never called your superiors by their first name. This was such an established convention that after more than 30 years of close friendships and acquaintances there remain only three Cameroonians who call me by my first name.

It was also just common and polite to refer to your equals by their family name. I grew to know many of my co-workers by their family name only. This produced some hilarious situations—we had both a "Yu" and a "Mih" working at our Mbingo Hospital—leading to endless fun whether it was Yu or Mih on duty today, and could Yu please check to see if Yu was there or if it was in fact Mih, etc. etc… In Cameroon, naming may signify an event that happened at the time of birth, such as "Conference" or "Sunday". One could also take a new name on reaching important milestones in life such as graduation from school. Names chosen at birth may indicate the mood or condition of the parent such as "money hard" (It is difficult to get ahead) or "Ah no sabby"(I have no clue). It takes a bit more imagination to figure out why someone might be named: "Author", "Omniscience", "Video", "Trabant", "Sixpence", "Expensive", "Sanitary", or even "Obnoxious". Others suggest more obvious explanation: "Waste time" may indicate a long labor, "Suffer you" a tough delivery. The hospital driver appropriately named his ever-hungry dog "Jealous".

Biblical names are common in Christian circles: from "Genesis" to "Revelations", with "Shadrach", "Abednego", "Ephesians", and "Phillipian" in between.

"What is your name?" I asked a young fellow: "Genesis" he replied. "So why not Leviticus", I asked half-jokingly, "Oh that's my brother", said he.

Twins would almost certainly be named "Jacob" and "Esau" or "Moses" and "Miriam", while a pastor's triplets were called "Peter, James and John".

Peculiar pronunciations would add their own humor: Bruno sounded suspiciously close to Blue-nose.

An illiterate proprietor grandly named his mismanaged high school "Christ the King College". The townspeople called it: "*cry de king*" (complain to the Chief) in derision.

Two events coincided in the year 1972. Man walked on the moon and we had a large number of patients present with "pink eye". It was logical then, that the two should be related. Patients would come and say: "*I get 'pollo*". They had "Apollo", and man's foolhardy venture into space was the cause of it.

One day "Hitler" came to ask for a job as a yardman at the hospital. There was no work for him. But then I remembered the time when his mother had come to consult me 18 years earlier, because Hitler was sick. I could hardly hide my disgust while briefly recounting history for her and my very own experience of that monster's legacy. Why had she labelled her son that way? "*no be e been get power?*" was her justification. Power is all-important. The daily greeting is not only: "what news?" but is immediately followed by the question: "are you strong?" i.e., Is your power increasing, is your spirit able to overcome all it's adversaries? Therefore it only made sense to be miles ahead in the power struggle— with a name like Hitler.

I also made the acquaintance of Einstein and Napoleon, they attended St. Augustine's College up the hill from our house. Cosmos was a local mechanic and Appollonia the apprentice seamstress. Ambrose Africa and Chinese lived in town.

What choice had I, but to join in the fun. I chose to inscribe my motorcycle with "*man no be God*", which stimulated a lot of wonderment and many a chuckle. This statement invites a whole host of philosophical considerations: Man isn't God! I am only a man. Don't expect me to be perfect, omniscient, omnipresent, omnipotent etc. I could be just like you, humble or dishonest; mischievous, but a unique creation, just plain me. Don't blame me for the way I look. I know my place in life. Don't expect me to compete with God either, I would obviously lose every time!

Townspeople are forever coming up with new names. New fads, in particular, do not escape the sharp eye of the market woman. When bell-bottom pants made their sweeping entry onto the scene they quickly got the name "*trouser keep town clean*".

One could buy any part of a freshly butchered cow on market days, from brain to intestines. The lower third of the leg, including the hoof was sold as "*salamander*", so named after the famous German shoe brand.

A large billboard in Nigeria advertised underwear: "Come and have your inners beautified".

Small two-door taxis, particularly VW beetles, are aptly named "*come-out-make-I-enter*" (get out of the front seat, so I can get into the back seat).

Modern Taxi Vans have rather bland group names such as "Amour Mezam" or "Guarantee Express" while the more thought provoking "Psalm 23", "Mark of Zorro", "Apollo 13" and "Here comes Winter" have fallen by the wayside, often literally. I miss them because they brightened my day. Still on the road are "Slide rule", "Toronto boys", "New Era", "God knows why", "Piccadilly Circus" and "Why worry". Many have a pointedly Christian message: "Love thy neighbour", "Lamb of God", "New Life" and "Prince of Peace".

"No food for lazy man" and "ask God—why" were certainly biblical admonitions, "No event—no history" just wistful African profundity and "I'll be right back" was probably to be interpreted in the widest possible parameters.

"Air Mezam" flew by in a cloud of dust and "Idea" was followed by "Son of Idea". But "Blackbirds fatten best in cold weather" really left me puzzled.

Drivers took meticulous care of their vehicles, certainly with regards to cleanliness. A complete one-hour wash-job at the "Submissive Washing Point" or the "7th formula washing point" could be had for about 50 cents.

Village market scenes are crowded with "*clandestines*", a gross and comical misnomer, because they are everywhere present and obvious. The bush taxis are in fact the only means of public transport between smaller towns and villages in the grasslands. These ten to fifteen year old four door Toyota Corollas are imported second-hand from European ports for their ease of repair and availability of spare parts. The clandestines got their name from the personnel who collect bribes at checkpoints all along the busy roads. These vehicles are simply unable to meet utopian safety laws and elaborate license requirements. Clandestines evoke fake disgust among the forces of law and order. They can barely hide their glee when another overloaded jalopy slinks into view. It is the traffic officer's main source of illicit income, particularly before festive occasions like Christmas.

Commercial enterprises have catchy names, while grandiosely proclaiming the owner's hopes and aspirations: "Kyrie eleison Bar", "The Final Chicken Parlour" and "The Boss-man's Stomach Controller Restaurant". There was the "Plan with God Barbing Studio", the "Perseverance Bar"(I would really like to go home now, but will suffer through one more beer.), and the "Family Planning Food Store".

I passed an enterprising young fellow walking barefoot towards Bambalang. The wooden box filled with succulent fritters balancing on his head advertised "Fast Food".

"Go to work on an egg and a chicken" was the name of the little shack that competed boldly with the "Vatican Restaurant", a slightly bigger shack down the street. Expatriates liked to eat at "Sister Rose's Apple Hot Spot" where charcoal broiled fish was the featured menu. Apples were nowhere in sight; of course, they don't grow in Cameroon. Yet apples seem to have a fascination for the general public, as they appear increasingly in modern folklore.

A number of young maidens were home for the holidays from their elite colleges in the big cities. They offered to sing a special number during the church Christmas program:

"I wish I were an apple, hanging on a tree;

My Jesus could come walking by,

And take a bite of me."

Over the years I acquired a number of names in this society. Some were honorary, just mumbled under the breath as I passed by, including: "*tadom*", the historically wise, powerful medicine man of the Nso people; some less flattering, such as when I missed a shot on the soccer field: "*sabolo*" (weak homemade black soap). To my close co-workers I became *Pa lim* (work-daddy).

I wish I had understood more of what I heard, and could have lived up to the flattering words of the Chief of the Warrior Society: "You should come back, You understand us!"

It made me feel good. I had a name among the Nso people.

      *   *   *

Linguists and lovers of languages can have a 'heyday' in Cameroon. The count of distinct dialects has recently been upped from 248 to 272 as more tribes with separate dialects have been "discovered". A tribe may have as few as two or three thousand people who speak a distinct language that is unintelligible to most of the neighboring village inhabitants. Ngoketunja plain, for example, with an area of about 30 by 50 km has 12 clans with distinct languages and borders, none of them numbering much over 25 000 people. Experts tell me that slave raiding parties, extensive migration, tribal wars, geographical boundaries, but especially the historical absence of the written word account for this amazing diversity ("perhaps unparalleled in any African territory" 2.)). With the spoken word assuming the major means to preserving history and heritage it is easy to appreciate the high value this society has placed upon the ability to express oneself publicly in elaborate oration. People also listen well.

The ability to learn foreign languages among Cameroonians is astounding. It is not at all unusual for *turntalks* (interpreters) to speak five or seven languages, and their ability to learn a new language is not restricted to African tribal languages. Most Cameroonian students studying in France, Germany, Russia or China are given only 3 to 6 months to learn the language of that country before enrolling full time in their course of study, and they do very well indeed. A certain amount of need may facilitate this phenomenon, but it does not excuse the amazing ignorance of Westerners who largely suffer from "monolingual myopia, a disease of the tongue that affects the vision".

I was never given a block of time for language study, although it was mission policy to encourage all missionaries to learn at least one tribal language. Only a handful made such attempts. *Pidgin* was just too handy when ten of our eleven original mission stations had different tribal languages, negating the value of language study in case of transfer. As a result, we never truly learned the heart languages of the people, though I was able to do simple consults in one language eventually. It was most gratifying to experience the ground swell of goodwill when one attempted to communicate in a native's language. It seemed as if people said: "he cares enough about us to make the effort to learn our language and our ways".

Exemplary literacy and linguistic work is being done in Cameroon by the "Summer Institute of Linguistics", an organization presently reducing many tribal languages into writing. Translation of Scripture, adult literacy programs, instruction of schoolchildren in their native written language and formation of language societies will help to retain valuable culture and history, but will also challenge the National Government's efforts to unify the diverse population and discourage tribalism.

Eight different language groups regularly attended Banso Baptist Hospital (BBH). Many others came from farther away, but sporadically. It is customary to consult in *pidgin*, which is the lingua franca through large tracts of the West Coast of Africa. It is amazingly similar to the *pidgin* spoken in Papua New Guinea, half a world away, according to my son Robert who visited there on a short term Youth Mission Project. He was able to communicate within days. Wherever British ships plied their trade, there evolved the need to communicate, and the Brits did not seem to mind the use of their language as the basis from which this "patois" evolved.

Pidgin is a non-written language with distinct grammar and syntax. It may sound like badly pronounced English, liberally sprinkled with native words and bits of Portugese, German and French, but it is well suited for trade and inter-tribal communication. Most men and the women from smaller tribes use it extensively in their daily interaction. In urban areas with multi-tribal communities and churches it is the language of choice, unless the level of education is so universally high that English or French can be used. It is highly frustrating to make a speech and have it interpreted sentence by sentence into two or even three local dialects, as it breaks the natural flow of a message, but thinking on one's feet is definitely made easier by the many interruptions. Children are forbidden to speak *pidgin* in school, because it makes the study of English more difficult. Since *pidgin* is not bound by the written word it mutates at a fast rate. We have noted marked changes in only 30 years, and have lately been complimented on our "beautiful pidgin" by the younger generation who increasingly adulterate their *pidgin* with *grammar* (English).

The beauty of *pidgin* lies in its crisp and pithy expressions. It is concrete and pragmatic, echoing the local inhabitants' upbeat mood and optimistic lifestyle and philosophy:

sick no be die. (Sickness is infinitely better than death)
small no be sick. (A man's height is not his substance)
ol' no be joke. (Getting old is no fun)
all ting de well. (Everything's dandy)
complain no de. (No worries!)

Occasionally it would take a sentence to translate a word, but would then become an almost philosophical statement: "Flat tire" became *"moto-foot we' brief no de".* (an out-of-breath tire).

Native languages recognise and use only three (or four) colors: black (includes brown, green, and blue) white (includes most light colors) and red (includes yellow, orange and pink). (Yellow may be the fourth color in certain tribes). One might think that the recognition of so few colors indicates a poverty of expression, but African English-speakers quickly learn and use names for all the colors that are so important to us in our Western world. One could also point out that Eskimos have 21 names for snow, and Cameroonians have many names for monkeys and birds that we don't use unless we study zoology and ornithology.

It all depends on what's important in life.

Culture and Art are closely related. Cameroon Art impressed us with its remarkable depth. Dancing, drumming, dress, carving, weaving and painting held us spell-bound. I regret not having had more time to take part in cultural festivals. I can close my eyes and experience again: the old men's sword dance, the wedding-gift dance and the gut-shaking full band drum-and-xylophone dances. There is nothing like it anywhere.

Of particular interest was the artwork displayed on human bodies. I still saw many instances of this rapidly disappearing art form.

Within the first week of life boys would be circumcised and girls would have their ears pierced. At puberty many girls used to undergo long painful scarifications of the face, abdomen and back with razor blades. The superficial cuts would be encouraged to form controlled scar formation by the application of wood-ash, palm oil and herbs. The commonest and still persisting mark of beauty is a very light form of scars in the style of cat's whiskers around the mouth. Intricate geometric tattoos of the face, neck and chest could also be seen frequently, especially among Aku women, a sub-tribe of the Fulanis.

In addition, a good number of older women had their nasal septum and the lower lip pierced in the midline, the holes were kept open with wooden plugs, sometimes of increasing sizes.

We inherited a "garden mammy" when we moved to BBH. She had been responsible for weeding and preparing the seedbeds in the garden, while she depended on us to pay the school fees for her youngest daughter and to supply her with soap, salt, sugar, kerosene and cooking oil as needed. There was no use arguing about this arrangement. Every household is expected to contribute to the livelihood of a number of local workers, from cooks and stewards to yard boys and gardeners. One day garden-mammy surprised us with a unique ornament in her pierced nasal septum. She had found a used Q-tip in our refuse.

Women's, and more rarely men's, upper incisors would commonly be filed to a point. The last remnant of this art form is the still practised filing of only the two upper central incisors to an inverted flat V. (I must admit that I found this particular attempt at beautification to be rather attractive, if it was done moderately). A new fad among rich Muslim men and women is to sport a gold-capped front tooth when returning from Mecca. A rarer variant is an inlaid star in one of the upper incisors.

Men occasionally had their two upper incisors split transversely down to the level of the gums. This revealed all the layers of the tooth in dramatic fashion, enamel, dentine and nerve. The last person I saw with this sign of beauty and manhood was the Chief of the Nso who ruled in the seventies.

With the majority of Cameroonian history preserved exclusively as anecdotal, and oral tradition spread through hundreds of tribes, it stands to reason that this history is shrouded in mystery and difficult to reconstruct with the paucity of literature before the arrival of Colonialism in the 19th century. The oldest book I could find on Cameroon recorded history was a biography of Alfred Saker, the first English missionary to Cameroon. 3.) It was a great source of information if one learned to read between the lines. Fufu corn, for example, is now the staple diet of a million or more grasslanders, yet was unknown before the introduction of maize over 100 years ago. Most of the delicious fruit and vegetables now freely available in markets all over West Cameroon: Papaya, mango, citrus, pineapple, carrot, lettuce, tomato, and members of the cabbage family have been introduced by foreigners and now thrive locally. Some of these were introduced in our time and enjoyed immense popularity within a few years of their arrival.

The main source of precious firewood (and increasingly a poor quality construction lumber) is the fast growing Eucalyptus tree. Our oldest missionaries can remember their introduction into West Africa.

Students of Cameroon history would be well advised to search the Archives of Colonial History in Berlin, the Portland Art Museum with the Gebauer collection 4.) and the archives at North American Baptist Seminary located in Sioux Falls, North Dakota.

There are a few isolated anthropological studies published as far back as the nineteen-thirties as well as some studies now ongoing in a few of the grassland tribes, but much of the unique culture and customs will soon be lost forever, as modern society evolves in the new Africa.

At least one fascinating record of tribal history has been uniquely preserved however, and we were privileged to experience it first-hand as a family. Unique, as it involved a **Native** historian who had to first invent an alphabet, then reduce his language to writing before documenting his-story.

The Nso and Bamoum people are neighbouring tribes with very different cultures. They were further separated by the old colonial border between French and English Cameroon. These two tribes fought a war about 180 years ago in which the Bamoum chief was killed. Since then there had been little communication between them until recently, when the Sultan of Foumban had dispatched a permanent "ambassador" to live at the Banso Chief's Palace. This courtly gentleman, Nji Musa, probably had multiple roles to play. There was no reason to continue hostilities in the new atmosphere of "re-unification" between French and English speaking factions of Cameroon. Trade and Commerce would benefit both tribes with the upgraded road from East to West Cameroon. And the spread of Islam would most certainly be facilitated by the new feelings of brotherhood. The old Fon of Nso had made a point of remaining neutral in the matter of favoring one faith over another. But his follower could not refuse the gift of a ticket to Mecca from the Sultan of Foumban, particularly as it was accompanied by a *dress-car* (limousine), a wonderful new status symbol for a man with lesser principles. Nji Musa became our valued family friend. He showed a wonderful openness, courtesy and strength of conviction that attracted us to him. The children loved him, though we struggled a bit to communicate in *pidgin* and lam-nso (the language of Nso). Nji Musa did not speak English or German; we could not speak French or Bamoum.

One day my friend surprised me with an invitation by the Sultan of Foumban (Chief of the 250,000 strong Bamoum tribe). With advancing political unification of East and West Cameroon the 85 km dirt road from Foumban to Banso had been upgraded. This led to an ever-increasing stream of Bamoum patients who liked the care at BBH, "the hospital with the red roof" or sometimes known as *melika* (crudely for: "America"). Although Foumban had two local hospitals, the Sultan was ever looking to improve the health of his subjects, as I was about to discover on our visit.

It was an unforgettable weekend for our family.

Foumban has been included in many West African tourist brochures because of its indigenous written history, probably unique in all of sub-Saharan Africa.

The Sultan's residence lies in the heart of a large village among gently rolling hills on the major road from Douala to Cameroon's North and on into Chad. A traditional covered gate marks the entrance to the old town. It is built of carved hardwood pillars on which the two-headed snake (one head at each end) the ancient symbol of the Bamoum tribe, features prominently. The main street is lined with schools, administrative offices, the court, small shops and modest mudblock-and-mortar homes with shiny aluminum roofs. Huge kola nut trees give pleasant shade to the compounds. The red fertile soil between the humble homes is tilled meticulously and yields rich green foliage of maize, cassava and plantain. As the walled compound of the Palace comes into view, a massive grey building dominates with its most unusual architectural style for the old West Africa. Gothic arches, massive one meter thick walls plastered with tree resin for durability, mahogany planks for stairs and flooring, and especially the 3 storey construction is most unconventional for a traditional grassland building.

Nji Musa waited for us at the iron gate to the Sultan's palace. He wore his traditional flowing blue robe and matching cap. His greeting was enthusiastic. Our friend explained that he would show us around the palace grounds, after which we would have our evening audience with the Sultan.

We entered the large courtyard in front of the old palace and were introduced to the curator of the museum, a little old man who spoke French, Bamoum, and *pidgin*. A small curio-shop to the left did not catch our interest as much as a number of hippo-skulls arrayed under a low overhang. They served as seats for the Sultan's councillors. In the centre of the courtyard a fenced burial site had the customary life-plant growing around a large marble slab. The German inscription read: "here rests in peace my dear mother, born 18?? died…1905.

The gravestone was a gift from the German colonialists who had arrived in Foumban near the end of the 19th century. There was also this King's genealogy of nineteen rulers reaching back to the fifteenth century, written on a large concrete slab that we were shown next. We would hear more about this remarkable man in the next hour or two. In studying the genealogy of Bamoum rulers we took note of Njoya's grandfather who had been killed in battle with the Nso people, a second ruler who was on the throne for only 20 minutes and a third mighty warrior chief who was said to have been 2.4 meters tall.

Next we entered the cool reception hall of the old Palace, now used as the museum and soon to be restored by a French historical society. The gothic arches of sun-dried brick formed 3 storey-high vaulted ceilings that echoed our voices. The large openings to the West looked out upon the sloping fertile gardens of the Chief's wives leading into a ravine. We climbed the broad steps to the second floor that housed the museum. It was dark and dusty, but soon aroused our fascination. Calabashes, each adorned with a number of human jawbones, pointed to a victorious violent history. The chain-mail suit of armour, three meter long spear and large sword of the giant King were there. Two elephant tusks, measuring 2.90 meters each, animal skins and personal carved wooden beds from former rulers were arranged together with other memorabilia of the chiefs in chronological order of their reign. King Njoya's era featured prominently in the displays. He had died in 1933 in the Yaounde jail, incarcerated for intransigence by the French Colonial Powers.

King Njoya had been a genius. We were awed to see that he had not only built this unusual palace and lived in it, but he had also designed a corn grinder that was manufactured by local blacksmiths according to his direction. He had further gathered all the skilled artists and craftsmen into a central location in the capital of his kingdom to learn from and teach each other. He had personally invented an alphabet with 34 letters (after discarding an earlier trial of 'symbols for syllables'). He had written books in this Bamoum script, at least two of which were on display: a history of his people and a medical text with a list of 80 diseases and their appropriate traditional treatments. Sketches of local medicinal plants punctuated the yellowed pages. Native practitioners were required to pass an examination before the wise chief granted permission to practice. The books were hand-written on coarse paper and bound with thick leather.

We were duly impressed. The more we asked, the more remarkable the story became.

German missionaries, upon their arrival in the late nineteenth century, were surprised to find a school of 500 children from the immediate area of the Chief's compound enrolled in a program where they learned to read and write their own language. The curator himself was still able to read the script, but it had since fallen into general disuse with the overwhelming use of French in local schools since 1917 when Germany was forced to give up it's colony to French and British "protection".

One other stately old man was presently introduced to us as we exited the museum's hand-carved doors: The former King Njoya's personal secretary, now well into his eighties, but still standing very tall, with a kind and regal bearing. Both he and the curator were members of the large local evangelical church, the only two male Christians out of the entire household of the Sultan. We enquired about the next day's church service as I was determined to find out more about the history of Christianity among the Bamoum.

Next we paid a visit to the "rue d'artisans" located a kilometer from the palace. We found an entire street lined with workshops of weavers, wood-carvers and brass-workers. Vigorous bargaining ensued and my wife bought a number of lovely carvings at reasonable prices because tourist season was long past.

The recurring theme in the hunting, harvesting and health scenes depicted in carvings and brass was the double headed snake, emblem of the Bamoum. (The significance of this totem intrigues, but remains obscure to me.) Some of the tablecloths, hand spun from cotton grown in North Cameroon, woven and embroidered in Foumban, still adorn our table from time to time.

The rapidly sinking equatorial sun found us hurrying back to the Sultan's palace where we cleaned up and were led into our host's expansive quarters while Nji Musa took his leave. At the entrance to the private home stood the "victory drum", carved from a tree trunk, near two meters in diameter. It exceeded a man's height and would need a platform to be played by the drummers. We could only imagine how the sound would have carried when flailing hands and clubs pounded it after a battle won.

We entered the Sultan's living quarters. Oriental rugs and antique chairs, table silver and ornate dishes pointed to their German origin from bygone days of glory. The Sultan's favourite wife began to serve my humble little family. Truly we had never dreamed of a ten-course meal waiting for us in Black Africa! With over-filled stomachs we were ushered into the Sultan's presence.

Njimole Saidu was a 66-year-old greying, obese friendly man of average height, unlike many of his tribesmen who are mostly over 1.8 meters tall. He had recently been to France and wanted my opinion on his ECG, laboratory test results and radiographs which most rich African patients carry with them for many years. He showed me his anti-hypertensive medication and the prescription glasses for his recently operated eyes, but soon led the conversation, in *pidgin*, to the purpose of my visit: "how soon could I open a hospital like BBH in the Bamoum area?" Land was already allocated. Patients would be plentiful. Trainees for nursing and midwifery likewise.

I was clearly unprepared for his proposal and tried to persuade him that I had only limited powers. He was not easily convinced. He was a man of considerable financial and political means, a friend of President Ahidjo. His numerous Mercedes trucks plied the roads to city markets with farm produce and timber from his vast land holdings. He had many wives (I estimated 150 plus) and many children and grandchildren. His father, King Njoya, had chosen him from among his many brothers as the wisest and best leader. As for me, he had heard many glowing reports from his subjects who were treated for cataracts and hernias at BBH. And as Medical Officer in charge of such a famous hospital, surely I could easily help him, if I only wanted to. I felt severely limited by my inability to think on my feet and could only outline the policies of our medical board at the time. We were hampered on all sides by lack of personnel and finances. Now, nearly thirty years later, our Health Board does indeed run a well functioning health center in the area then designated by Sultan Njimole. The large village is nearly 100% Muslim but has enthusiastically welcomed a Christian health facility, even supplying all buildings and considerable start-up funds.

The audience ended. Soon we bedded down in a huge German "Himmelbett" and had a wonderful night of rest but were awakened rather rudely at five a.m. by what seemed like a cannon shot fired just outside our window. It felt powerful enough to lift the roof off our guest-house. The following gun shots were not nearly as frightening, but we were now well motivated to rise. One of the many daughters of the Sultan was getting married that day and the appropriate expressions of joy had to be universally made known. Our involvement with the significant event ended there, however.

There was time for a brief tour of the two local hospitals. Both places did not impress me with their level of cleanliness or services offered. I had to agree with Nji Musa, that BBH was much to be preferred.

Then we were off to the much-anticipated church service.

More than three thousand people crammed into the large brick building where the service was conducted in French and Bamoum. It lasted a good four hours with the inclusion of five weddings on this particular

Sunday. Nji Musa interpreted in a low voice, and we did get into the spirit of worship with the harmonious singing, but missed the rhythm of drums now so dominant and familiar in English speaking services of Cameroon.

We took our leave from our great friend with many thank you's and promises, finally heading home to Banso. Did we have stories to tell, suddenly realising, we had not seen a single white face all weekend!

Much later I learned how Christianity had come to the Bamoum, how King Njoya had welcomed the German missionaries, how he had torn down the mosque, embraced Christian teaching and encouraged his family to follow the New Way. Then the missionaries had committed a critical error. They asked the King to dismiss all but one of his wives and renounce polygamy. This made the brilliant man very angry indeed. The missionaries had to flee. The King's household became officially Muslim. A number of wives remained Christians and hosted very occasional secret visits by Christian clergy from coastal areas of Cameroon.

Today there is a vibrant growing Christian community in Foumban, as we experienced on our short visit, but the Muslim "Feast of the lamb" and the "End of Rhamadan" is celebrated in front of King Njoya's palace. Tens of thousands bow to Mecca, an awesome sight that fills me with strange melancholy.

There is an interesting postscript to our Foumban visit.

The long-standing feud between the two neighbouring tribes finally came to a formal end with the visit of Njimole Saidu to the Banso Fon on the third of February 1976. The Sultan surprised me with a request for a personal tour of the hospital, which ended in the private ward where my dear wife had just delivered our fifth son on that very day. The Sultan insisted on visiting her and giving our son yet another name, Russel David Keafon Saidu ("Prince") Lemke.

Apparently God's special blessing rested on this day, for against all odds we had a heavy downpour in the middle of the five-month long dry season which is a most unusual occurrence at Banso. The locals always interpret dry season rain as a special blessing. No doubt about the blessing, but was it upon the reconciliation between two tribes, or the birth of our son?

*   *   *

I was removing a small rubbery nodule from the forehead of a 7 year old Fulani-boy. It contained the usual threadlike filaria worms that are the cause of the dreaded "river blindness". The tall, slender father stood beside the "kitchen table" which served as our O.R. gurney in this remote clinic. He was firmly holding the child, though it really was unnecessary, as the boy did not flinch, exhibiting the typical stoicism of the tribe. I was engrossed in my work when, suddenly, my patient was gone. The father had fainted, falling backwards against a clattering patient screen and yanking my little patient into an upright position. I don't know who surprised whom the most among us three.

The Fulani or Fulbe are a tribe with easily distinguishable features. Their tall slender bodies and narrow faces with thin lips and aquiline noses are easily recognisable as different from the other 90% of the population in the Northwest Province. These cattle herdsmen were originally nomadic and exclusively Muslim.

Historians date their arrival in the form of slave raiding parties in the early nineteenth century. There is practically no intermarriage with other tribes as Fulanis consider themselves superior "white people". Their skin colour is a bit lighter on average, but some almost black Fulanis can also be seen.

As a tribe they have several peculiar characteristics in their attitude to illness, but they are not spared most of the afflictions of other Cameroonians, from malaria to AIDS. They often suffered most severely from onchocerciasis, a filaria-worm infestation that could lead to grotesque thickening of the skin resembling elephant hide, and infestation of the eyes leading to "river blindness". (Dr. Duke, a British researcher who lived and worked in Cameroon's rain forest for more than 20 years described 10 distinct pathological lesions of the human eye in his excellent publications). In recent years a generous offer by the pharmaceutical company Merck has provided world-wide free treatment for the 40 million patients with onchocerciasis which could eradicate the disease within a few years. 5.)

Fulanis bear their pain and sickness with stoicism and accept death with typically Muslim fatalism. Their cyclical attendance at the hospital seemed to be influenced more by their cattle's needs and their religious festivals than by the severity of their illness. They certainly suffered from high perinatal mortality, as most of the wives still delivered their babies at home. Schooling has gained some ground among male children, but I have met only a couple of girls who finished secondary school.

Fulani girls usually marry shortly after puberty, usually in clan-arranged polygamous unions, which rarely remain stable for life. "I divorce you" repeated three times by an angry husband is sufficient grounds for dissolving a marriage, whereas an unhappy wife can only "run away" to a distant compound in order to escape ill treatment in a marriage.

Many Fulani *guynacos* (cowboys) have to remain single because they are poor. The typical pay for a year's work as a herdsman is one young calf, whereas the dowry for a good wife may be four adult cows. It was a matter of some pride to be referred to as "*an eight cow woman*", though my wife definitely preferred other terms of endearment in my introductions of her.

The wealthy owner of many cows will try to follow an old Muslim tradition that proposes four wives as the ideal number. That does not leave enough females to go around, according to my estimates.

Life in a Fulani compound is simple and regulated. Men are busy with cattle or with business, usually travelling by horse. There are drawn-out meetings and celebrations of colourful religious festivals. Women do marketing, prepare food, tend the children and may milk a few cows. Very rarely have I seen girls or women riding horses. They walk long distances from their hilltop compounds to the markets where they do their weekly shopping for staple foods. A few Fulani families now try to grow crops near their neat compounds, but they are often frustrated in these attempts by voracious destructive cattle in the dry season. The husband inhabits the largest and most elaborate house in the compound. Each wife has her own, usually circular sleeping hut, which is always swept and tidy. Her wealth is prominently displayed in the form of many colorful enamel dishes resting on clay shelves. The thick, low mud walls may be decorated with white, black and red clay plaster in geometric designs, and the thick conical grass roof keeps the hut warm at night and cool during the day.

There are now a handful of Christian converts among the Fulani tribe. They face severe hardship, often being disowned of all possessions upon conversion. They will be shunned by family and sometimes even killed by fanatical relatives. Most Fulanis adhere to the five pillars of the Muslim faith: Recitation of the creed, prayer five times a day, giving alms to the poor, the hadj to Mecca, and fasting during daylight hours in the month of Rhamadan. Only the more devout follow the Koran very strictly in the area of alcohol use and sexual continence. Fulanis near our hospitals have not held onto their old native remedies for illness as closely as have other tribes. They make up roughly 5 percent of our hospital population.

A young Fulani brought his wife for delivery in the days when few Fulani women even considered a hospital delivery. She had a serious hemorrhage and needed a transfusion. Expecting the usual response when we asked the Fulani husband to bring relatives for donation of blood, I nearly fell off my chair when he stuck out his arm and said: "Here, take my blood."

Fulanis were particularly hesitant when it came to blood donation. Many Fulani men seemed to rate their cattle higher than their wives. Had this particular couple, against all odds, experienced something that the Bible calls a mystery? Had they experienced that "One-ness" of their very being that God built into that very first human love-relationship. A One-ness that He grants mysteriously even to people who instinctively follow his plan though they may still be in a state of rebellion or ignorance of Him. Then why was I surprised to find this thing we Westerners call 'Love' among an unsophisticated couple?

Several Fulani men considered me their friend. A few invited themselves into our home for a meal or a bed, and one even offered us a son to raise in western ways. One lady I had cured of particularly stubborn tuberculosis honored our family with periodic gifts of a grass container filled with butter.

This tribe may have seemed aloof, remote and stoic, but they certainly added another captivating dimension to the richly diverse cultural mosaic of Cameroon.

We do not claim to be more than superficially acquainted with Fulani culture, however.

A British anthropologist lady married a wealthy Fulani from the Bamenda area. She became his fifth wife. The husband developed acute appendicitis leading to rupture while he was travelling in Nigeria. He was treated conservatively with a lifesaving drainage procedure in a remote area near the Cameroon border. Several months later he decided to have the definitive operation to remove his diseased appendix at another hospital. Unfortunately he died from complications, and his widow returned to England. Her cultural insights would be considered invaluable.

*   *   *

Most of my cultural knowledge was gained from admiring or disparaging remarks of my uninhibited African co-workers while on long clinic trips, and from dinner conversations with close friends like "Tarzan".

His family name was Ngoran and his father was Shu-Fai Nzengwef, one of the seven kingmakers of the Nso tribe. The Dutch Catholic Priest gave him the name "Henry" at his infant baptism in the large Kumbo Cathedral where his mother was a member. Both Henry and his father functioned as members of the "Ngiri" secret society who advised, monitored and even censured the Fon (chief) in all his dealings with the Nso people.

Tarzan had had a miserable childhood by my standards. When he was only six years old his father had offered him to the Fon to learn the role of a "*nchindah*"(servant in residence) where he would remain until age seventeen. Tarzan's old polygamous father was but a remote figure in the young boy's life. But worse by far, he was not allowed to ever lay eyes on his mother again until the end of his service at the chief's palace. Tarzan had to learn all about the numerous traditional customs regarding ancestor worship, sacrifices, taboos and die-cry festivals. He knew the history of his people, the roles of all the members of the large palace family and the spiritual significance behind many obscure symbolic actions that continued to mystify me. I never asked him outright, but I strongly suspect that he had functioned as a masked "*juju*" on many occasions. Jujus could be encountered on the roads of our town on a regular basis when they were running their traditional errands to ancient sacrificial sites. Their hooded "heralds" would warn the populace of the juju's approach with characteristic melodious chants and shouts. Women and girls had to hide, for a single glance at the powerful "Kibarangko" juju could effect a miscarriage or worse. Men would have to kneel or bow low, or else sustain a vicious blow from a thrown wooden club or spear. These messengers of the Fon have a sinister role in ancestral rites, law enforcement and mock terrorisation of the population. I suspect they also served as executioners in the days before the Colonial era. On my introductory visit to the old chief of a powerful mountain tribe I was shown a 500 meter high cliff which served as a "mountain of truth" for anyone suspected of adultery with a chief's wife. The accused man would be thrown over the cliff (by masked jujus?) and was proven innocent if he survived the fall. I was quickly convinced that few would have qualified for innocence when I cautiously peered into the abyss.

Tarzan knew the ways of his people well, but he never learned much about establishing and leading a family of his own. He had but few models to imitate, and his few attempts at conjugal happiness failed miserably. Was that why he enjoyed the few moments of family life he observed in our home, and why he often dropped in for a family meal with important little bits of news and rumors?

For me, Tarzan was more than the wiry little left-wing forward on our soccer team. He became my friend and cultural confidant.

Great secrecy always surrounded the death of a Fon, since the first Nso male to sit on the throne after the chief's death would automatically become the new Fon. The seven wise elders of the tribe were not themselves eligible for Fon-ship, but were secretly summoned to the palace the moment the old Fon died, while a specific old woman called "Yah"(titular mother of the Fon) physically occupied the throne during their deliberations. The Shu-fais' selection of the new Fon was made from among a few eligible families. It was based upon the candidate's perceived wisdom in judging clan disputes, strict adherence to ceremonial tribal customs, and the ability to add many children to the Fon's household. The Fon was therefore the supreme Judge, High Priest and "Father" of the tribe. The new Fon was physically forced to assume his role after being apprehended by a delegation of nchindah's who would fetch the candidate under cover of darkness and utmost secrecy before any commoner could possibly be aware of the old Fon's death. Refusal of the honor to become "Fon of Nso" was not an option. Suicide would be the only way out if the Fon failed in one of his three major roles.

As personal physician to several Fons, it was important for me to behave gracefully and appropriately in culturally sensitive consultations. Tarzan was indispensable to me in this regard. He was my main source for reliable and accurate information about the intricacies and nuances of Nso culture, dedicated as he was to the traditional values upheld by the chief and his advisors. A real "nchindah".

9 to 5 in the Armpit of Africa

It would take a lifetime to discern the subtle, yet important cultural differences among the tribes who regularly visited our hospitals. "Trial marriage" was unique to one tribe, maternal lineage to another. A very high dowry was expected among the Nsungli, while the neighbouring Nso people did not pay a dowry at all, the bridegroom's only obligation was to build a small hut for his mother-in-law. Among the Yamba it was legitimate to marry a half-sister, as long as certain rules were followed, including the placing of an up-side-down cooking pot on top of the conical grass roof under which the newly married couple resided. (Was it the fear of the tribe's extinction that led to the weakening of the taboo against incest?)

Certain other customs, such as polygamy, and elaborate death celebrations were universal. The traditional approach to medicine and healing seemed also quite similar for most of the tribal groupings in the Northwest Province.

Historically, the extended family of a clan lives in a compound of 20 to 200 members with a senior male given the job and a title such as Quarterhead or Shey, Fai or Shu-fai, in order of increasing rank.

It was the senior male of a compound who was ultimately responsible for everyone's health and well being. He would use the best herbal medicine known to him, seek help from appropriate native specialists for more stubborn afflictions and determine when sufficient effort had been expended and treatment had to cease, so that nature would take its course.

A very common explanation for a delay in seeking medical help for a sick infant was, "the father was not at home". Nothing could be done without his sanction!

The traditional "specialists" were fracture experts, male or female birth attendants, mental health practitioners and *ngambe man*, who could determine by spider divination or witchcraft the cause and person responsible for an illness or calamity. There were also experts in the preparation of various "medicines", herbal poisons really, that can be smuggled into an enemy's food or drink to test his claimed innocence. Our cook assured me that those medicines would surely never work on me. I had nothing to fear, as my own medicine was demonstrably stronger. I thanked him for that assurance, hoping that my reputation would dissuade anyone from testing my cook's theory.

There were a good number of shrewd pop psychologists among the native healers and it cannot be denied that they had a certain amount of success, particularly in the treatment of mental illness. There is no doubt, that power corrupted a number of them (as it does in the Western World). Even "Tadom" the great Nso healer who lived about 100 years ago would occasionally use his superior knowledge to harm rather than heal.

I had great difficulty discerning who among the traditional healers was actually adhering to a code of ethics I could relate to. Some hung out elaborate "shingles" advertising all manner of skills and cures, from treatment for "veneral" disease, rheumatism and epilepsy to "Vaginal douches for infertility." Others used herbs and fetishes to consolidate their power and fame. Two of them occasionally accompanied certain patients into my consultation room when they considered my treatment superior to theirs. But they were the exception. Since I only saw the end results of the native healer's work I can easily criticise their practise, just as they undoubtedly inherited my treatment failures. There are some modern academics who hold rather lofty opinions of traditional medicine, but what I saw of native treatment usually did far more harm than good, ripped people off and delayed prompt, appropriate treatment for serious illness until it was too late. These unfortunate patients would then arrive at the hospital in extremis and usually die within hours or minutes, in which case I did not usually blame myself much. But it nevertheless upset me enough to lecture the accompanying relatives upon arrival. Unfortunately they were probably the least to blame, as they had just won the argument within the family that *white-man medicine* was superior and ought to be given a try.

The payment for the native doctor's ministrations was usually couched in the form of animal sacrifices, with the meat ending up in the healer's pot. (Nothing ethically wrong with that!)

For any particularly vexing dilemma a client would have to bring large amounts of cash or goods to solve the problem. Even rather difficult ingredients, such as body parts of man or ape were sometimes needed. It was rumoured that certain mentally ill village denizens had disappeared inexplicably, or that their remains were found without the head when such "strong medicine" was required.

This pattern of dealing with illness has not changed all that much over the last thirty years in spite of considerable efforts on several fronts, including mine.

Sometimes I have been tempted to muse. Had I arrived at Nso before modern medicine was introduced by others before me, I might have tried a different approach: working with and through the native healers; involving them in the distribution of western medicine, rather than competing with them and destroying their livelihood and prestige. But this argument is highly speculative and futile, now that the pattern has been set. Besides, this speculation violates late Dr. Paul Gebauer's dictum: "do not criticise the work of those before you, there will be ample opportunity to make your own mistakes". He was right.

A well-muscled man presented in severe pain. He was unable to void and his bladder was highly distended. While preparing for a quick catheterisation of his bladder I noticed his flailing thigh going into repeated painful spasms. The broken leg was shortened by several centimeters from a fracture of his thighbone. I offered to put him into traction and relieve his pain. "No, I am going to the native doctor with the broken bone, just fix the other problem", was his reply. I was annoyed and refused to treat the minor problem while leaving the challenging one to the competition. He left with both problems. I had the uncomfortable feeling that I had failed badly. Hippocrates wouldn't have been impressed.

The traditional fracture specialist at Nso had such fame that we hardly saw any fractures, dislocations or sprains in my first few years at BBH. Our own casts where somewhat superior to the splints that he fashioned out of animal bones and twigs, but patients were very impatient with our lengthy immobilisation. I was told that the native healer broke a chicken's leg when someone consulted him with a fresh fracture. The patient was expected to use his broken limb as soon as the chicken began to walk again. That period of immobilisation was grossly incongruent with my "Adam's Book of Fractures". I had no choice, but to shorten the suggested times by half. And still the patients preferred their countryman's treatment. It took an orthopedic specialist and expert in appropriate therapy to finally bring the population around.

Dr. Coleman's weight-bearing cast-braces gained much better acceptance than our conventional traction and cast applications in the 70s, as his treatment allowed almost immediate mobilisation. It also helped that the native expert had no competent successor at the time of his death.

A group of mountain villagers arrived at the BBH maternity with a sorry load. They had carried a pregnant young woman for eight hours in a lawn-chair like contraption, after she had spent five days with the native doctor, unable to deliver.

The uterus rarely ruptures with a first pregnancy, although I was told about powerful native medicines that can cause tetanic contractions that will either deliver the baby or rupture the uterus. This was not the first botched delivery attempt from that mountain tribe and I was determined to do something about it this time. But first we had to help the girl in her distress. Intravenous fluids and antibiotics got her out of shock. The destructive delivery of the long-dead baby resulted in such a horrendous smell, that doors and windows in the maternity ward had to be opened for five hours, with only minimal improvement. Both bladder and rectum had broken down because of the unrelenting pressure of the baby's head on the tissues. Without successful surgery she was condemned to remain a social cripple to the end of her days, with a constant trickle of urine marking her for instant recognition wherever she went. Surgeries to repair these fistulas were without question my most difficult surgical challenges in Africa. This patient underwent no less than eleven attempts at repair before she left the hospital with a tiny defect that closed spontaneously—denying me the satisfaction of finally having cured her. I have met the short lady from the mountain tribe on several occasions since. She informed me that she now works as a prostitute in the market. This is perfectly understandable in the local culture: A "trial" at motherhood before marriage had failed. The "garden" was useless. It was never going to bear fruit. There were no other options for this woman to make a living. I somehow felt trapped with her in this cultural conundrum, but I still had something to settle. On my next visit to our clinic in her home village I asked to be led to the native birth attendant's home. I found him in his smoky grass-covered bamboo hut. He was a tall lean bearded man in his sixties. We had to communicate through an interpreter. I tried to get into his mind by asking a few questions about his practise of obstetrics, but he remained suspicious and monosyllabic. I could see his heart pounding under his torn shirt. But I could not get any kind of admission of a problem with his unfortunate patient. He denied having unloaded her at our nearby clinic at the last moment and feigned ignorance of any complications whatsoever. I then dropped all pretence and threatened him with police action, which both of us knew was unlikely. But I left him with the distinct impression that I would definitely be on the lookout, and take any opportunity he gave me to report him to the authorities, should I hear of any more attempts of his to help women in need of delivery.

My effort actually proved to be entirely superfluous, as the council of elders in the area soon passed a resolution. Any woman not delivering in a modern maternity would be faced with a fine, which would be equal to our modest delivery fee of three dollars. ($3.50 for boys, as it included circumcision.)

We did in fact see a complete reversal of practise in maternal-and childcare in this area. It changed from 40% of women delivering in maternities and hospitals to near 100% over the span of a few short years.

The most common form of acquired heart disease among the Young in Cameroon is rheumatic valve disease. It is rarely seen and recognised in the acute stage, but the devastation of ruined valves and ensuing heart failure is all too common. There is no heart surgery available in the country, if one discounts the visits by a French cardiac surgery team to the Capital that may occur for a short two or three weeks a year. The team may operate on a few fortunate children, but I have met only one such patient after successful surgery, though I have referred a number of them for the lifesaving procedure of open-heart valve replacement.

Memuna was a beautiful 7-year-old Fulani girl with large eyes and long braids. She was a very quiet, sad little girl. Her chest heaved as it was pounded by every beat of her powerful heart muscle. But it was a largely futile work, for the valve in her aorta failed to prevent the large amount of blood just ejected from her heart from rushing back across its ruined valve leaflets. So there was little energy left for walking and tending the calves and running with the other children in play. Her slender long fingers could be busy with weaving and seed sorting, but she wanted to run outside her hut in the short kukuya grass of her mountaintop compound.

I explained the need for surgery to the father and wrote a letter of referral to the cardiologist in Yaounde. The family promised to *find money* and make the 3-day journey by bush taxi.

Eight years went by. I worked in a far away modern emergency department and forgot about Memuna. Then I returned to the remote village near the Nigerian border, and that's where I recognised my handwriting on Memuna's consultation card. Yes it was the same patient. She was now a tall beautiful young maiden. But her face was marked by impending doom. What had happened? The father told me her story. The clan had been shown my referral letter and had been told of the need to travel to the Capital. They had decided against it. Instead they would take Memuna to a famous native doctor who lived in Tibati, a two-day journey away. There she had stayed for several years. The father had paid for the difficult treatment until all his many cows were gone. There was "not even a fowl left in the compound". The family had returned quite recently. I was struck by their sadness and commiserated with them. I examined Memuna's chest and heart, there was little else I could do. She was in end-stage cardiac failure. No one would operate on her at this late stage.

I mumbled something about an emergency evacuation by helicopter, but in my heart I knew it was all so futile. It did not help my own sadness that I had had little hope of getting Memuna to the surgery eight years earlier, nor could I even muster much anger towards the "native expert". It was one of the saddest moments of my life to see such a beautiful young body lie in the arms of her mother awaiting certain death. It claimed her two days later.

Just when I thought I had seen it all, native doctors would come up with another surprise. It was in 1998 that I saw my first patient whose treatment for a sore throat had been a uvulectomy. The patient was unable to eat or drink for several days following the barbaric act. He regurgitated liquid through his nose every time he tried to quench his great thirst, and his throat was a mess. The uvula is a highly sensitive and intricate part of our swallowing reflex. It takes weeks to retrain a patient to swallow when surgery has been necessary in that area of the throat. Not to speak of the pain and infection that the crude amputation without anesthesia produced in these victims of "native medicine". My patient improved with intravenous and antibiotic therapy. His swallowing problems were persistent but manageable at the time of his discharge from hospital. Unfortunately this "operation" seemed to gain popularity, and I saw several of these patients without being able to mobilise any action against the perpetrators.

In all of the above cases one could, I suppose, argue in favor of traditional medicine, especially since modern medicine could also have had an unfavourable outcome, and practitioners of these ancient skills may have believed in the validity of their methods. The following cases, however, reveal a rather different motivation for some of the practise of traditional medicine.

A foreign commercial enterprise had been allowed to continue operating after Independence from British Colonial Rule. It employed about a thousand Cameroonian natives in a tea plantation that needed our medical care for their workers and families. The manager and engineer were British citizens.

A new maternity centre needed to be built, as many of the workers could now afford more than one wife to work the family farms, and the population grew rapidly.

The time came for the grand opening of the facility. Employees made the strong suggestion that native medicine needed to be buried ceremoniously at the corners of the maternity to ward off evil influence. "Rubbish" was the manager's curt reply to the request. And there the matter rested.

The first 50 deliveries went well. Then a set of twins was born and mysteriously died within hours. Another set of twins showed signs of acute distress shortly after birth. The concerned midwife requested transfer to our hospital an hour away. One baby died en route, the second showed signs of atropine-like poisoning; widely dilated pupils, a racing heart, dry red skin and mucous membranes. The baby died shortly after my examination. When a third set of twins was about to be born at the Tea Estate maternity and the mother heard the midwife's diagnosis of twins, she became hysterical and demanded immediate transfer to the hospital. She delivered living twins who thrived. I tried to involve the police in an investigation of these deaths but met a stone wall of disinterest and ill-disguised fear.

In fact I could not get anyone very interested or even upset that four babies were killed just to prove the power of native medicine. To me, this was naked evil, straight from hell.

A prominent religious leader arrived with clinical jaundice. He claimed to have been poisoned by his houseboy. I stood by impotently as this man developed successive liver failure, kidney failure, bone marrow failure and heart failure as he succumbed over the next few days. Perhaps an internal medicine specialist with a modern hospital laboratory could have made a diagnosis and maybe even attempted treatment. I was impressed with the power of native poison.

There is yet another set of circumstances where "native medicine" is subservient to human greed and manipulation:

I attended one of many football games at the divisional stadium together with a crowd of one or two thousand happy spectators. Everything went well until half time, when a fan from the visiting team was seen to be digging behind one of the goal posts. He was in the process of transferring "native medicine" from one goal to the other, to ensure his team's victory, because of the customary "change of ends" at half time. The spectators, including the forces of law and order, turned into a furious mob. They ran across the field from all sides, converging on the culprit with a howl of anger. I am not even sure if the man escaped with his life; and if he was arrested, what the official charges might have been.

Another time there was a commotion when a first division goalkeeper accepted "medicine" from a fellow player at half time. The angry crowd could hardly be restrained as he surreptitiously hid the powerful fetish under his cap. It was difficult to see the outcome of this episode from the sidelines, as players and officials gathered quickly, hotly arguing and gesticulating. The palaver was settled after many minutes of "extra half time", but I noted that the goalkeeper had to perform his duties without his cap.

So patients continue to arrive at BBH and MBH with the evidence of native treatment on their ailing bodies: protective amulets around the neck of babies, woven grass bracelets on their wrists, multiple superficial razor blade cuts over swellings and sites of pain, and fertility belts of various nuts and beads about the waists of women.

*   *   *

"Couching for cataract" is a skill that has been widely practised for several thousand years and has also been handed down through the centuries to the Hausa people on the West Coast of Africa. In Cameroon the price for the procedure was one adult goat. The Hausa man skilled in the craft would come into a village and set up shop. He would invite all the blind people to gather on a certain day when he would select suitable candidates: people past middle age with pure white pupils indicating "ripe" cataracts. If he were really skilled he would cover one eye with his hand and observe the pupil upon removal of his hand. If the enlarged pupil would contract briskly when exposed to the sudden change in light, the patient was a good candidate to benefit from the couching.

On the selected morning the operator's assistant would line up the blind patients, give each one detailed instruction and collect the goats. The old Hausa would place the blunted end of a small wooden peg near the limbus of the blind eye (where the clear cornea meets the white sclera) and strike a very judicious blow to the end of the peg with a tiny brass hammer-like instrument. Just enough to dislodge the lens, but not enough to rupture it. Should the attempt succeed, the lens would now float free in the posterior chamber of the eye and give rise to immediate, though blurred, vision. I have had occasion to meet a few of these patients, some only needed a pair of +10 lenses to bring things into focus, while several others were not so lucky. Their lenses had ruptured during the couching procedure and that had initiated an extremely painful inflammation of the eye that responded poorly to my late treatment and inevitably led to permanent blindness.

When I started doing cataract surgery I was sure to charge exactly the price of a good-sized goat.

I found it remarkable that I met no colour-blind men and very few myopic people in our area of Cameroon. Presbyopia, however, and the need for reading glasses in middle age, seemed to afflict patients five years earlier, on average, than in Canada.

The use of glasses of any kind is often more a status symbol than serving any useful function. Many educated young people came asking for sunglasses or blank lenses. Photochromic lenses are the newest rage, but I really have no sympathy for people so vain as to endure the nuisance of spectacles for any reason, especially if ill fitting and useless to boot.

There are thousands of people with perfect vision and many with remarkable night vision. Here is yet another area of interest for the budding medical researcher.

I do not remember seeing any blind patients during my first year in Cameroon. Perhaps I had a blind spot for them? Later I did see a few patients with curable cataracts that seemed to beg for extraction, but there was no chance for referral. I knew of only one ophthalmologist in a country of 7 million people, and he worked in Douala, 500 difficult kilometers away. That eliminated referral as an option for practically all of my eye patients.

I also knew that the basic cataract extraction in people over the age of fifty was not a technically difficult surgery, just very different from general surgery. Of course, one would have to take care of a few details such as adequate training, suitable instruments, equipment, medications and local anaesthesia.

During my furlough year in 1971 I met Dr. Hugh Maclure who had done such work in Sierra Leone. He encouraged me in my plans. The ophthalmology department of my training hospital in Edmonton granted me a three-month training period. The seven eye surgeons allowed me to see all their patients pre and post-operatively, and to watch all of their surgeries. I observed 7 slightly different techniques, learned a lot about general principles, and saw nearly all the complications that could occur. I tried to understand the surgeons' hesitancy to let me operate on their patients, as I did not fit any of their categories for training. ("It takes four years to train an ophthalmologist!"). I was, however, able to scrounge up a few basic instruments and supplies to start on this new and exciting endeavour of eye surgery at BBH. I must admit that my hands were shaking a bit more than I had hoped. So I stopped drinking coffee and it seemed to help.

By restricting myself to certain eminently suitable patients my initial success-rate was comparable to North-American standards and this attracted many patients. Had my first and second patient been seen in reverse order, however, I think I would have stopped doing cataract surgery.

The first surgery went smoothly. I got a good local anesthetic block and the patient held perfectly still throughout the 40 minute procedure. The lighting and instruments worked well. I remembered all the many steps and precautions, though I had no one at my elbow to coach me. There was no bleeding, no undue pressure on the open eye. The critical lens extraction was exciting, but easier than anticipated, and the suturing of the cornea gave me a watertight anterior chamber. Of course I perspired profusely from the intense concentration, but I was elated and deeply satisfied. This blind man was going to see again.

The second patient was sent to me from Nigeria. He was a gardener, but no longer able to do his work for a missionary employer. Because he was in his twenties, the suspensory ligaments of the lens were tough, and I struggled with the small suction cup when trying to extract the opaque lens. The end result was acceptable, but I knew that I had to have the expensive enzyme to dissolve the suspensory fibres of the lens for any young patient in future.

At any rate, I continued to gain more and more confidence and satisfaction from the eye work. Was it because these patients had a non-lethal affliction, or because they paid me so richly with their smiles every time I first slipped the correct test lenses into the frame, and they could SEE? Curiously, every single one of the newly bespectacled patients bumped into the doorframe with their shoulders as they left the consultation room. They had not yet learned to allow for the considerable distortion of vision that was caused by their thick cataract glasses.

Soon one of my classmates who practised ophthalmology in Edmonton followed my invitation and became the first in a long line of Volunteer-specialists of different kinds, who, over the years, have given valuable time, advice, donation of instruments, and a ton of goodwill to our cause.

Dr.Gary T. Leitch brought his young wife and child, a few medications and a number of used cataract glasses with him. Among them were the five spectacles of the recently deceased Dr. Marshall, Edmonton's pioneer ophthalmologist. Gary operated on 40 patients while I observed. He watched me operating and gave suggestions and encouragement. He also had a whale of a time on our bad roads with my VW Kuebelwagen.

Dr. Marshall's glasses soon adorned 5 different patient's faces. One of them was a 20-year-old village woman who had gone blind with cataracts quite recently and would have faced lifelong misery without the surgery. Gary's small family enjoyed the social and medical challenges so much, that they repeated their cross-cultural service elsewhere in later years.

Gradually the curable blind began to come out of the woodwork. People who had lived within shouting distance of the hospital finally found the courage and the money to come for eye surgery.

We kept a stock of used spectacles that corrected the optical errors sufficiently for many illiterate old men and women to become independent again. One such old man kept coming to my house year after year to present me with a large rooster. And every year I found it necessary to clean his incredibly dirty glasses and repeat the cleaning instructions. Another brought 40 eggs, most of them of the non-floating i.e. still edible, type.

One day a man came with his six-year-old daughter. I had operated on her congenital cataracts shortly after birth. That was the last I had seen of her. But now she was ready for school and could I please help her to see better? I was able to find a suitable small frame with +13 lenses in my big box of old spectacles. The little girl beamed with the discovery of suddenly focused vision. And that is the very last time I saw her. I gather that some people do not have very high expectations of ongoing care by a physician.

A high-school student began to gradually lose his sight. He was one of my first glaucoma patients. I had only seen the Scheie iridectomy once but I knew that lifelong medication was not the answer for this young man. His pressure stabilised with my successful operations. Follow-up visits ceased when I left Cameroon. But upon my return in '86 he came to see me again. He was now a married high-school teacher, needed no glasses and still had adequate vision. His pressures were perfect. He just came to express his gratitude. He was one of the few fortunates while thousands of fellow countrymen were going blind from a variety of causes, most of them preventable.

Dr. Helen Marie Schmidt, general surgeon, introduced the Africa-pioneered trabeculectomy to BBH as a more suitable treatment for the many glaucoma patients who neglected to take their eye-drops for one reason or another. In time Christian Blind Mission (CBM) sent Dr.

Taylor from East Africa to our hospital to assess our need for better instruments and equipment and so began a wonderful liaison with a service mission that does admirable work for the disabled all over the world.

CBM upgraded our equipment, supplied us with eye sutures and medications, and helped us begin a school for blind children. They also arranged for training of personnel and the building of suitable facilities. Today Mbingo Baptist Hospital has joined BBH in providing the service of an eye department that is attracting patients from far and wide, continuously improving its services, and bringing a smile to many a patient with the new-found freedom of sight. The most recent advance at MBH includes cataract surgery with intra-ocular lens implantation under microscopy.

Friday morning was reserved for eye cases at the BBH operating room. Our staff learned the routine so well, that on one morning in 1995 I was able to complete 8 cataract extractions before the 10 o'clock coffee break.

Not every day went that well. On another Friday morning I recorded 2 patients with vitreous loss, one failure of an extracapsular extraction attempt in a child and an intra-ocular hemorrhage among 9 scheduled patients. On top of that the electricity failed at a crucial moment, which it so often does, interrupting the light from my 150-watt OR lamp, so that I had to finish suturing the cornea in the unsteady beam of a hand-held flashlight.

There was great excitement on men's ward one Friday. An old man had become confused shortly after an injection of Demerol was given for postoperative pain. He tore the bandage from his eye and escaped towards the hill behind the hospital grounds with nurses in hot pursuit. Only with great difficulty could he be coaxed out of an avocado tree in the nurse's garden where he had fled from his imagined enemies. Fortunately, his operated eye did not suffer any damage.

Not every patient was fully aware of the gravity or urgency of our ministrations. An emergency glaucoma patient could not be found in the ward at the time of his scheduled operation. "He has gone to market", was the message relayed to us, while we waited impatiently in the OR.

Another time an elderly cataract patient struggled to get off the O.R table in the middle of the procedure, without giving us any warning. He needed to go to the bathroom now, and it was urgent. No matter that his face was draped, his eyeball open and his surgeon having a major anxiety attack. Only with the greatest effort were we able to calm him down for a few minutes to complete at least the most essential steps of closing the anterior chamber of the eye, before letting nature take its course. These kinds of situations could be tricky, especially when no one in the O.R. happened to speak the patient's language, which did occur occasionally.

"Doctor, it have finish"! I heard those dreaded words once again one fine eye surgery day when I asked for the routine 8-0 suture for the cornea, halfway through an operation. A few anxious moments later we were able to finish the surgery using some samples of 10-0, the smallest diameter suture in existence and much finer than human hair. It was not really visible to the naked eye, and only barely discernible with the magnifying loupe clamped to my glasses. Adaptability is both a learned skill and a virtue.

Even though I had no part in the planning, creation or operation of the Banso School for the Blind, I thoroughly enjoyed the 30some children attending this boarding school built during my absence. The dormitories adjoined the local primary school. The children were fully integrated into the public school system, many graduating with secondary school certificates, but especially enjoying the care and attention of trained, devoted staff who knew how to guide these severely handicapped children into a fuller life. I liked visiting the dormitories in my spare moments to enjoy the children's singing and playing. We had some great discussions, and every visit gave me a real lift. Here is where

I met four boys from one family, all born with undeveloped eyes. I suspect an X-linked recessive gene because their two sisters had normal vision. The oldest two boys, Richard and Oliver, were twins. They had been at the school for several years. Oliver enjoyed singing and playing the Autoharp. It was particularly moving to hear him sing: "I have seen the light, the light of God, shine in my heart." At the time of his baptism at age fifteen he gave an unusual testimony. He thanked God for having been born blind, for otherwise he would not have been given a chance to attend such a fine place as the School for the Blind. Samuel, the younger brother, had an excellent singing voice as well, and imitated his brother's songs to the t. Emanuel, the youngest at age six was a pitiful little bundle of misery when he arrived at the school during my time at BBH. Like his brothers he had been sitting in a corner of his mother's hut and had rarely ventured forth from there. He was considered totally useless and un-teachable. What a joy to see him flourish within his new family. He particularly enjoyed the teeter-totter I had built for the children together with old Davido, the maintenance man. The older children liked the wind blowing in their faces when they used the new swings we built, or when I gave them joy rides on my motorcycle. But none of the children liked the new merry-go-round as it left them disoriented. But it was in constant use as a handy sitting area on Sundays when the children gathered for impromptu group singing with Oliver leading on the Autoharp.

One day we discussed their confident way of walking about in the dormitory area. I asked how they would know, if there was a car or motorcycle suddenly parked in unexpected places. "Oh, that is easy", they all agreed, "you can smell them".

One of the young boys was particularly bold and a bit headstrong, for he liked to wander beyond the boundaries of the compound. That is how he fell into a newly dug 7-meter deep pit-latrine, which, thankfully, was not yet in use. He came away unscathed but wiser for his wandering.

Several of the blind high-school graduates have been able to find useful employment. One is a travelling evangelist in Esimbi, a most remote and primitive area of Cameroon, another teaches Braille at the school. Several more attend the seminary in preparation for the pastoral ministry.

*   *   *

I purchased a new Tropical Disease textbook shortly before leaving Canada for Cameroon. During the Trans-oceanic flight I read up on Hansen's disease (leprosy) since I was going to be in charge of a 350 patient leprosarium and the supervision of leprosy inspector's clinics in the Northwest Province.

I also knew that I would have to treat other diseases I had never yet seen: malaria, Wucheria bancrofti, Loa loa, onchocerciasis and the occasional case of schistosomiasis. What surprised me, however, was the fact that many of the so-called "tropical" diseases, though now found mostly in the tropics were really diseases of poverty and ignorance.

I had never seen tetanus, kwashiorkor (protein-calorie malnutrition), cancrum oris or sickle cell disease until I reached Africa, but these weren't tropical diseases at all. They are now largely confined to the tropics because the First World has not been able to share its advances in medicine very well. Nevertheless, I needed to learn all about them, especially since my family would certainly catch a few of these diseases over the next few years. Three of our sons had to be treated for onchocerciasis and all of us suffered bouts of amebiasis and other gastrointestinal afflictions. I myself tested positive for both hepatitis A and B on my final return to Canada. Some of us had serious malaria, but we all recovered without long-term ill effects, which is somewhat remarkable, since together as a family we spent over 83 man-years "in the arm-pit of Africa."

To be adequately trained for solo medical practise in remote Africa would ideally require training in a minimum of 2 or 3 specialities plus a course in tropical medicine. This training would simply take too long, and one might never get to Africa at all. It is much more reasonable to complete training in General Practise or one speciality and have on-the-job training with someone who has been on site for a number of years. The pattern of disease rarely changes much in a given area, and the best training cannot adequately prepare one for all eventualities. During my work in Africa I met graduates of medical schools from all around the globe. I was able to assess my basic training in the light of their work. I became convinced that I had been adequately prepared for my practice in Cameroon. My medical school could not be blamed for the absence of referral specialists, or for the paucity of instruments, diagnostic facilities or medical equipment. Visiting specialists can often teach valuable new procedures. Short refresher courses and surplus equipment can do a world of good where one has to start from scratch. Adaptation and innovation does not have to mean substandard care. Many procedures and even a few discoveries originated in Third World medical practise. Overall, the care we provided and the rate of cure in our patients compared reasonably well with results in the developed world. The surgical treatment of chronic glaucoma by trabeculectomy was begun in Africa and suited the African situation. Medical missionary Dr. Dennis Burkitt pioneered the diagnosis and treatment of Burkitt's lymphoma while he worked in Kenya and Tanzania.

Dr. Burkitt's findings were also confirmed in our experience. All of our patients with the peculiar tumors that bear the doctor's name had come from low-lying areas with heavy mosquito infestation. The tumors were usually of the highly disfiguring facial type, and most responded beautifully to a single anti-cancer drug. Sometimes a single injection seemed to cure these children.

One day a very concerned 16-year-old boy brought his 13-year-old sister from Mbaw plain, located only about 400 meters above sea level. She had been paralysed below the waist for several days. There were large growths in her lower abdomen that had apparently spread to her spinal canal, compressing the nerves to her legs. Without a rapid pathology report there was but slim hope to even reach a diagnosis. Besides, we had only one anti-cancer drug in stock at the time. The rapid onset and progression of the disease made me suspect Burkitt's lymphoma. We had little to lose with a trial of therapy.

I was deeply touched to see how lovingly the boy cared for his little sister, especially when our treatment began to shrink the ovarian tumors within days. His joy knew no bounds when she started to move her legs and gradually regained strength in them. He followed the nurses' instructions faithfully and did the exercises of the recovering muscles day after day until the girl took her first few wobbly steps.

Burkitt's tumor patients often responded dramatically, up to 60% could expect permanent remission. An orange sized tumor could be melted away in a mere three weeks. But this was the first patient I saw with such a dramatic recovery from paralysis and with such a beautifully devoted caregiver.

In 1967 I examined over one hundred girls on their admission to a secondary boarding school and found a total of only 5 small dental cavities in the entire group.

Only two tribes of my acquaintance had significant tooth decay: the honey eating Oku and the Fulani people. The habit of kola-nut chewing may have been a factor as it was particularly prominent among both of these groups.

Overall I was pleasantly surprised to meet thousands of people with 32 perfect teeth. With generous room in people's mouths, mal-alignment and impacted third molars were unusual. Once I even encountered an Oku patient with 34 teeth. I am sure my dentist friends have an easy explanation for that.

A marked change in eating habits was first introduced in the secondary boarding schools who began to serve heavily sweetened tea and bread made from imported wheat flour for the students' morning meals. Some "better" schools added chocolate bars to the menu. Tooth decay increased among the young.

I am reluctant to admit that I acted unethically by venturing forth into my colleagues' territory when I began to pull teeth. But West Cameroon with its 1.2 million inhabitants had only one dentist in the late sixties. Someone had to do it.

We had a fair collection of dental forceps at each hospital, which gave us an unfair advantage over the native healers. I was not breaking new ground, so to speak, nor was I planning to pursue this activity a moment longer, once qualified professionals came on the scene.

Jerry Fluth, M.D. showed me his extraction technique on a few patients and I was off in my newfound calling. My tall instructor had the advantage of a very long shinbone that served as the patient's backrest when Jerry placed his foot on the stool behind the patient. The patient's head rested comfortably on the doctor's knee. I felt disadvantaged with my average height and inadequate length of leg.

Dental anesthesia was not very difficult, especially when I used a human jawbone for an anatomy refresher lesson once in a while. One of my predecessors had obtained the specimen from a cave in the Banso area (an artifact of the Bamoum-Nso war?).

Patients with dental problems were offered a visit to the dentist in coastal Victoria, 2 days of travel away, or they could opt for our extraction. Most chose the latter, with fear of pain being the major influence in their decision. My expertise had been limited to a few extractions per week-and it was not until that first encounter at Jickijem with dozens of long-rooted Oku teeth that I learned just how much lateral stress a root will take before breaking. Once my fame spread with many painless extractions, the course was set. In eleven years I extracted teeth from over six thousand patients.

Off and on we enjoyed the generous two-week service visits of an American Presbyterian Dentist from Yaounde during the early seventies. Dr. Sandilands used an ancient dental chair and the low-speed dental drill located at BBH to help the missionaries with their dental needs and always treated a large number of Africans as well. His denture production was particularly popular. (It was rumored that several edentulous folks would share one set of dentures during a meal.)

Dr. Sandilands graciously gave me a few more hints on extraction techniques with particularly difficult problems, like impacted third molars (wisdom teeth) and broken roots.

I did not really enjoy working in people's mouths, but was empathetic with those who needed relief from horribly abscessed teeth or unbearable toothaches.

An elderly lady came with a special problem. Patients scattered from the waiting area as she approached. She did have quite an odor about her. I asked her to open her mouth and was nearly knocked over by the foulest smell I had experienced so far in my life. Quickly I adopted the mouth-breathing, decorum-saving technique to be able to examine her dentition. She had suffered a root abscess years ago, which had turned part of her mandible into an immovable sequestrum of dead bone encased in her jaw. The surgery proved not particularly difficult, and the iodoform packing quickly substituted a different smell to the relieved patient. Her gratitude was genuine. People would no longer shun her.

But I wondered, as in so many other cases, how could she have waited so long before seeking help?

With increasing numbers of dental patients we needed to offer better service. Isaac Lontum (also called Shingo), a trained nurse, assisted a number of visiting dentists during their short sojourns with us. Each of them taught Shingo a few more skills. He showed interest and aptitude for further training, and his chances for advancement in this specialised field improved with a unique and unexpected opportunity.

The Eigners, a young couple of medical/dental students from Oregon had applied to some fifty mission organisations for a chance to explore Third World practise during their elective time. Ours was the only mission willing to give them an opportunity for service. Frank was a cheerful and capable senior medical student always eager to try a new procedure or get involved in a practical joke.

Toni had only finished her first of four years in dentistry training. We had many a good laugh in future years about how a bush-doctor in Africa taught her the rudiments of dental extraction. Up to that point I had been sure that a woman would never be strong enough to pull an Oku tooth. She convinced me otherwise and for 2 or 3 months I was freed from any dental involvement.

Our investment in the Eigner couple paid rich dividends after they completed their training in the U.S. three years later. They gave a full year of volunteer service to BBH, a First, and still lingering in its overall impact on dental services offered at BBH, MBH and their affiliated health centres.

Toni spent one entire year intensely teaching Shingo all she could about her newly acquired dental skills. She had prepared well for this endeavour. Generous U.S. dental supply companies, whom she convinced of the merits of her plan, had donated brand new high-speed dental units, filling material and denture making equipment for her cause.

Today the M.D.s at our hospitals have not pulled teeth for years, if ever.

The dental department at BBH has become a recognised school for the training of dental assistants.

Drs. Charles Sijyeniyo and Liberata Uwantege applied to work with our Health Board. They had spent a year in Goma refugee camp after fleeing their homeland of Rwanda. All four of their parents had been murdered in a single night of the Rwandan massacre. Dr. Charles had studied oro-facial surgery in Moscow. He spoke Russian, French, English and two Rwandan languages, and had taught at Kigali University Dental School. He began teaching small classes of dental assistants at BBH. His wife Liberata was the first and only ophthalmology student in her final year of studies at Kigali Medical School. She took over BBH eye surgery. Rwanda's loss was Cameroon's gain.

*   *   *

The unconscious state of a loved relative is powerful motivation for a family to seek help urgently. Arguments about cause and blame are silenced by the universal fear of death and the overwhelming need to do something before it is too late. The physician must balance scientific objectivity with compassionate care in his effort to help a malfunctioning mind re-establish it's tenuous direction of a body out of control.

Three common causes of sudden "unconsciousness" were cerebral malaria, meningitis and mental stupor. The collective local expression for these calamities was: *"sick de fo head".* I have already mentioned the cruel calamity of cerebral malaria earlier.

Though I have been spared the experience of a meningitis epidemic, even isolated cases of this frightening illness induce fear in people who have been in close contact with the victim, at least in North America. None of our hospital workers in Cameroon ever took prophylactic antibiotics when treating meningitis cases. (Meningitis is not very contagious in the non-epidemic forms. Only once in my career have I seen two children from one family affected by meningo-coccemia). But meningitis always ranked among the 10 top causes of death in our hospitals, and many survivors of meningitis were left with serious damage and crippling disabilities. There are two main reasons for the high morbidity and mortality from meningitis in the developing world, aside from the fact that many patients present late with an illness where mere hours of treatment delay can make the difference between life and death. First, fever and headache are so typical of malaria, the most common illness around, and neck stiffness is not uncommon with cerebral malaria. So it is easy to miss the diagnosis of meningitis for a day or two while treating only for malaria. Second, our personnel working in remote health posts were not equipped to diagnose this illness for lack of laboratory facilities and lumbar puncture skills, at least in earlier years.

An 18-year-old Fulani girl arrived on a native stretcher with a grotesquely arched back. She was unconscious, severely dehydrated and incontinent. The flies were walking on her open eyes. She had been ill for 5 days. I could easily believe that part of the story. Though I had little hope for her life I was willing to give it a try. The needle entered her spinal canal, but I had to apply suction as the normally "spring water"-like cerebrospinal fluid had turned into thick pus. We used the then common triple antibiotic regimen of Penicillin, Streptomycin and Sulfadiazine with good effect in this quickly confirmed case of meningococcal meningitis. To my utter amazement the patient improved over the span of a few days and completely recovered her health. Only the lower third of her corneas remained permanently scarred.

I chanced upon her compound some years later while my sons and I went on a hike in the Mbinon hills, (looking for a family of baboons). The lady had married in that area and had borne children. There were no permanent sequelae to her illness, apart from her corneal scars.

Not so with our hospital laundry man who was treated promptly when he fell ill with meningococcal meningitis, but ended up *mumu* (stone deaf). In his case it may have been the use of the streptomycin that led to the complication, but we saw cases of deafness even after switching to the more modern antibiotics in later years. It was for these serious infections that we tried to reserve the very expensive new antibiotics. We could never dream of regularly stocking the cephalosporins and other modern antibiotics in the hospital pharmacy, but hoped to keep them replenished from visiting volunteer's supplies and well-meaning friends on the home front.

During one of my last tours of service I kept track of a small drug donation from a pharmaceutical company. With the use of 500 tablets of Ciprofloxacin I counted at least six lives literally saved with this relatively new drug that most of our patients simply could not afford.

One of them was the ten-year-old son of a belligerent Bikom man from the Belo valley. I ran out of ideas when my patient's fever did not respond to any of our stock antibiotics. After two days of high-dose intravenous antibiotic treatment he was clearly getting worse. It was time to try the donated Cipro tablets! The fever came down promptly, the boy began to respond and demand food. His neck stiffness was the last to improve, but he was definitely going to be well. I was not impressed with the impatient father who would not wait for the discharge day. He did not seem to be properly aware of his son's precarious state. A few days later I met the father again while I was cooling off on my motorbike along the beautiful newly paved road to Fundong. He demanded a ride to his nearby home. Too late did I recognise that he was drunk. He told me that he operated one of the many bars in the area. His son was well, thank you.

It was in the treatment of severe acute illnesses such as meningitis that we became most drastically aware of our impotence in battling disease with limited resources. When a missionary contracted meningitis and developed a brain abscess she was evacuated and treated in a tertiary care facility in North America. This option is not open to the Cameroonian native unless he is very rich or has relatives with political clout. But even then, evacuation by Air to Paris, Zurich or London will often be too late.

Cerebral malaria or meningitis could readily be confused with the equally feared sudden attack of *criss man* (mental illness). The similarity of the presenting signs is perplexing to the untrained eye.

Every society has been forced to deal with the mentally ill in its midst, and modern man has not done a very good job of it. We may have vastly more psychiatrists in North America (Cameroon has one or two), but we are mentally no healthier than West Africans.

In the absence of institutions or hospitals for the acutely and chronically deranged, practically every village may have one or two schizophrenic patients in need of care. They are readily identifiable as they often wander aimlessly, down the middle of the road, usually entirely naked, or else attired in grotesque ways. If a *criss man* was minding his own business and not stealing too much raw food off the neighbouring farms, he would be ignored by all but the children who would throw stones at the mental patient, forcing him to withdraw physically. In his mind, he had withdrawn long ago.

Curiously, a mental patient could play unique roles in the community: A *criss man* was caught cutting down a greedy man's coffee bushes, a foul deed which nevertheless met with general approval among the many people this crook had cheated in town. Perhaps the mental patient was sensing the collective anger in that village but knew he would be immune from punishment.

If, however, a psychotic episode was spectacular or violent, relatives or townspeople would take action to protect the patient or the public.

Some schizophrenic patients languish in special sections of local jails while others walk "free", restricted by permanent ankle chains. Traditionally, forceful restraint was used to keep a mentally ill person confined in a native doctor's hut for many months.

The incidence of frank psychoses is probably roughly equal among all communities around the globe, if it does in fact have a neuro-chemical cause, which I believe will be proven sooner or later. Patients with a genetic make-up for mental illness may be pushed over the edge of normalcy by experiencing severe stress, such as childbirth, severe emotional trauma or by taking "recreational drugs".

A good number of patients in acute psychosis were taken to the native doctor first, or transferred there by the relatives once we made the diagnosis in our hospital. We would try one or two anti-psychotic drugs and encourage close family involvement, as we often could not communicate with the patient in his native language. This was a distinct disadvantage for us. We never recommended native treatment, but the relatives would collectively decide to transfer the patient to the native practitioner, especially if our treatment was slow to produce results.

The bizarre behaviour of a florid psychotic seemed hilariously entertaining and occasionally frightening to the layperson, but it is not of primary concern for the therapist, generally. Someone banging his head against the wall or acting out bizarre fantasies attracts a lot of attention, but will often respond dramatically to moderate doses of anti-psychotic medications.

I have sometimes been asked about my experience with demon possession, (since I worked in the "domain of the devil, darkest Africa"?). I admit that I have never recognised such a case, be that because of a blind spot in my spiritual eyes or because I never went out of my way to specifically look for these kinds of afflictions. I have certainly seen enough evil perpetrated by men that could be classified as having a most intimate connection with the "father of lies", but I have always been hesitant to assign cause to unexplainable phenomena in the psychological realm. It was interesting to me that the natives of Cameroon consider the devil himself as definitely having white skin color. Their fiercest, most powerful jujus have whitened arms and legs.

A small tribe of about 10 000 people had the misfortune to be ruled by an intelligent but paranoid schizophrenic chief who had good insight into his illness while on medication. He functioned adequately except for the common vice of Chiefs, inordinate greed for power and wealth. When the Chief would run out of his Largactil, he could present a formidable challenge for the anxious villagers. Once he burned down the huts of his numerous wives, another time he threatened our resident midwife with a gun.

One day this chief suddenly burst into my consulting room, prostrating himself before me and "worshipping" me. My father was on a visit from Canada and became the alarmed witness to the spectacle. With appropriate medication, however, the chief was back to normal within a day or two. He then sent my father the gift of a beautifully carved wooden stool, which did not impress Dad nearly as much as me. He much rather wanted no part of this chief.

The villagers had no such choice. Tradition dictates that a chief's position can be vacated by death only. There are, no doubt, ways to help nature along, but it would be particularly difficult when dealing with an intelligent and paranoid chief. Fortunately the chief's son has since inherited the throne, and our health centre has enjoyed enormous growth and favor among the population, though not without trials. Several boundary palavers have made work so difficult for our staff that we decided to close the health centre temporarily. But we had not counted on the villagers. When the old Land Rover was loaded to the hilt with our departing staff and their belongings the road was blocked by a mass of sitting, protesting humanity. Two or three thousand chattering, gesticulating women simply would not agree to the loss of their beloved health centre. The driver resolutely rammed the transmission into reverse and found a trail over which he exited the village backwards. A very large *palaver* (meeting) soon followed to which I was invited along with 3 dozen dignitaries of traditional, civil and hospital authorities. I was easily convinced to attend, as the picturesque two-hour Honda ride was a welcome relief from my hospital duties. The chief was given the first chance to speak. His address took exactly 2 hours and 45 minutes. Fortunately, I detected some very large black clouds gathering on the horizon and was able to excuse myself at the end of the chief's speech in order to make it home before the rain.

The centre is functioning again and is as busy as ever, although the palavers will re-surface as certain as the new grass at the coming of the rains.

A young teacher's wife suffered a severe psychotic episode shortly after the birth of her child. Irrational, she fled the confines of her home and began to climb the newly erected high-tension electric pole in the centre of town. She came too close to the wires and was flung down by a terrific jolt. A telephone cable halfway down snagged her foot and there she hung, suspended between heaven and earth till they rescued her and brought her to BBH. She behaved entirely normally at this point. I could not find any serious damage of body or mind and she very meekly accepted our medication. Her minor burns healed, and she was able to take care of her baby. I wondered if she had had just the right amount of electroshock therapy in her near-death experience.

The epilogue, however, was grimmer by far. A couple of years later she presented with numerous hard lumps surrounding her trachea that were spreading into the chest. She had developed carcinoma of the thyroid gland for which we could not find the correct treatment in the country. Radioactive cobalt was unavailable. She died an agonising death, choked by the tumor. The grieving husband later married again and on my last visit was doing an excellent job, while in charge of a large primary school in a remote area of Mbaw plain.

A very tall, broadly grinning man dressed in rags was pushed into my consulting room by his relatives. He held out his problems in front of him. Both hands were black as tar with dry gangrene. The native doctor had tied his hands when the patient could not be controlled in his mental frenzy. That was customary. But, instead of using the traditional locally made rope the native healer or his helpers had used the more modern rubber straps cut from inner tubes. These straps are the universal fasteners so readily available in the market at 30 cents for a 2-m length. They had acted like a surgical tourniquet, cutting off the vital blood supply to the mental patient's hands.

I am an excitable person, which is a character trait more suitable for operatic tenors than surgeons and for performances in theatres of the non-operative kind.

I got excited. No, I could not treat this patient. I had amputated single hands and even entire arms before. But **both** of his hands? Even though I was assured by the patient and his relatives that it was OK, I could not believe what I saw and heard. How was this man going to open his zipper, drop his pants, feed himself, wash, touch, hold, caress...

I felt cornered. Still excited, I demanded that the patient be presented to some higher authority, the Senior Divisional Officer perhaps. The relatives kept coaxing me, asking for the unthinkable. Finally I settled for pictures, to prove, some time in the future, that I could not be blamed for the horrendous misdeed of robbing a man of his hands. But there was no other solution, so I amputated both of his hands.

The deed was done. He healed quickly. However, the man gave further insult to my sense of pride: the patient demanded a picture. It was to be just the two of us, with him, grinning broadly still, holding his stumps out in front of him for all to see.

*   *   *

As a medical student I experienced a variety of emotional reactions to the various disciplines of medicine during each of my first clinical rotations. I found myself swinging wildly from intense dislike of one speciality to the wish to work in another speciality exclusively. These feelings were influenced by a number of hang-ups, by difficulties encountered and overcome, by the teacher's personality and example and, to a lesser extent, by the quality of the teaching program.

I felt no attraction to obstetrics. I flunked my first clinical exam in this subject on the question: "how do you deliver a breech presentation". I do not remember how I was allowed to continue my studies. I disliked obstetrics. When I witnessed my very first birth one dark and dreary night during my second year of medicine I had to rush outside and vomit.

Things have changed, I have changed.

One physician cannot possibly be equally adept in all the specialities. But since I was so poorly motivated towards this discipline, I guess I learned the most in obstetrics, but not without real tears. In no other field have I come as close to total exhaustion, total-person challenge, and intense feelings of failure as I have in obstetrics.

To start with, as the only doctor assisted by one midwife and one ward-aid in charge of the 35-bed maternity I found myself dealing with two patients at once. In turning my back on the delivered patient, trying to resuscitate a depressed non-breathing infant, the mother starts to hemorrhage; Not a trickle, not a gush, but a torrent of that precious red stuff. Hardly have I persuaded her uterus to contract properly or have sutured her laceration when the baby starts grunting or turning blue or whatever. Arrrrgh.

Obstetrics at the BBH maternity ward was a huge challenge. The appropriate pidgin expression for the speciality is *"born palaver"*. I took over from Dr. Peter Fehr, whose training and interest lay in obstetrics and gynecology. Eleanor Weisenburger was a very wise and experienced matron who had the maternity humming. Over the years we had an average of 1400 to 1900 deliveries per annum. But with referrals from surrounding maternity centres one doctor could easily be presented with all the complications from over 3000 deliveries a year. The midwives handled all "normal" deliveries, including multiple births and breech deliveries. In Canada one would expect several obstetricians to be involved for a caseload of that magnitude.

I learned in a hurry. We tried to keep the C-section rate low. It was below 3% in the first few years and has since risen to near 15%. In earlier years one could not trust all women with previous C-sections to return for future deliveries, and that still holds true for some patients and certain areas. I heard of a physician practising in a remote corner of neighbouring Nigeria who ligated the Fallopian tubes on all his C-section patients, thus preventing any further pregnancies. He simply would not take responsibility for the entire obstetrical future of his operated patients. Such a radical stance may no longer be necessary, but I can sympathise with that physician in his quandary.

I too saw women coming at the very last moment, or with ruptured uteri and in deep shock following previous C-sections because "there was no money for the repeat surgery".

We kept the section rate low by using a variety of alternate management schemes. We often tried internal or external versions of the baby (turning a baby that is lying abnormally by inside or outside manipulation-a risky procedure hardly practised in North America any more). I learned about symphysiotomies (surgical division of the bony pelvic ring) from the "Tropical Doctor" magazine and found it a useful procedure in certain specific circumstances. Other options were vacuum extraction and forceps deliveries. Our patients did not expect or receive narcotics and our midwives were taught to assess progress of labour with as few internal examinations as possible. We did, of course, have the typical African woman coming for delivery: young, strong, muscular, intent on proving her fertility. Obesity was extremely rare. The patient walked to the delivery table when the event was imminent and walked to her maternity bed thereafter. The lone stretcher in maternity was used solely for transport of C-section patients to and from the operating room. Post-delivery patients were kept until the dried stump of the umbilical cord fell off the baby's navel in three or four days. This long a stay was clearly unnecessary, but it gave us an excellent opportunity to educate young mothers about childcare and a host of public health issues. And they learned eagerly.

The midwives delivered with bare, well-scrubbed hands up until the scare of AIDS came upon us. Gloves were expensive and hard to obtain in large quantities. The delivery room was sparsely equipped. All efforts were made to prepare the students for future service in outlying areas where they would have to make do with inferior equipment and supplies. Nitrous oxide (an excellent pain-control drug) became unobtainable. Open drop ether and Ketamine were the only two general anaesthetic agents available. A limited variety of delivery forceps and a vacuum extractor, bottled welder's oxygen and oxygen concentrators, a heat lamp, suction and a few old incubators for communal occupation (three or four babies per incubator) pretty well completed the equipment in the delivery room. Until 24 hour electricity reached us in the late seventies most deliveries were done more by feel than by sight, as the kerosene lantern often gave more smoke than light. Even minor surgical interventions had to be done without electric light.

Though the incidence of low-lying placenta (a major cause of heavy bleeding in late pregnancy or in early labor) was equal to the Western world's, other complications were not. Eclampsia was so rare as to be considered a special event, whereas multiple births and late referrals of horrendous obstructed labours were common and unfortunately still are.

With the introduction of an excellently run "high risk clinic" and a lower threshold for C-sections, infant mortality has improved over the years.

I have been asked about the need for therapeutic abortions in a setting such as ours. Abortion for any reason was against Cameroon law during Muslim President Ahidjo's reign. The law is still in effect. But I can truly remember only one case of severe cardiac failure due to rheumatic valvular disease that I saw close to delivery, when I might have considered recommending a therapeutic abortion, had I seen the patient early in her pregnancy. The patient delivered a live baby and had a sterilisation procedure thereafter. The delivery was assisted with forceps. The mother's heart failure was controlled with some difficulty. So-called medical indications for therapeutic abortion must be very rare indeed, if I saw only one in over 10 000 deliveries!

Africans have a twinning rate of about one in fifty births. At BBH it is now about one in eighteen deliveries. In 1998 I met a mother of ten children, five boys and five girls. She told me proudly that all her births had been twin deliveries! We also saw triplets being born nearly every year and recently one of our outlying maternities had a set of quadruplets, only three of whom were viable and survived.

A thoroughly competent male Nursing Aid/Midwife with a total of two years of training brought a patient from his remote health centre in Kouhouat, in the Foumban area. The woman had delivered dead premature twins and a large retro-placental clot indicating premature separation of the placenta. The nurse had treated the patient's shock with intravenous saline and two units of blood drawn on the spot from relatives. He then bundled her into a taxi and accompanied her for the two hour ride in a dusty ramshackle "clandestine". Her Hb (blood count) on arrival was 1.8 (about 15% of normal). She was bleeding uncontrollably and had to undergo immediate hysterectomy (removal of the uterus) while the third unit of fresh blood was given. While I was suturing the incision I noticed that her blood was failing to clot. I began to experience a familiar and distressing feeling of doom. This was turning into the nightmare of DIC (disseminated intra-vascular coagulation) which I was not prepared to manage with our limited facilities and medications. A fourth unit of blood was "squeezed" out of a relative who had just given the first unit hours earlier, and with earnest prayer she was given 10 000 units of our small reserve of heparin.

The family was Muslim. They followed all of our efforts with intense interest and fascination, as this kind of care was unheard of in their neighbourhood. The patient herself never showed any signs of alarm. She observed my expressions of concern with amused smiles. Her quick recovery amazed us all. God had heard prayer, again.

Other days in maternity could only be termed indescribably bad. March 3. 1980 we recorded 5 infant deaths from the last 8 C sections. A case of sepsis, a baby from 12 hours of labor in second stage, arriving on the back of a 4x4 truck, another referral with 5 hours of second stage, a premature baby from a placenta previa C-section and an anoxic brain damaged baby. It was a day one would rather forget.

Exactly 27 days later I was summoned to maternity **now**. Abandoning my busy outpatient post I rushed to the rescue. The delivery room was filled with midwives, students and ward-aids. A chorus of: "April fools day"! Was followed by happy laughter. What a relief, but why was I not amused? The midwives must have felt that I needed to relax.

There was considerable excitement the day a Siamese monster was born in our maternity: One underdeveloped head, two arms, and four legs. Within minutes the Chief of Nso heard of the event, and he sent secret strict orders to me: "do not let this child live". There was no conflict of interest, as "it" was stillborn. But I was curious, obviously the chief played more roles than I had suspected.

I had been wondering whether I would ever diagnose a case of intra-abdominal pregnancy (a baby growing outside the uterus), so when "prominent fetal parts in the presence of a good fetal heart" was reported to me, I rolled down to maternity on my motorbike. I soon became convinced of the very rare diagnosis, but since the baby was kicking lustily, and the mother was not distressed, I scheduled the surgery for the next day when a small group of visiting nursing students from the Provincial Government School could observe this very rare event. The surgery revealed a baby free in the abdomen, among coils of intestine, but NOT an ectopic pregnancy. Instead it was a rare case of "placenta increta", a placenta grown inseparably into uterine muscle, which had weakened the uterus enough to burst next to the edge of the placenta, expelling the fetus into the abdominal cavity where it was finding considerably more freedom. There had been very little bleeding, as the placenta remained inseparably attached to the wall of the uterus, which had contracted adequately to stop bleeding without jeopardising the blood supply to the baby. The lady had a good recovery with her near full-term infant after the necessary hysterectomy. I was a bit disappointed that my preoperative diagnosis was wrong, and that I had not even considered this oddity in my differential diagnosis. (Vanity of a diagnostician?) And to think that I had wasted precious hours of the night wondering about management of the placenta, should it be stuck to various vital structures, instead of sleeping, as any **real** good doctor would have done.

In my efforts to avoid unnecessary C-sections I was confronted by tough decisions. We could rarely count on more than one or two units of blood for any patient, usually from relatives or staff. So when I was called for a prolapsed cord one day, we went into our usual mode of high gear preparation. I gave the spinal anesthetic. One last check of the cord led to disappointment. No pulse from the baby's heart...too late! Slowly the team dispersed, the patient was sent back to maternity to deliver the dead fetus spontaneously. Minutes later I was called urgently. "Doctor, it is pulsating again". Sure enough, there was a pulse in the prolapsed umbilical cord, the baby was still alive! In fact we got lusty twins out of this one. There was joking and merriment all around.

I suspect that the feeling of immense relief after a difficult delivery is just the feeling obstetricians cherish. But I can do without all that excitement!

For me the outstanding characteristic of obstetrical practise was it's total unpredictability. I was nearing the end of my first four years of missionary medical practise and realised one day that I had seen many problems and complications of pregnancy but had been spared the disaster of a ruptured uterus until then. Just as I began wondering how to explain that to my colleagues in Canada, I had to face two such patients within one week, in the very last month before leaving for furlough. And there have been several more since then, yet none resulting in a maternal death, if the patient reached the hospital alive.

The 35-bed maternity was a generally happy place, with many wonderful and joyous surprises. The surprises were not restricted to maternity, however.

*   *   *

One of the most frustrating aspects of my work in Africa was the recurrence of preventable "accidents" with identical causes. What surprised me about these injuries, was the fact that the concept of preventive strategy seemed foreign to the culture.

It finally drove me to write my one and only academic article for publication with the title: "Ten common health hazards in West Cameroon". 6.), but I don't think it helped much.

I still saw the "die cry eye" and the "corn grinder finger" with unnerving frequency in the nineties, in fact new modes of accidental self-mutilation were invented in more recent years.

Hazard one: "home-made guns". It was very difficult to import weapons into Cameroon. Even hunting guns were very hard to find. Local craftsmen worked around the ban on importation with dane-gun replicas fashioned from the steering arm of Land Rovers (a reasonably adequate shotgun barrel!) or from half-inch galvanised pipe (much less desirable). These crudely made weapons were muzzle loaded with a mixture of gunpowder and either sharp basalt stones or chips of steel. When loading for the hunt of the fiercest African animal, the buffalo, the bullets needed to be of good size. For smaller "ground beef" (edible small animals living close to the ground) a shotgun type of effect was more desirable.

A fifteen-year-old hunter was accidentally shot in the face with two rough 12-mm balls of steel intended for a "*bush-cow*" (buffalo). He was blinded by the horrendous shock as the two bullets smashed through his maxillary sinuses and lodged in his head. He arrived conscious and walking, a day later, from his hunting area 50 km away. The Xray showed one bullet resting just in front of his right ear canal. It had missed his facial nerve and was easily removed under local anesthetic. The other bullet had come to rest a millimeter in front of his second cervical vertebra. I was able to remove it relatively easily through his open mouth with a small incision in his posterior pharynx. The lucky hunter even regained some vision in one eye once the blood in the vitreous humor cleared.

The most frequent injury from dane-guns, however, was to the hand that tamped the explosive mixture into the rear of the barrel through the muzzle. The contraption would often explode unexpectedly. Picking hundreds of stones or iron chips from a mutilated hand, trying to salvage a couple of remaining fingers, and amputating, always amputating, was a most distressing job. All the more since it seemed so senselessly stupid.

With the increasing population, for which our superior health care was partly to blame, land disputes between the hundreds of language groups in Cameroon flare into armed combat now and then. These land disputes eventually became the commonest reason for gunshots fired in anger, but they were not frequent.

Two patients stand out in my mind.

A young man complained of having been shot in the head with a 12-gauge shotgun at close range. He had a very swollen head, shaved and ready for my inspection. One eye was ruined, and there were multiple black punctures on the left side of his face and scalp, but I was not prepared for the X-ray revelation: I stopped counting the 2 mm lead pellets when I reached one hundred. We did not attempt to remove more than one or two pellets. There were just too many of them. He recovered uneventfully, though his head still "felt a bit heavy".

The other victim was from the same tribe and arrived with a dane-gun bullet in the dominant hemisphere of his brain. Our treatment consisted of "masterful inactivity and watchful expectancy", just as I had been taught in medical school. He was ready for discharge in a couple of weeks with (fortunately?) only the total loss of speech and some muscle weakness of his right limbs as residual damage. We relied on the searing heat of the bullet to have created a sterile foreign object that could safely be left in his brain. Alternatives were not really considered. ("Above all, do no harm!" was the other lesson I remembered from medical school).

Hazard two: "the die cry eye". Another use of dane-guns seemed even more senseless to me: their regular use and prominence during die cry celebrations. "Good" spirits of the ancestors had to be appeased or "bad ones" scared away (I forgot to ask, which). With the enthusiasm of alcohol-fortified valour the guns would be loaded without shot, but with extra powder, to get more bang for the buck. The eye closest to the gun would get a good dose of gunpowder from the backfire, and the other eye would not always escape. Once I treated six such patients within a two week span. One of the six remained totally blind in spite of my treatment. Many a brave warrior against the spirit-world lost an eye in this way, especially if diverted to native treatment for first aid.

Hazard three: "the corn-grinder finger" regularly belonged to curious toddler's hands that just **had** to find out what made such beautiful fufu flour out of ordinary corn. It was always the right index finger that was "educated" and subsequently and regrettably shortened proportionate to the degree of curiosity.

Hazard four: "The cutlass hand". Women occasionally tolerated the help of young men in their farms. I suspect it was below the men's dignity to use the women's customary shovel. But since the cutlass was a typically "male" tool, it was sometimes used for purposes other than cutting.

When one tries to grasp the cutlass handle with two hands to dig into the soil, there is not enough room for both hands on the handle. And when the broad end of the cutlass hits an unsuspected stone hidden in the soil the lower hand may slide down the recently sharpened blade with devastating effect. Some young men escaped with just a couple of cut tendons. Others cut six or eight tendons in an area of the palm called "no man's land" by plastic surgeons, (because even they have difficulty getting good results when tendons are cut in that region of the anatomy). Most of these hands were permanently disabled.

Hazard five: "Use of sharp tools by children". All children are given responsibility within the family rather early in life. This develops a good sense of community. One can see a group of pre-schoolers fetch water in buckets from the stream. Three or four of them will lift a 20-liter bucket till one of them can get his head under the load. The strongest will have the last bucket to wrestle with alone, before they all march off in regal procession. Carrying bundles of grass for roofing, sun-dried mud-blocks for building and baskets of farm produce at harvest time are expected chores for school-age children. Small children are expected to gather twigs for the evening cooking fires.

One nine year old had the job of cutting firewood with the family axe. His seven-year-old sister helped by holding the wood. It was the cleanest amputation at the wrist I had seen since the customary one practised by strict Muslims when dealing with persistent thieves. Children use sharp iron tools regularly. In the absence of lawnmowers, school field grass is trimmed by hordes of kids swinging cutlasses in close proximity to each other. Why more children don't get hurt I don't know.

Hazard six: "Inappropriate storage of toxic products". Empty beer bottles are a handy storage container for a wide variety of liquids. Corrosive battery acid, delicious palm oil, bitter malaria medicine and new engine oil is all marketed in beer bottles.

I met a heartbroken acquaintance of mine who had just forced bleach down the throat of his child, convinced it was the recently purchased cough syrup. The child died while being held in the arms of a sobbing father.

Hazard seven: "Road barriers" are a necessary evil when daily heavy downpours in the rainy season turn the laterite-covered roads into mud of varying depths. Overloaded trucks can quickly ruin any such road by grinding out deeper and deeper ruts that may eventually be 1 to 2 meters deep. The local solution to this problem is the rain barrier ("barrier du pleut" in the bilingual Cameroon) established at every major intersection. This limits the movement of trucks to short periods between rainshowers on semi-dry roads. Unless, of course, a bribe is paid.

There are also other barriers erected randomly for the purpose of municipal tax collection, control of coffee transportation out of a "co-operative union" district, and the inevitable military or gendarmerie checkpoints for "traffic control" (collection of bribes). Most of these barriers have no advance warning signs posted, are often erected in the most unsuspected places such as tight curves, and often consist of heavy iron pipes mounted at eye level (to inflict major personal damage). The checkpoints are, of course, unlit for greater shock value to the unsuspecting night traveller.

Increasingly, highway robbers have also adopted this method of bringing travellers to a sudden halt. They often use massive steel cables with similar effect.

Hazard eight: "Indiscriminate parking". The custom of parking on both sides of the road has been readily imported from Europe, but a distinctly Cameroonian invention seems to be the *"packing"* in the middle of the road, for any and sundry reasons. There might be the announcement from the rear of a nineteen-passenger taxi: *"driver, driver! I wan go pis"*, or the sudden joyful meeting of a long lost friend coming from the opposite direction who needs to be greeted with the latest news and much laughter from the parallel parked cars in the centre of the narrow road.

Combined with an almost total lack of seat belts, deplorable brakes, tires, and suspensions, and a host of inexperienced drivers driving at unreasonable speeds, it quickly becomes clear that travel on Cameroon's roads is far more hazardous than any disease, tropical or otherwise. It is "health hazard number one" for expatriates and kills an inordinate number of natives.

Hazard nine: "Common poisons". Rat poison became available in the nineties and was sold in small unlabelled plastic bags in the market. I presumed it was the old Warfarin, but my first experience with its deadly nature took an unexpectedly fortunate turn, precisely because of my previous encounter with the substance while working in the emergency room of the Royal Alexandra Hospital in Edmonton. So when I saw a "rat-poisoned" suicidal patient with pinpoint pupils, excessive salivation and writhing with abdominal cramps, there was no room for doubt: organo-phosphates! Within hours of aggressive atropine therapy, which depleted our supply considerably, the grateful young lady could be released to her humbled husband who promised to refrain from beating her in the future.

I tried to reinforce that noble intent by referring the couple to our chaplain for marriage counselling.

After that first episode we were able to save several children who ate poisoned rat-bait accidentally. But I never found the original commercial container, or the entrepreneur who divided and prepared the small packets for sale in rural markets. My investigative efforts led nowhere.

"Cassava poisoning" had to be a rare but well-known occurrence among local manioc consumers. I learned that some African adults imbibe up to 150 mg or 50% of a lethal dose of potassium cyanide daily without ill effects; and it makes sense, as humans are able to excrete the poison rapidly. The dose is all-important, however, and native manioc consumers around the world seem to know that.

Children are more prone to this poisoning due to their low body weight and ignorance of the warning: "you can't eat too much of it, if it's bitter". We saved several poisoned children with conservative measures of rapid stomach aspiration and charcoal administration, (in the absence of the antidote amyl nitrite and thiosulfate, which was unavailable).

"Thorn apples" with their high cyanide content figure prominently in many rituals and "native medicines" in Cameroon.

Textbooks describe a "characteristic bitter almond smell" on the breath of cyanide-poisoned patients. Here my African experience came in handy in a case back in Canada.

The ambulance delivered an elderly man to an Edmonton emergency department. He had become disoriented and began to vomit while eating porridge prepared by a lady living in his house. The man was rapidly losing consciousness, had difficulty breathing, looked blue, and smelled funny. Bits of porridge were retrieved and I scurried about the corridors of the department asking people to give me their interpretation of the peculiar odour. No one identified it as bitter almond-like, but I started IV administration of the antidote for cyanide nevertheless, and transferred the patient's care to the

ICU staff. I also notified the police who began to search the man's premises. The next day I was informed of the man's death, and the detection of a bottle of cyanide buried in his garden. The lady who had prepared the porridge was charged with murder.

Hazard ten: "Baker's hands". The newest health hazard in the Northwest Province is surely the new bread-making machine. Two rigidly fixed metal rollers reminiscent of the wringer washer of grandma's laundry were spun rapidly via gears and crank by a sweating baker's apprentice or, alternately, by a small electric motor. The 12-mm space between the rollers did a nice job of kneading a 2-kg lump of dough flung into its shining whirl.

The confidence and speed with which the second apprentice would gather up the dough and fling it into the rollers repeatedly was something to see. The total lack of any safety device or shield resulted in roughly one mangled hand per month seen at BBH. The human hand is a marvel of divine engineering, but not after it has been randomly rearranged into a twelve-millimeter thick mass of bone, muscle, tendon, vessel, nerve and skin.

I located one manufacturer of the infernal device and tried my best to persuade the machine shop owner to improve the machine's design with a view to safety.

It is easy to criticise a government or regulatory body for negligence in our developed world. It is very difficult indeed to even begin to create the likes of: "Workman's Compensation", "Guaranteed Minimum Wage", "Child Labour Legislation", "Safety Standards" and their enforcement in a country that is rushing from the stone age into the twenty-first century in a short 50 or 100 years. "Long range planning" and "pollution control" are foreign concepts in a hand to mouth society. So much to be learned, so few teachers, and a lot of people getting hurt while waiting to be taught.

*   *   *

Northwest Cameroon has only two seasons. From November to March the prevailing winds bring the harmattan, a fine hazy dust from the Sahara, partially blocking out the sun, drying out all but the hardiest vegetation, and parching the land and it's people. Near the end of the dry season water becomes precious. Children and hunters set fire to grassy slopes to aid in flushing out *ground beef* (edible rodents). The brown grass disappears, leaving lifeless scorched black hills in its stead.

The winds begin to turn in March, bringing clouds, thunder and finally refreshing, life-giving rain. For a few weeks the battle of the elements mirrors the struggle for subsistence below. Women prepare for planting, heaping the powdery barren earth into mounds or rows with their broad short-handled hoes, burying last years shrivelled vegetation, and burning it to produce ashes, hoping to increase the soil's fertility.

There is an odd fascination for the burning of the grasslands. Agrarian reformers and foreign advisors have effected little change to this farming method.

And every year the victims of grass fires arrive at the hospital.

A farmer from the Oku hills was caught in the raging inferno of his grass-roofed hut. He suffered second and third degree burns to all but the soles of his feet and his crotch. The outcome appeared inevitable to everyone who met him on his arrival at BBH. It was only a question of hours or days before he would leave this earth. But he surprised us all with his courage. He had little pain, because the flames had destroyed most of the skin's sensory nerve endings. His burned skin became a thick leathery brown armour that began to restrict his movement and life. My short-term volunteer-friend Andy agreed to do the necessary escarotomies, (longitudinal incisions of the burned skin on his limbs), to enable him to move about. Incredibly, in his desperate condition, he insisted on getting up from under his mosquito net every morning, walking stiffly down the hallways of the hospital and greeting everyone cheerfully. He said he was not afraid to die! He knew where he was going, and there was no reason to be sad. Eating and drinking was difficult, but he could still talk and laugh with the horrified visitors sitting on the hospital verandas. His incredible testimony to the human spirit and un-dampened hope in the face of death finally fell silent after a long ten days. He had done much more for us than we could do for him with our limited resources of torn up bed-sheet bandages, honey compresses, and limited antibiotics. We never even started an IV, as he had no veins for access.

Many others tested the very limits of our burn care skills with long-neglected scar contractures, non-healing wounds and crippling deformities.

A Nsungli man brought his 10-year-old son for consultation. A turban-like cloth covered his head. There seemed to be a problem with his scalp. I lifted a corner of his unusual head-dress. Pieces of dried mud fell to the floor. The father helped me to remove most of a thick mud poultice with the cap. *"Na whatee been make um?"* *"E been fall fo fia"*. *"Whose kine time?"* *"After one year Sah"*. (He fell into the fire one year ago? Then why did he wait so long?) First he had to be sent for a thorough saline soak and cleansing. On a hunch I got an Xray. The presence of a 10-cm circular defect in his skull proved this to be a very deep original burn indeed. But the burn had failed to kill him. Native medicine had not succeeded in healing his wound nor controlling his epileptic seizures.

It took less than a week of saline compresses to clean the scalp area in readiness for a split thickness graft, which took successfully on first attempt. I had to ignore the large defect in his bony skull, of course. Phenobarbital controlled his seizures while in hospital, and he was discharged in record time. Would the family be able to refill his lifelong prescription of one of our cheapest drugs? I never saw this child again, like so many of our patients.

There was a commonly held belief that epilepsy was contagious during a convulsive attack. Epileptics would therefore never be pulled away from open kitchen-fires in the event of a seizure. One could almost presume the diagnosis of inadequately treated epilepsy whenever these pitiful patients appeared with their grotesque scar contractures or chronic wounds. A head could be seen frozen to the shoulder in a permanent severe tilt, a hand pulled back by the contracting scar until the fingers touched the back of the forearm. Fingers would be fused together after deep burns to a hand that lacked medical first (and second) aid.

I was deeply gratified one day while attending church. An elderly man who stood next to the pastor as his *turn talk* suddenly collapsed and had a seizure on the elevated platform in full view of hundreds of worshippers. The first people rushing to his aid were our nursing students. Their obvious change of beliefs resulting in fearless action was a powerful testimony to everyone present. An attack of seizures did not need to result in massive burns because fearful relatives failed to pull their loved ones from the fire.

Little Magdalene came to us from the Capital. She was a fine upstanding girl of twelve. In fact she never sat down. Lying flat or standing up was the only option she had since the severe burn injury to her back. The National Burn-unit Referral Centre had not yet been opened and she had been told to return, when it would, in a couple of years! Huge ropes of scarring covered her entire back. Forget the textbook dictum, that human skin can only bridge a maximum defect of two or three centimeters. She had healed an entire back without skin grafts. True, it had taken most of a year, but she had healed. Now all that remained was the challenge to get her to sit, squat and separate her knees. Our MBH physiotherapy staff began the task with its usual energetic verve. But there was the puzzling immobility of the poor girl's hip joints. An X-ray revealed the enormity of her problem. Both joints had been dislocated completely out of their sockets by the relentless force of the contracting scars on her back. The balls of the hip joints were frozen a good five centimeters above their normal position. This problem would challenge even the best orthopedic and rehabilitation clinic in the world. It was certainly too big for us. I will never forget the picture of a smiling slender girl standing at the rear of Mbingo church throughout a long service. She was leaning onto the back of a chair someone had thoughtfully placed there for her. And later, to see her walking stiffly, swinging oddly along the grassy path. A gigantic human spirit trapped in a pathetic body; another victim of inadequate Third World medical care.

Cameroon has been able to supply its own oil and gas from a few offshore rigs for some years now. One day two gasoline filled railway cars derailed in the Capital. The ruptured tank attracted dozens of opportunists who filled their pots and pans with the escaping precious liquid, until something, a cigarette? a passing car? a malevolent spoilsport? More likely an ignoramus ignited an inferno. 60 people burned on the spot, most beyond recognition. The 3 hospitals serving the million inhabitants of Yaounde tried valiantly to cope, but the death toll climbed to 150. The local news media praised the fire department for its speedy containment of the blaze. They had taken **only** 45 minutes to get to the site.

WAWA

WAWA stands for "West Africa wins again". It is the resigned expression of a suffering people against the impossible odds of circumstance, harassment and fate. Long range planning has a low priority in a hand to mouth society. In a tightly knit community it is "One for all and all for one", whereas "saving for a rainy day" is frowned upon as unreasonable hoarding. "How can you sit on your money while your nephew needs 159 000 cfa (C$450) for his annual high school fees right now?" There are endless tales of misfortune that come to those who save and hoard. It's the rats or the relatives, the rain or the rot, that will ruin your best-laid plans. Not to speak of new government decrees, witchcraft, illness or death. West Africa is winning constantly, and WE are the losers. Better to acknowledge it and make the best of any given situation with humor and zest.

People's vitality lies in their never-ending optimism and willingness to constantly battle Wawa and win at least sometimes.

We had just pushed and wrestled the Land Rover out of another deep rut on our way to Mbem clinic when we could hear the snarling engine of a Land Rover approaching from Nigeria. Overloaded to the hilt, it parted the 3-meter tall elephant grass rounding the bend in the road ahead. The mud-covered 4 wheel drive half-ton had *moto boy dem* hanging from various precarious hand-and footholds ready for the next push and attempting to steady the top heavy load as it leaned perilously into the deep rut. Our driver stopped to give the lurching vehicle a chance to pass. I shouted a concerned enquiry: *how road de fo befo?* (How's the road ahead?). The busy driver grinned broadly: *rood e fain bad, coltar daso* (perfect, paved all the way!) was his response as he manhandled his aged wreck through the deep mud beside us. *Wawa* may in fact win a few, but when Cameroonians pull together with verve and humor it can't win them all.

I received an invitation to join a missionary couple on a trip to Jos, Nigeria in their VW beetle. Our children attended boarding school there from grade 4 to grade 11. The hospital was not terribly busy, I had the necessary papers, and it was dry season, giving us a reasonable chance to make the 1000-km trip in one continuous drive. Yes, I badly needed to see my boys!

We would go Southwest through the equatorial rain forest of Cameroon, cross the border at Ikom and head north to the Jos Plateau where the children would get a huge surprise, as I would appear unannounced. Communication was slow, with Airmail going via Douala-Paris-London-Lagos, usually taking 3 weeks one way. Phone service was non-existent.

Because it was dry season we hoped to reach the border in about four hours, descending into the rain forest, carefully manoeuvring the low-slung "beetle" over the rocky, narrow road. Once in Nigeria, we would enjoy long stretches of paved two-lane highway.

Dry season indeed. A rare tropical downpour had descended the night before and gave us a nasty surprise. A Peugeot 404 taxi was stuck halfway up a hill in deep mud. The 9 passengers were valiantly trying to push the top-heavy station wagon while the driver flung big chunks of mud at them with his spinning tires. How could we possibly get through this mud, let alone pass the taxi?

We made a deal with the people blocking our way: we'll help you, you help us. Five hours later we had literally carried the two vehicles up that hill. Mud to our knees, we were shouting and laughing, heaving and pushing, and finally joining in the communal foot washing in a small stream. We had a story to tell our children when we arrived in Jos after the 26-hour trip.

My sons told me of a motorcyclist in Jos, Nigeria being stopped by Police shortly after the new helmet law came into effect in that country. He had done a good paint job on a calabash (half a gourd) and tied it over his head. The Policeman was not fooled, but there were plenty of appreciative listeners to the story. *No be e done try?* (He's done his best) was the laughing affirmation of the common struggle against insurmountable odds.

A surplus Army truck was hired to carry a rather large family to a *cry die* from Bamenda to Ngoketunja. The driver refused the honor of driving as he had doubts about the brakes, which would be sorely needed in the 800 m winding descent from Sabga village into the plain below. A willing volunteer driver was found and the inevitable happened. Thirteen died on the spot and many more suffered severe injuries as the truck lost its brakes, left the road and overturned, flinging passengers among the boulders on the hillside like so many rag-dolls. Several patients were transferred from the Provincial Hospital to our facility. One had major fractures in all four limbs. In North America this accident would have led to a number of lawsuits. Not so in West Africa. It's just another battle lost. *Wawa!*

Certainly, one needs to carry insurance papers if driving on public roads. But they are inexpensive, probably because it will be very unlikely to actually collect insurance when one is involved in an accident.

The usual advice to expatriate drivers on the narrow, heavily travelled roads is: "when colliding with one of the many pedestrians sharing the road, it is best to keep going to the next police station". Otherwise, the nearby relative's anguish could turn into violence and no one could guarantee the survival of the driver.

A curious animal-like mischievousness is ascribed to vehicles and inanimate objects: *E done heave me* (it bucked me off), the bleeding Suzuki rider will complain.

Moto done spoil! The passengers will woefully explain their 4-hour late arrival.

Driver bin djomp! (The driver jumped out the door when the brakes failed), the injured passengers explain why their taxis left the road and rolled down a hill.

Sitik been nuck me! (A tree hit me). *Situn been nuck me fo mai top head!* (a stone hit my head), without a word about the guy who threw it.

Moto been nuck e lass oba! (The rear end of the car kept bottoming out), never mind the careless driver and the overloaded vehicle.

"Economic crisis" has become an overarching excuse for dashed expectations.

It is sadly true that two salary reductions totalling a loss of 65% hit all Cameroonians on the government pay roll (except the Armed Forces) in the early Nineties. It dropped Cameroon from its lofty second place in per capita world beer consumption, parked the shiny Mercedes and Peugeots of the rich and established motorcycle taxis in the capital. Retirees and entrepreneurs went back to subsistence farming. The struggle continues.

The new political party "Social Democratic Front"(SDF) was quickly and optimistically nicknamed *Suffer Done Finis*. It was premature hope. Heavy-handed military brutality and general strikes led to bloodshed. International observers documented widespread election fraud by the party in power in 1992 and 1997. *Wawa*! Given the choice between peace with injustice and bloodshed with elusive justice the people have settled into an uneasy choice for the former.

I marvel at the patience and perseverance, the resilience and humor in the African soul. The outstanding and attractive characteristic that I came to admire is the people's indefatigably positive outlook on life.

The African's making do, attempts at repair, and long-suffering patience in the face of cruel odds are exemplary in the face of the throw-away, instant-gratification society, which ours has become.

The blended African and Christian virtues of patience and long-suffering were aptly demonstrated to me in David Kayuh, affectionately known as "Davido", our hospital maintenance man whom I met at my arrival at BBH. One of Davido's first jobs under my direction was to re-wire the entire hospital. Electric wires had simply been hung on nails until then. A new 3-phase generator had to be installed and integrated with the old single-phase army surplus unit. My previous career in steam engineering and maintenance now came in handy. We congratulated ourselves when the new 30 kW Lister diesel lit up the hospital compound for the very first time. Now we could expand and use more of our donated electrical equipment.

Davido was one of the many Africans who surprised me. His single-minded devotion fit my ideal of a maintenance man perfectly. He had come from a small village in the Rom valley as a youth and found a job with the Tea Estate where he proved his willingness to tackle any task that needed doing. While he was digging one of those 7-meter deep narrow pit latrines, the walls had caved in, killing his partner and breaking Davido's hip. He was treated at BBH, but his severe injury left him with a permanent limp. He was offered a job at the hospital when he could not pay his bill and impressed Dr. Peter Fehr with his attitude of service and innate mechanical talents to be hired on permanently, after his hospital bill was paid. Davido had no training whatsoever. He could barely scrawl his first name and he spoke a *pidgin* that was unintelligible to most of us. Many thought him incorrigibly simple and accused him of ruining rather than repairing the many broken implements in the hospital. I found him a kindred spirit in more ways than one. He was an improviser par excellence. He had a nose for impending maintenance problems. He would appear out of nowhere whenever there was a blown fuse or a seized motor, a leaking water pipe or a major power failure. No machinery under his care would ever be found to be lacking oil.

There was no way a man of his low stature could be assigned one of the few staff dwellings on the crowded BBH compound. Nurses and midwives with call-duty had obvious priority. But he weaselled a minute piece of land out of a chiselling Nso landlord right next to our property line, directly below the generator house, to build his mud-block family-home there—so he could be close to the heart-throb of the hospital. The slightest change in the old generator's thumping growl would bring him on the scene. He was forever suggesting ways to improve "the system" and took any rebuke of his impractical ways with humility born out of a servant's heart. Usually he would persist with his solutions to impossible problems at least until I would give him my full attention or had a better idea, and would then tackle stubborn mechanical problems with inadequate tools but sensitive fingers and patient persistence. We had overwhelming odds against us. Through its evolution, the various hospital buildings and installations were blessed—plagued, actually—with fully five different kinds of threads on the hundreds of nuts, bolts and pipes around the compound. Besides the universal pipe thread there was Whitworth's thread from the jolly good British Empire, left behind with equipment from colonial times. Replacement bolts and nuts of this kind were to be treasured as gold, for they became ever rarer and irreplaceable, should someone ruin a thread of that type. All of our North American medical equipment was, of course, blessed with either coarse or fine imperial thread. At least we could often scrounge up nuts and bolts from unusable precious North American junk that seemed to be spread all over our compound stores. Those bolts couldn't be found in any hardware stalls of Banso market either. All one could possibly hope to find there were a few metric bolts of the poorest quality imaginable. But metric thread was our last resort. Japanese and European cars came with metric thread. One could always search for some of these high quality used bolts among the many mechanic shops along the roads to the market. At least we had metric taps and dies to re-thread any other type of bolt for which we couldn't find a suitable nut in our large box of unsorted leftovers. Davido could tell the type of thread and their origin at a glance. He also seemed to have a phenomenal memory of previous problems.

As the years went by it became hazardous to contemplate retiring good old Davido. No one else could be trusted to know the exact location of the many shut-off valves, improvisations and installations that he had been part of. Nevertheless, more formally trained maintenance personnel, who took a dim view of the limping, illiterate simpleton and his intimidating foreign partner, eventually displaced our two-man team of intuitive improvisers. Davido longed for the good old days when he and I would tackle big projects together. After years of pleading, I had finally listened to him and purchased a welding machine for the hospital maintenance department. Time did not seem to matter when we built a merry-go-round for the blind children out of an old Toyota truck axle unit. Davido seemed to see exactly what I was designing in my head. I measured and cut while he welded, and together we improvised until the wonderful new toy was firmly anchored in the ground. And all the while he was telling me about his many family problems. Davido was the epitome of a good man who was being taking advantage of. His wife's family demanded never-ending dowry payments even after his five children had grown into adulthood. Again and again she was obliged to return to her family village for many months until he paid up some more of his precious salary. Davido's father seemed to have had similar problems, as his mother's family approached Davido to pay his father's unpaid dowry-debts decades after he had died. (Davido showed me the farm-plot one day, where they had found his father, dead from a snakebite.)

I was short on advice for any of Davido's convoluted marriage palavers, but could relate better to the problems that he had with his children. They did not seem to share Davido's deep commitment to God or the church, though he tried his best to give them a living example of devoted faith and sacrificial service. Davido's heart was broken when his only son died of AIDS and his daughter in law followed a few months later, leaving him to care for the two grandchildren. One daughter was killed in a traffic accident and another is chronically ill with immuno-suppression, leaving even more young grandchildren for old Davido. It seems that he will never be able to retire, especially since the National Pension scheme has fallen on hard times. Even my own puny plans for Davido's retirement have fallen flat. I purchased a beautiful second-hand Stihl chain saw from a Canadian farmer and gave it to Davido to secure his livelihood in retirement. But his relatives took it from him, and a scoundrel "borrowed" it with a promise to make some necessary repairs. Davido is very nearly without hope for the future. Wawa has seriously afflicted him.

My own troubles with WAWA were not nearly as serious but annoying enough.

When I planned to visit my children in Nigeria I had to attend no less than 9 separate offices in Cameroon to clear my exit and re-entry. Nor would a single visit to an office ever suffice. The Chief of a department would rarely be "on seat" and none of his underlings were authorised to sign the necessary papers. But I could hardly complain, as my African brothers would fare even worse when dealing with public officials. A bribe or favor would be routinely expected of them. VIPs would be served preferentially and one could count on waiting several hours for something as simple as purchasing fiscal stamps.

Since power has such a high cultural value in Cameroon, this may be the reason why even minor office-holders are tempted to engage in a show of power, even at the risk of looking ridiculous.

Politicians and administrative officials were generally kind to us. Petty theft, occasional harassment by the forces of law and order and an exasperating bureaucracy were much less annoying for us as missionaries than for the local population.

Native citizens were often harassed mercilessly by tax collectors, police, gendarmes and military controls.

A taxi-driver had run out of the customary bribe of the one thousand franc note (about 2-3 dollars) when stopped once too many times. The entire load of passengers was forced to swing cutlasses to "mow" a near-by school field in a bizarre form of "community service".

During the political unrest that followed a fraudulent election a grey-haired pastor was forced to lie face down in a mud puddle for hours while armed militia terrorised the population.

A large Catholic congregation was made to pay for the humiliating but non-violent take-over of a Gendarme post by political opponents of a village. Women and children were released while all the men were thoroughly beaten as they left the church.

There was the occasional shock for us as well. Marlis, my wife, has an exceptional eye for photography. She had the patience and foresight to take pictures of unusual perspective. It occurred to her that it might be nice to illustrate her deputation speech with some pictures of local **currency**. I was oblivious to her thorough work, as well as to the potential hazard of her activity. Some sharp eyes in a photo-lab in France alerted the appropriate authorities in Cameroon and soon we found ourselves in very hot water. Our normal routine was suddenly and forcefully interrupted one day without warning by warrant-wielding detectives in civilian clothing. We were told to sit quietly while they searched our house, not knowing what law we might have broken. With the investigating officer's special attention to Marlis' photo equipment my anxious wife's memory was jogged in the right direction. The police asked her for a written statement and the search ended for now. A few days later we were summoned before the National Chief of Judicial Police in Yaounde-"**now**"!

I had the idea to include a good selection of Marlis' famous and less famous photo slides in our hastily packed suitcases. It took a good day and a half of travel to appear before the French speaking Police Chief. No charges were ever read to us, but by this time we had gathered that we had broken a law against the production of counterfeit money. I scoured the Canadian and American embassies for a projector to be able to show my wife's pictures in her defence before the official in a black suit and tie. Daringly I interspersed some of our gory surgical and post-mortem slides with pictures of sweet children and spectacular scenery to convince the man that **nothing** was safe before my dear wife's documentary thirst. He asked: "Does that include pornography?" I hastily assured him otherwise.

When he finally broke out the wine we knew that I had successfully saved my sweet companion from jail.

Unfortunately, things did not quite end there. For several years I was reminded at appropriate times that I was under close surveillance. All our mail was opened at the local Post Office, and we had to be careful to maintain our foreign worker status. But it did not particularly worry us, since our conscience was clear.

Certainly we needed to live in greater dependence upon our Lord. The props that we in the West have come to lean on were simply not there: Insurance, first class medical care, grandparents, hardware stores, TV, videos, regular mail, working telephones, privacy, holidays, experts and advisors, extravagant hobbies and toys, public libraries, movie theatres and symphonies. Instead, a rich family life with games, pets, adventures and cross-cultural friendships more than made up for most of such amenities. The home church-family was thousands of kilometers away but One with us in spirit—a strangely palpable Presence.

*   *   *

The Canadian Government has a reputation for effective Foreign Aid. Not only people of Christian persuasion or heritage make large contributions to a number of relief organisations working in disaster areas and countries with chronic needs. Although overall grants from our Canadian national government have fallen to less than one half-percent of the annual budget, a large number of non-governmental organisations (NGOs), church missions and para-church organisations are the unsung heroes of Third World development.

I had opportunity to be personally involved in several foreign aid projects and observed others closely over the span of many years. There have been some changes in policy which have proven beneficial. Instead of giving funds to foreign governments, most Canadian aid money now goes to NGOs with proven track records of philanthropic work in developing nations. Many other well-meaning projects have misfired badly. The fault lies mainly in the assumption that people in the developing world think the way the donors do, and in the widespread practise of corruption and misappropriation of funds. I recall a number of examples—of shining success, and those in which I saw Foreign Aid succumb to WAWA.

In the early seventies the people of Kumbo (Banso) town applied to the Canadian Government for aid to supply about 20 000 people with clean drinking water. Engineers from Canada surveyed possible sources and selected a small stream 6-km away. This brook ran clean water all year round and could be garnered and gravity fed to two steel tanks the size of large houses located above the town. Altogether 100 public water points were planned for an area of about 20 square km. The pipes were made of Canadian asbestos, from 10 to 45 cm in diameter. The fittings and valves, concrete water points and taps, catchment and storage tanks were donated at a total cost of $250 000. The community supplied all labour to dig the trenches by hand, and gave substantial contributions for the project. The Chief of Nso oversaw the work by the population. Unfortunately, two thousand people had to be moved forcefully from the intake area in order to prevent possible contamination. Compensation for their resettlement was grossly inadequate and late in coming.

Several years later the National Water Board shouldered into the scheme, built a filtration and chlorination system and began charging for the water. During the 1992 political riots the chief took advantage of the rebellious mood of his people. He re-appropriated the water system and its administration, "because it had been a gift from Canada, and thus it belonged to the people". 7.)

25 years later, the water is still running most of the time, though it is inadequate near the end of the dry season due to the increase in population. Maintenance is acceptable. There are increasing numbers of direct lines to homes and businesses and the charges are reasonable. About half of the original public water points are still accessed free of charge, the rest are not functioning.

Shortly after the taps were first opened we noticed a marked change in disease patterns. There were now far fewer cases of water born diseases, particularly amoebic dysentery and typhoid fever.

Soon other smaller villages followed the lead. Most of them were helped by a superb organisation in their search for clean water: the engineers of

Swiss Association for Technical Assistance (now "Helveta"), who built hundreds of well catchments, trained hundreds of local maintenance men, and probably saved thousands of lives in the decades since the sixties. In any given year as many as 40 to 80 small villages have received help from this outstanding foreign aid organisation.

In contrast, I saw a Belgian Foreign Aid scheme fail miserably in its effort to supply water for two large villages of about 10 000 people. The Belgians made an agreement with the Cameroon Government: 90% Belgian Aid, 10% National Government contribution to the project. First, roads had to be upgraded over the very challenging mountainous terrain to the project site. Two large diesel pumps were delivered and installed in one village. A storage tank was built on top of a hill. Pipes were laid and the catchment constructed. But the Cameroon government never came through with their part of the bargain, just as we had seen in other foreign aid projects. Whether corrupt officials siphoned off the money, or there simply was no money allocated in the budget will never be known. The Belgian engineers left with the keys to their project and have not returned for over 10 years. Meanwhile the people continue to drink from contaminated streams.

During my last tour a close friend of mine in that region died from infection of the bowel while his wife became very ill, but survived. Many people who attended the funeral became ill with severe dysentery and six more died following my friend's burial in the village.

A political solution is needed, but who speaks for the population whose apathy born of powerlessness seems overwhelming?

Banso Baptist Hospital needed more bed space yet again. A surgical ward with 30 beds was proposed. The cost was about $200 000 for a two storey building containing X-ray, laboratory, eye department and optic workshop, central supply store and staff conference room on the ground floor, with 2 open wards occupying the top floor.

The Cameroon Baptist Convention Health Board applied for Canadian Aid since Canadian citizens had worked at BBH for many years.

Eventually a large percentage of the cost was granted by two agencies: The Canadian International Development Agency (CIDA) and Christian Blind Mission. Upon completion of the building (within budget), the final inspection and opening ceremonies so impressed the Canadian foreign embassy staff that another offer of funds was made on the spot. It was decided to upgrade the hospital water system. Five small springs located near the hospital had supplied us with gravity fed water since the fifties. The new grant enabled us to add two more spring catchments and construct a large holding tank.

Opening ceremonies of the surgical ward took place in the early nineties and occupancy rate usually runs over 110 percent (extra beds and mattresses are spread in hallways).

Measles has a high mortality rate among non-Caucasians. This is as true for the Inuit as it is for West Africans. Centuries of exposure have probably given us Westerners relative immunity, just as Africans seem to have at least some immunity against malaria, which is often rapidly fatal for untreated Caucasians.

A new measles vaccine was developed in the United States of America. The governments of Cameroon and the US agreed upon a joint pilot project. For five years the US would supply four-wheel-drive Dodge trucks, mobile refrigerators, modern inoculation "guns", and the new expensive trial vaccine. Thereafter the Cameroon Public Health System would take over all of the above. Our province was included in the pilot project. Our measles isolation ward was soon used for other purposes as the usual one to two hundred cases per year fell to near zero. Then the team from the US left. The Dodge trucks broke down soon thereafter. There are no American-made trucks and no spare parts for them available in that part of the world.

The National Public Health team arranged for an inoculation clinic on our hospital compound. Over three thousand mothers showed up with their children, ordinarily a three-hour job as these jet guns could easily handle a thousand patients an hour. But not on this day. The single remaining operational gun jammed. As the sun grew hotter people grew restless. Eventually everyone left, as the crew was unable to repair the gun.

Our number of measles cases stayed low for a couple of years, until a new crop of susceptible youngsters grew up. Then the epidemic hit with a vengeance. One day I counted 80 children in the 30-bed children's ward. Cross-infection was inevitable. It was a provincial disaster. We prided ourselves on a mortality rate of "only" 4% while some government hospitals reported 8%. Eventually a newer vaccine became available on a more regular basis and was distributed through existing channels of the public health network, but I count that pilot project of measles prevention among my Foreign Aid WAWA nightmares.

A German biogas-engineering firm explored the possibility of introducing modern concepts of waste management to rural Africa. Their research was thorough. The German Government gave large amounts of money with stringent guidelines and conditions. Pilot projects proved workable. The company approached BBH with the proposal to collect all human waste in plastic pipes gently sloping to a methane digester. The end products of soil enriching fertiliser and methane gas would help to defray the ongoing costs of the project. The proposals were approved. In the past we had had problems finding sites for our 7 meter-deep pit latrines near the hospital. They were being filled in record time, while the growing number of flush toilets used up inordinate amounts of precious dry-season water.

The German proposal seemed to have the solution for our problems. Not only would the systems take care of all our sanitation sorrows, there would even be enough biogas produced to run a couple of stove-burners or sterilisers all day. As a volunteer working at BBH I asked many questions. I followed the construction and initial operation with great interest. The first year of operation was relatively smooth. MBH too, saw the installation of a much larger system, because the decades-old self-help cattle project there provided a much greater potential for biogas production. The manure from over 200 cattle could be harnessed. I have reasonable hope that these projects will continue to work well. Cost effectiveness and "appropriate technology" are still to be assessed.

Foreign Aid must be one of the most difficult tasks in international relations. It takes the utmost in diplomacy, shrewd caution and cultural savvy and still there is no guarantee for lasting success. What appears as a victory of progress and goodwill may turn into embarrassment in a few short years. The monuments to many a well-meant effort stick out of the landscape as rusty remnants of foreign power and goodwill, appearing not unlike the modern art sculptures that grace many North American City centres.

In view of the very high potential for failure among even the most well-meaning foreign "gifts" to Cameroon, I felt justified in doing all in my power to remain culturally and technologically appropriate in my practise of cross-cultural medical missions.

*   *   *

Medical practise in Africa is not boring. During the first ten years I could count on an almost daily challenge. A huge growth filling an abdomen, a rare skin condition, a disease I had never expected to see **here**, a life saved by rapid action, a daring improvisation in treatment. In later years the excitement came more often from recognising something I had seen before, something I might tackle with a different surgical approach, or from recognising a rare disorder for which there might be a treatment somewhere in our hospital stores. I also derived great satisfaction from teaching anyone interested in unusual presentations or rare diseases. Hundreds of medical, nursing and midwifery students have had the unique challenge of working with us over the years. Not all of them shared our enthusiasm or showed a burning desire to serve, but those who did have not regretted their efforts. "What will I have to do to be able to work in this setting?" "Do I have to become a Baptist to work here?" or "I will return!" were typical parting words from students who came for brief electives from the western world. Graduates from the BBH Nursing School and the National Medical School worked alongside us and grew into capable conscientious leaders in health care both in remote and sophisticated settings.

Mrs. Rachel Tawah was the first African midwife posted to a newly opened health centre. The number of deliveries exploded to 400 in the first full year of operation. Steady improvement in buildings and facilities followed, a laboratory, an ambulance (a Suzuki Samurai, nicknamed "motorised Pogo-stick"), running water, new wards, a public health program, and finally, electricity. Not a single mother died under Mrs. Tawah's care in the first 8 years. Eventually, we experienced the first maternal death at that health centre, though with an eventually strikingly positive outcome.

The native doctor had predicted a twin delivery and certain death for the mother and both infants. The concerned husband had brought his wife to deliver at the health centre. The babies were born prematurely, each barely a kilogram in weight. The mother expired immediately after the birth of the second twin, to the shock of the attending midwife. There was no discernible medical reason. Due to lack of transport the relatives began the eight-hour trek to BBH. One twin died on the way. The second arrived with the father. It survived the first night in the customary zinc washtub with a kerosene lantern placed beneath it to provide marginal heat.

I had an outlandish idea. Would the father agree to give me this baby, in case it lived? The idea was novel and totally unacceptable culturally, as the child belongs to the clan. But to my joy the father agreed to my request, as he had been told that the child was doomed to die anyway! Had not the traditional birth attendant said so? I drew up an agreement and the father's thumbprint gave the transaction a legal appearance. The child's weight dropped to 950 grams, but then gradually responded to the loving care given by our maternity staff. When the baby weighed 2 kg my wife was allowed to try her hand at mothering this little girl in our male-dominated home. The name "Ruth" had been in reserve for the five consecutive male births in our family and could finally be applied to a worthy candidate. Ruth drank the home-pasteurised Fulani cow's milk enthusiastically. Soon a childless couple received this wonderful gift into their life. Their joy was unending as the little girl grew exceeding all their expectations in character, physical development and academic achievements. She married a good man and had three sons, whom she named: "Doctor Lemke", "Desmond Tutu", and "Leslie" (Chaffee). Illustrious company indeed!

It was a Saturday. Clinics were held on Saturdays, and since the grassland week had always been 8 days long, market day and clinic day would coincide every 8 weeks. This suited the mission doctors well, as Sunday would give them a bit of a break after these rather exhausting clinics with 3-5 hours of travel and patient loads of 200 or more.

When we arrived at Bangolan clinic at 8 one morning the crowd began to stir in anticipation. These stoic patients never failed to expose my own foreign ways. For me the lengthy greeting was something to be endured.

When could I start? "Oh doctor, there is one patient here who has been waiting since early morning."

He had an obstructed hernia. What a quandary; were we to return with him to the hospital, rush through emergency surgery and then return to this large crowd to attend to their needs? Many of those waiting were quite ill. Several children needed immediate care for their malaria or dehydration. It was not uncommon during those early years to have a child die right there, while waiting to be seen.

I decided to procrastinate. The patient had only started vomiting a couple of days earlier, perhaps his bowel was not yet rotten. So he was asked to lie down, the foot of his bed was elevated, a narcotic was given, and after he was comfortably half-asleep, I succeeded in pushing the offending gut back into his relaxed abdomen from whence it had come. There was relief for both the patient and myself, for now. The day wore on with the heat rising, the complainants jostling and the medicine shrinking. Finally we loaded the patients, carers and cargo to begin heading home, only to be met at the gates of the hospital by the news of another patient with an obstructed hernia, waiting for the doctor since morning. I was tired and hungry. Why not try the same reduction? This patient too, did not show signs of peritonitis yet and his story sounded favourable. Again the reduction was accomplished and both patients were booked for elective surgery the next day. Just as I sat down for supper with my wife and sons, the food not yet in my mouth, the *watch night* brought a note from men's ward: "Please doctor, we have a strangulated hernia, just arrived".

This one I could not shrug off, as the patient was seriously dehydrated from 5 days of vomiting. He needed emergency bowel resection after appropriate intravenous re-hydration.

All three patients did well.

We lived in *muntuli* (hernia) country, and some tribes had an inordinate number of them. It is no wonder that I learned a lot from the 1500 repairs that I did and taught over the years. It is generally expected that an untreated bowel obstruction from a strangulated groin hernia would lead to an agonising death, and we were witness to some who reached the hospital barely alive a full 7 days after the obstruction. But I also recall 2 patients who arrived in the same week, from the same remote village with the same story of bowel strangulation in a groin hernia. The only difference: they were not of the same sex. So they drained small bowel contents from scrotum and vulva, respectively. After the initial calamity of prolonged vomiting and terrible bowel cramps they had formed abscesses which turned into draining fistulas in their groins. Both had regained a reasonable measure of health. They had walked a long distance to the nearest motor-road. After finally arriving at BBH they both underwent routine repair of their bowel and hernia sites from inside the abdomen and both went home well, in about a week, confounding the odds.

I was tempted, on occasion, to raise the fees for patients with neglected illness such as strangulated hernias. After all, it was well known that traditional medicine could not cure this common affliction and only our surgery could help their condition. Our waiting lists for elective surgery were getting longer. The extra cost of intravenous fluids and antibiotics were a heavy burden for the patients who were already overtaken by the sudden surprise attack of pain and vomiting that signalled a strangulation. An expensive unexpected trip to hospital followed, with both taxi driver and lender of the hospital fees taking cruel advantage of the poor victim. Interest rates on emergency loans of 100% per **week** were not unusual.

So I never got around to raising the fees for emergency hernia repairs.

Much has been told about the sizes of some of these neglected surgical challenges, and comics among my surgical colleagues have had a hey-day with the classification into "above knee" and "below knee" hernias. I have had to inject the abdomen of one such patient with air (rather than the safer but unavailable Carbon Dioxide). The procedure was done over the span of several days, trying to stretch the abdominal cavity, so that it would be able to accommodate the bowel, which had been hanging outside the abdomen for years. No wonder some people had to borrow a wheelbarrow to transport their hernia to the hospital.

I don't know what kept some patients away so long, but I know about one fellow's reason for delay:

The patient was shaved and washed, dressed in the usual flimsy hospital gown which was approaching the colour of the red African earth from its many sessions in the laundry. He was led to the theatre and asked to remove his slippers, an act to indicate his acquiescence as much as our attempts at general aseptic technique. He climbed the OR table and was aided in baring his back for the spinal anaesthetic. As I approached with the 9-cm long, thin spinal needle, he glanced over his shoulder and struggled for freedom. *I no fit take chook!* (I cannot take injections). This struck us as very odd, since most patients not only expected injections, but actually came to hospital demanding them, as they demonstrably had far greater power than mere pills. However, in this case the native doctor had assured our surgical candidate of certain death, the day he would subject himself to an injection.

No amount of reassurance, reason or advice could persuade our patient. He suddenly gathered his meagre cover about him and crashed through the swinging doors of the OR, never to be seen again. My insulting *"go back fo bush na"* (return to the backwoods!) dissolved in my assistants' laughter.

Both men's and women's ward had a six bed "isolation room" where open pulmonary tuberculosis (TB) patients were hidden behind curtains until they showed definite response to the three (or four) drug treatment scheme. This was certainly inadequate care by First World standards, but it was the best we could offer under the circumstances. Patients would not be discharged unless they gave us reasonable assurance that they would be able to buy the minimum 6-month supply of triple therapy. Still, there were some patients who stopped treatment as soon as they felt better and later showed up with recurring tuberculosis. One such fellow remains vividly in my mind.

Musa was a personable 35 year old Hausa man from Ntumbaw who received a month or two of TB treatment before failing to show up for his regular follow up visits. Soon he became terribly ill with severe cough and alarming weight loss, which brought him back to BBH. By now his lungs showed massive damage from the now resistant strain of tuberculosis. My trial of three second-line drugs did not check his raging fevers. I was at my wit's end. On a bright and sunny afternoon an excited hospital worker summoned me "stat". Musa was in trouble.

I will never forget the spectacle of a man drowning in his own blood. Musa sat up on his bed with terror-filled eyes while everyone fell silent and watched the unfolding drama. Between gasps of breath the man coughed up massive amounts of frothy bright red blood which he tried vainly to catch in a large washbasin held in his shaking hands. The basin filled in an awful hurry and another basin was sent for, and then another. On and on the blood-gushing coughing spasms persisted with no sign of letting up as I stood by helplessly. I lacked both the courage and skill, even if I had had the bronchoscope and balloon catheter that could possibly have stemmed the bloody tide. It was by now liberally sprinkled all over the bed, the nurses and me as we supported the frightened patient by the shoulders until he mercifully slipped into unconsciousness. The German name

"Blutsturz," (bloody crash) kept coming into my head as I signed the death certificate.

With close contact of exposed skin in a tropical climate it is not surprising to see a lot of skin disorders. Ringworm fungus infection was particularly common, and when extensive, might point to severe underlying systemic disease.

A police inspector supported his staggering brother into my consulting room. The man was covered with ringworm and gaunt as an inmate from Auschwitz. He had been treated elsewhere for tuberculosis, but his cough was getting worse. No, the sputum was not really productive of blood, in fact "it tasted more like liver". A light went on: **liver**! Could he be tasting his own liver? Minutes later we had the diagnosis from our small laboratory: Entamoeba histolytica. This was a broncho-pulmonary fistula from an amoebic liver abscess. He was in fact coughing up his own liver, as the liver abscess had burst through his diaphragm and lung.

The patient needed two full courses of the old toxic drug Emetine before he began to recover. We did not yet use the far superior and much less toxic drug Flagyl until years later. The flattering letter of thanks from the policeman-brother went into my collection.

Here is another letter from said collection that will challenge armchair diagnosticians:

"Please doctor,

I want that the putuitre (his pituitary gland) on my head should be scatter. I am too tall. And an injection to make me healthy and have power. I am very weak."

I do not recall my diagnosis, but I know it was not a case of acromegaly and the letter was of little help.

Another young man complained of a long list of genito-urinary difficulties and suggested the problem originated from his **carburettor**. I scrambled out of my consulting room chair to adequately vent and share my laughter with the outpatient staff.

We were returning from a busy Saturday clinic in the lengthening shadows of the primordial mountain forest. The Land Rover swayed with its load of staff and patients, food staples and cooking gear. A terribly thin young girl of 14 had puzzled me particularly. She travelled with us because I could not reach a diagnosis at the clinic, but it was clear that she needed urgent hospital care. When we made a "pit stop" near a cool ravine, the girl bolted towards a small waterfall to quench her thirst, and then I had my diagnosis! How could I have missed it? But worse, the disappointment of her hope for medical help hit me hard. Juvenile diabetes is a death sentence in all but the most fortunate of patients. There is the cost of insulin, testing, storage, control, education, diet, each presenting an insurmountable problem.

True, BBH eventually established a monthly clinic for diabetics, but modern ideas of control were utopian. One wealthy Fulani man stored his insulin in a thermos bottle in a cool mountain stream. A few teenagers moved close to the hospital to get their daily injections. Several patients worked full-time just to pay for their insulin. No one had more than a monthly blood-sugar test. More than once customs bureaucracy blocked our insulin importation and the costly drugs were ruined by lack of refrigeration in the customs offices. There were times when there was no insulin in the Pharmacies of Yaounde or Douala, the two major cities. I even tried to keep a few people alive on oral hypoglycemics, an entirely unscientific endeavour. It was all so futile.

The "Indomitable Lions of Cameroon" proved to the world what we had known for a long time; that soccer is played well in many a small African country. The game is played with any object approaching a globular shape, with or without boots, but with great individual skill. Injuries are rare because of the high value attached to finesse, skilful dribbling and artful dodging. Occasionally someone does get hurt trying a particularly acrobatic feat, such as the 14 year old goalkeeper who turned a somersault while attempting to catch the ball. He was paralysed from the neck down.

His friends brought him to the hospital even before his parents were aware of the accident. I was extremely concerned, as these types of injuries have a devastating outlook. More than 95% can expect permanent, severe disability. Besides, no one had taken precautions during transport to prevent further injury to his spinal cord, and our treatment options were far from ideal. I had fashioned some skull tongs by welding a cross-brace onto a knee-traction bow for an earlier patient with a broken neck and we had this boy in the proper neck traction within a short time. Later we received 2 surplus Stryker frames from the Royal Alexandra Hospital in Edmonton via a Canadian military transport plane visiting the Canadian Embassy in Yaounde. I do not remember how we prevented bedsores in the days before the Stryker frames arrived, I remember considering a sand bed.

Our young patient had excellent care. Within hours his bodily functions were taken care of and the family took an active part in providing for his needs. His many soccer friends hovered about the bed all hours of the day, and whenever nurses would allow it. About the fourth day he surprised me by being able to move the fingers on one hand ever so slightly. This was NOT a complete trans-section of his spinal cord! Or was it a small miracle? My interest was stirred. I examined his progress daily. Soon he made giant strides in movement, and his sensation came back as well. The day came when his neck traction could be removed, and he began to sit up with help. Eventually he was able to walk and he left the hospital entirely unsupported. It was *"just too wondaful"*.

I have not been able to determine why even the slightest stumble of my feet always evoked great expressions of anxious vocal concern from anyone nearby. It must have had some spiritual significance that escaped me. People did not seem to fall very easily. Yet when they fell there was often serious injury.

An elderly man arrived in deep trouble. The clothes on his back were soaked in blood and he was on his last legs. He claimed to have walked from a village eight hours distant. I suspected foul play when I saw two broad knife wounds to the right of his thoracic spine. But he assured me that he had fallen onto his own two knives that he was carrying in a woven grass bag slung over his shoulder.

This man was tough. He had punctured and collapsed his right lung. This I was able to deal with by inserting a chest tube, but the second knife had cut his right kidney nearly in half and it had to be sacrificed. This was my first ever nephrectomy. Another one of the many operations I only knew how to do in theory. His recovery was uneventful.

The operation for suspected appendicitis would, more typically, yield a typhoid perforation, an amoebic inflammation or some other rare surprise. (Crohn's disease was very rare as well.)

A twenty-year-old man presented with a small pus-draining wound over the right 12th rib in his back. I thought he might have a chronic osteomyelitis, which I had seen in many bones, from skull to jaw, to rib, to hands and feet, but especially in the long bones of the lower limb.

My exploration led to disappointment; it was not osteomyelitis. He returned a few months later with his fistula still there and draining. It was then that I took a better history: His trouble had actually started with abdominal pain and vomiting, had led to a big swelling in his back, which had given rise to much fever. The boil had burst, and things had settled down, except for the annoying draining fistula.

My second surgical attempt was much better. He still had his appendix lying behind the Cecum in the right para-colic gutter. This time I was able to cure him by removing his long-ago ruptured appendix.

A ten-year-old removed his cap to show me two good-sized knife wounds draining thick pus from the dome of his shaved scalp. His father had incised a "boil" about 2 months ago, was his explanation. I could make out the faint outline of a roughly circular indentation of his scalp and began to wonder if this could be a loose piece of skull bone. In the absence of a working X-ray machine and films I decided to operate, for if it was in fact dead bone, the pus would never stop draining, and antibiotics would be useless. At surgery the scalp bled briskly, keeping me busy for a while. The skull bone looked dull and grey, not pink and living.

Carefully I lifted an edge of the 10-cm diameter loose piece of outer table of the skull. The defect of the inner table was 5 cm in diameter and revealed the healthy, pulsating dura mater covering the entirely unaffected brain. I shivered. This boy needed a silver plate or some other inert substitute to close the defect in the skull. But the body would reject any such foreign body in the presence of infection, even if I could scrounge up a substitute. So I removed the dead bone, closed the incision, placed a small drain and stopped the anaesthetic. The boy went home as the scalp wound healed rapidly.

Who can imagine my alarm to meet him again on one of my clinic visits to the remote village where he lived, **playing football**. The defect in his skull pulsated vigorously like the giant fontanel of a new-born baby. He looked at me quizzically when I told him he could be killed easily when trying to head the ball. I could not even suggest a helmet, as such a thing had never yet been seen in this remote area of Cameroon.

Snakebites were uncommon above 1500 meters elevation, as snakes preferred the heat of the plains. I did not gather much expertise in the treatment of these injuries, but copied the treatment methods of doctors before me. Anti-venom was rarely available and probably not even specific for the vipers, adders and cobras in our area.

A pattern seemed to evolve: If someone was inoculated with the neurotoxic type of venom, the victim would not survive for more than half an hour. So I never saw any of these unfortunate people, and might only hear of their demise. If the venom was of the cytotoxic type, the patient would arrive with a rapidly swelling, painful limb. We would remove the tourniquet (which the natives always applied) submerge the limb in ice water, give adequate pain relief and order absolute bed-rest. The ice in the bucket had to be replenished regularly from all the available kerosene refrigerators on the compound. The worst result with this treatment would rarely be more than a few square cm of skin-loss that could be treated with grafts.

If, however, the family would procrastinate and the tourniquet was left in place for more than three or four hours the tissues began to die from lack of blood supply and the limb would have to be amputated. I saw this unfortunate situation at least a half dozen times, always after a delay of several days.

I remember one 12-year-old boy in particular. His uncle unwrapped the unsavoury spectacle of the right, dominant arm in an advanced stage of wet gangrene, yet causing no discomfort, because the only connecting link to the boy's body was the bare upper arm bone, the humerus, but it wasn't funny. Maggots were busy keeping the healthy stump clean. It was one of the easiest yet most distasteful operations of my career.

It was amazing to see how quickly the population would learn of a new service offered in our hospitals, whether it was a visiting specialist who began to offer modern prostate operations or it was us beginning to cure the blind. The blood bank proved a great advance. X-ray, Dental service, Endoscopy and Ultrasound attracted numerous patients. They would soon come from the remotest corners of the country or even cross national borders to present their neglected and diseased bodies. Many, of course, only wanted to try the wonderful new machinery.

In the years before 24-hour electricity, before the beautiful Ultrasound now present at both MBH and BBH, before X-ray films and various serum tests now available, most of our diagnoses were reached by clinical deduction. We developed a greater reliance on our five senses, since even the history was more often misleading than not. Tumors that must have taken months to grow were usually claimed to have arisen "last week". But the patient was not always wrong in his effort to be co-operative and tell me what he thought I wanted to hear. The 4-year-old with the classical sign of a kidney tumor relieved me greatly when, at surgery, it was "only" a huge tense pyomyositis, a muscle in his abdominal wall that had turned into a huge bag of pus. So the father's story was accurate this time, it had indeed arisen "only last week"

A 20-year-old lady presented with the history of a sore throat for 2 weeks. She had no recordable blood pressure but an egg sized, vigorously pulsating mass on the right side of her neck. Her blood tests indicated a severe infection. She did not even give us a chance to pursue a diagnosis, as she expired quietly shortly after arrival.

And years later, there was that 15-year-old girl with the huge tumor that almost certainly was an inoperable cancer of the liver. But it turned out to be just another very ordinary amoebic liver abscess, eminently curable, just so very tense and adherent to the abdominal wall that it fooled this old experienced doctor. She was cured, though it took a few weeks.

And then there was the very concerned father of a 14-year-old girl who looked highly pregnant. Both father and daughter assured me that my diagnosis was wrong, and that the girl needed an operation. It turned out to be a huge dermoid cyst that arose from multi-potential ovarian cells and contained teeth, hair and cartilage. These benign tumors always stirred up great wonder among our theatre staff.

My young African colleague asked me for an opinion on a 3-cm lump projecting from a little boy's shaven head. It felt like a Wen (a cyst filled with dead skin cells), removal of which would have been an office procedure, but since the little fellow would be frightened he was taken to the operating room for a brief general anaesthetic. This one was a bad surprise: A rapidly growing brain tumour had eroded through the skull, leaving a punched out hole through which this ugly tumour now showed its killing intent. Our resident internist decided on a trial of chemotherapy. The biopsy result would not return from the far away pathology laboratory in Calgary for several weeks, where some of our puzzling cases were diagnosed gratis. I was unable to follow this little patient's progress, as I neared the end of my short-term service. All I could offer was to act as a courier of the pathological specimen to my home country.

Very occasionally a western medical magazine would come across my desk. One day I read about the routine inoculation of East African children with BCG (an old Vaccine developed in France) which gives partial protection against tuberculosis, and how it had had the unexpected result of cutting the incidence of new leprosy cases in half. The article also mentioned the use of BCG as an adjunct in the experimental therapy of advanced malignant melanomas. I had seen melanomas occasionally on the palms or more often the soles of my patients and treated them with radical surgery. But shortly after reading the above article I came across a young lady patient with a small melanoma on the cheek, in the region of the infra-orbital nerve. Unfortunately the cancer had already metastasized to the brain, as evidenced by an unresponsive dilated pupil and half-closed lid of the eye above the small skin tumor. I recalled the recent article and decided to try a local injection of the readily available BCG vaccine from our weekly maternity inoculation clinic. It might just prolong my young patient's life, as surgery was clearly too late for an attempt at cure. I was considerably impressed when I saw the young lady a month later. The third cranial nerve palsy had completely disappeared. It would have been interesting to follow her progress, but she never returned again.

A well-dressed educated woman brought her 12-year-old son to me after he had been living with his grandmother for a few months. It was a consult that raised me out of my chair. I was still fairly easily aroused in those days, and these kinds of problems always got me excited. Eric was a classical picture of kwashiorkor (an eminently preventable nutritional deficiency state): thin shiny skin, pallor around the eyes, puffy belly, hands and feet, weeping sores on his ankles, cracked corners of the mouth and, when he reluctantly removed his cap, yellow wisps of "eider-down" doing a poor job of hiding his shiny scalp. All he had had to eat for the last few months, and not much of it, was fufu corn. I could hardly believe how quickly he had progressed to this sorry state. The rapid growth spurt of puberty with its increased nutritional demands had accelerated his severe deficiency state. His mother was easily convinced of my diagnosis and treatment plan. She was as angry at her mother-in-law for starving her son as I was excited about the challenge of curing him. She and I made a pact. I would provide only Vitamins and she would supply the exact diet I would advise, and together we would prove to ourselves that this child could be cured with just food, not medicine. Avocados, soybeans, peanuts, the occasional meat and fish, an egg a day, beans and rice, and fufu too, all available locally and not expensive. This was not a problem of poverty. Pure ignorance had been at work.

Eric responded beautifully. I saw him at intervals. The one thing he lacked, however, was hair. It just didn't seem to respond to our prodding. I left the country when it was furlough time.

Eight years later, as I wrestled the Land Rover along crowded Commercial Avenue in the Provincial Capital, a tall young man ran up to my window: "Are my eyes deceiving me, or is this Lemke?" The imposing African male stooped to look into the Landrover's high window. He was towering over his lesser-muscled cohorts on the busy street.

"It is me, Eric!"

"Which Eric?"

"**the** Eric".

Surprise, delight, vigorous expressions of hearty greeting in the midst of heavy, now obstructed traffic. The hair! I couldn't believe the hair. It was all there. What a triumph. What a meeting.

I was sitting under the bougainvillaea bush in the late afternoon dry season sun when an emergency needed my attention. A two-year-old had been eating peanuts and had begun coughing and showing signs of respiratory distress. It was now two days and the child was getting worse. This was out of my area of skill. Besides, we had practically no suitable instruments for looking into the trachea of so small a child. Knowing that the girl was probably going to die if the peanut remained in her windpipe, I started looking for help from the theatre staff. Alex had years of experience and a heap of patience, combined with quiet determination and wise counsel. He found a box of bronchoscope parts and pieces that I scrounged through. I found a small bronchoscope, but only one tiny light bulb remained, and there were no suitable forceps to grasp the peanut. Perhaps I could grasp the foreign body blindly with the adult forceps and withdraw it together with the scope? Alex urged me to give it a try. I had the advantage of having at least seen a bronchoscopy, if not ever done one.

The child was put to sleep, wheezing and coughing. The oxygen was at least turning the lips a little pinker.

This was tough. Once I actually got the scope through the vocal cords, but it slipped out again. Alex kept urging me on: "Try it again doctor, just try it".

I got the scope in. And there was the piece of peanut sitting right on top of the bifurcation of the trachea, where it divides into the two main bronchi. My excitement was tempered. Now what to do next. Oxygen, give it some puffs of oxygen! Looking again, the child gave a cough, I felt something hit my right cornea and Alex was on the floor in a flash. "Here is it, doctor!" Relief, joy, a "flare-prayer" of thanksgiving. I did not have to use those terrible adult forceps. Quickly the scope was withdrawn. What a change in the toddler's breathing. Complete victory. Then the usual public health talks. Urging mother, grandmother, nurses and carers who listened with interest: "No fresh peanuts for children under 4, unless ground up or processed in food".

A few weeks later almost the same scene, another patient—a three-year-old girl—had been taken to several hospitals over several days. No one had a bronchoscope. The child was blue and exhausted. She died on the table while I tried to repeat our recent success. My dejection was not helped by the generous gratitude of mother and grandmother who thanked me over and over, *no be yu don try?*

(You have done your best).

I am not sure how our nursing school allowed the term "pale" to slip into their list of clinical signs, when over 99% of our patients where various shades of brown to black. Our staff loved to use the word "pale" and used it liberally in their reports. Severe anaemia can, of course, be clinically discernible in Africans. One such young man presented with a large bloody bandage around his left thigh at MBH one morning. He was rather reluctant to give a history. He had grown tired of the large swelling in his thigh and had tried to reduce its size by a courageous stab with his pocket-knife. The resultant flood of pulsing bright red liquid had surprised and motivated him to pursue an alternate plan of action. His hemoglobin was 4.2 (25%), his pulse a rapid hyperkinetic 140 beats per minute.

I was sure there was a lot left unsaid between us as I started my examination away from the obvious focus of his concern. The blood in his arteries seemed to be in a particular hurry, and the veins on his left leg were swollen abnormally.

When I placed my status symbol (stethoscope) on his abdomen and groin I was startled by sounds reminiscent of a steam engine from the fifties. "Aha….so what was the original injury….might as well tell now…was there a gun?" At this point the nurse in charge found an urgent duty for me outside the ward. Yes there was a gun, and the boy had been seen at MBH a few months before, when he had had a run-in with the forces of law and order. There was a bullet in that leg and it had been left inside, as it was causing no harm at the time.

This fellow had a huge communication between the femoral artery and vein that short-circuited vast quantities of blood back to his heart without doing any useful work. No wonder his heart was busy pounding in his chest, while he was just sitting quietly.

I had had a very difficult time with a similar case about 25 years earlier and was not about to attempt this surgery without some fancy X-ray pictures to guide me. These were the Nineties and there were plenty of specialists in the Capital, I decided much to the disappointment of the mother who eventually came on the scene. The pair left reluctantly with their referral letter and the patient was "lost to follow up".

Petty theft of fruit, chickens, household items, money and tools is extremely common and not particularly serious in all but the victim's eyes. However, to steal eggs, corn or plantains in your home village is universally considered evil. Eggs, because they represent future chickens, corn and plantains because they sustain a person's very life during the seasonal food shortage.

To steal habitually is widely believed to be an inherited disorder that cannot be changed by ordinary family discipline. National laws exist against robbery, which is defined as "theft with the use of weapons, such as a screwdriver or a get-away car". Proscribed punishment is very harsh, from the Muslim's amputation at the wrist to public execution of notorious thieves. Bribery to escape punishment is, however, even more common. With the recently very active International Human Rights Commission linked closely to International Monetary Fund loans and grants the government has been reluctant to carry out executions of criminals for some years now. Prisoners are overcrowding ancient jails left over from colonial times. Death-row inmates mingle freely with general prisoners, their only identification: permanent ankle chains. I saw several prisoners with tuberculosis and other signs of terminal AIDS on my visits there. Relatives are responsible for supplying food to all prisoners. The young man with the bullet in his thigh had been a thief.

There has been quite a shift in the way Cameroon Society deals with its thieves in the last few years.

We were driving along a very crowded main road in the Provincial Capital when we had to swerve rather abruptly in order to avoid a corpse lying near the centre of a very busy intersection. Clothed in rags and covered with only two or three small leafy branches the body was sprawled where it had fallen when the angry mob had beaten the thief to death. What amazed me, however, was the fact that no one seemed to even acknowledge him as being something other than a foreign body in the way, barely avoiding him with their hurrying feet or rolling tires. No relatives acknowledged or retrieved him, no officials investigated. Justice had been done.

But these were peaceful, friendly people. Many of them were Christians. What was happening to our beloved Cameroon? The laws enacted under President Ahidjo in the sixties seemed harsh. Thousands had gathered in the football stadium on each occasion when a thief was executed by firing squad. Mothers even brought their small children to impress them with the consequences of theft.

Law and Order seemed harsh and cruel then, but the recent trend to anarchy is far more worrisome. People seem to have lost all faith that official government procedures will deal impartially and fairly with the rising crime and hardship they are now facing. Their frustration may boil up in mob violence.

The medical profession prides itself on its ethics. When a doctor knows the patient's problem is outside his or her area of expertise, he/she will not only admit it, but also refer the patient to the appropriate specialist.

There were practically no medical specialists in Cameroon in the Sixties.

Later, when some of the young Cameroonian specialists returned from their overseas training, we tried to establish a professional relationship with them. Most of these highly trained specialists were severely hampered in their practises by lack of instruments and high-tech equipment that they had learned to use during their overseas training. They tried to adapt to the reality of their country's limited resources, but were severely frustrated by stringent import and foreign exchange legislation, which prevented them from building up their instrument and equipment roster. Further troubled by the lack of infrastructure, a total lack of pharmaceutical manufacturing in Cameroon and the paucity of competent assistants and technicians, many of these doctors gave up the dream to serve their country. They either did little clinical work at all, or tried to leave the country to practise in any one of a host of other nations. Sixty Cameroonian doctors were said to be practising in Paris in the Seventies.

The neurosurgeon in a large Cameroon hospital refused to open a skull electively, as he could not be sure of the sterile technique in the operating room. The newly trained ophthalmologist posted to the Provincial Hospital could not operate for cataracts because his only pair of corneal scissors was dull (I gave him a sharper pair). The radiographer could not use the new CAT scanner after a few months of use, because the rigorous maintenance schedule could not be followed and there was no money to bring in a competent technician.

A few specialists have made a go of private practise, but their service is restricted to those patients who can pay their relatively high fees.

A referral system such as we know it in Canada is simply non-existent. The few times our referrals actually achieved a measure of satisfaction must be considered a miracle.

Is it possible that the Cameroon Government welcomes the continued presence of private (former mission) hospitals because they set a high ethical standard for the medical and nursing professions?

A young Pastor dragged himself to the hospital with the help of a cane. His face was contorted with pain. It was not difficult to make the diagnosis of a protruding intervertebral disc in his lumbar spine, he had all the classical signs. He needed a myelogram (a special X-ray with radio-opaque dye) and a neurosurgeon. The closest accessible place where he might expect to get this kind of help was at the University of Ibadan in Nigeria, a thousand kilometers away. I wrote a referral letter and bought him an airline ticket (Pastors are among the lowest paid workers in the country). Three weeks later he came back with a note: "Sorry we could not do the myelogram, as we are out of dye". This was so exasperating, yet typical, that it was easy to develop the attitude: If we cannot help the patient, it is very unlikely that anyone else can. The referral system worked only for the rich, the relatives of the powerful or the lucky ones.

There were, however, not a few instances where God mercifully enabled bodies to heal themselves against formidable odds.

One of our senior nurse/midwives experienced a sudden complete paralysis of both legs from an L2-3 midline disc protrusion. Conservative measures of physiotherapy, traction and medication had not made a difference in the week before I left for Canada. But six months later I found her back at work, aided only by a rarely used cane, and pain-free. The hospital staff family had rallied around her in prayer, and she had recovered very well indeed.

I was often amazed how eagerly patients and their families agreed to all surgical procedures, unless it was an amputation, when most of them would balk. But abdominal explorations, especially, seemed to enjoy a reputation that was simply astounding. One of the letters in my collection was brief and to the point:

"His Ruyal Highness, the Doctor of Nso.

This Christian man needs operation, Sir."

I suspect that centuries of untreated abdominal emergencies with their violently unpleasant deaths had something to do with this universal belief in the value of laparotomies (surgical opening of the abdomen). And the great fear of dying with a swollen abdomen added urgency, as that phenomenon signified a spiritual problem; the patient had "eaten someone's spirit". The swollen abdomen was proof of his malevolent greed. And now he had died. The relatives would plead, could I at least reduce the size of his abdomen to curtail the sizeable accusations of his enemies?

With our limited facilities for diagnosis we felt justified to be rather liberal with diagnostic laparotomies, often with great satisfaction.

A four-year-old had a growing mass in his abdomen. With accompanying weight loss and lethargy it looked like a rapidly growing malignancy. His Mantoux test for tuberculosis was negative, yet at surgery he had widely spread tuberculous growths filling his abdomen, like knobbly hills and mountains rising out of a clear yellow sea. We started anti-TB drugs immediately after surgery and he enjoyed a remarkably brief recovery time. We would have missed the diagnosis without the exploratory operation.

A youth from Wum presented at MBH with signs of intestinal obstruction. I was greatly puzzled by his operative findings. Hundreds of tiny hard white globular swellings of varying sizes were fixed to the outside of most of his small bowel wall, and in three or four areas extensive scarring and stricture had developed where these small nodules were particularly concentrated. I relieved the obstruction with conventional surgical procedures, and obtained a couple of the nodules for laboratory analysis. I mailed these to the highest authority of my training years, the Chief of Pathology at the University of Alberta. I had to look up "meiosis" in my textbook when I finally received a reply many weeks later. The fellow had eaten uncooked meat exposed to flies, not an uncommon habit in the area. The white nodules each contained a fly-larva. Unfortunately, the young man had died by this time.

Mrs. "Coffee" was a respected village woman who consulted me with a persistent fever and weight loss. (Her husband was a progressive cash crop farmer who had successfully introduced arabica coffee into the Banso area.)

I quickly ran through my limited lab tests. Nothing but a few white blood cells turned up in her urine and she had some kidney tenderness when I gently pounded her back with my fist. When all my trials of antibiotic therapy failed to improve her persistent fever, I asked for acid fast stains of her urinary sediment, and we hit the jackpot. Never before or since have I diagnosed tuberculosis of the kidney. She responded to treatment and for years thereafter this lady's gratitude shone in her radiant smile whenever we met in town or market.

A family living near Mbve market brought a slender boy of about twelve with abdominal pain and fever. He was in terrible shape. He had been ill for several days and had been treated at home with herbal medications and an enema. Then he suddenly got much worse, and it was decided to give Western medicine a try.

The grossly swollen abdomen, the dull sunken eyes, the high fever and the slow pulse suggested that he could have typhoid fever. The textbook suggested surgery for the complication of a perforated small intestine but also warned of a 50% death rate in such cases. With a sense of foreboding I decided to operate.

My diagnosis of typhoid was indeed confirmed. The small bowel had the feel and fragility of wet toilet paper and there were 12 raggedly punched-out holes in his last half-meter of small bowel. Perhaps the enema had precipitated this terrible complication?

It was easy to excise, but difficult to reconnect the friable bowel. The sutures kept cutting through the mushy bowel wall.

And now we faced the challenge of a stormy postoperative course with our little patient hovering on the brink of death for several days. His abdominal wound broke open and drained bowel content. (So my connecting job was leaking!) He was terribly weak and the fever responded only very gradually to the antibiotics. Several times I expected to see his bed empty when making rounds in the morning.

Well, he did pull through and even closed his fistula without repeat surgery, but his abdominal scar resembled a three-dimensional geography map.

When a fourteen-year-old Fulani boy arrived from Mbem with an even worse clinical picture I decided to try conservative treatment. Somewhere in an old textbook I had learned about this option. I was certain that an operation would kill him, so I simply relieved the awful distension of his abdominal cavity with repeated needle punctures, gave intravenous fluids and oral Chloromycetin, the antibiotic of choice. (We had no intravenous Chloromycetin). The bacterial toxins weakened his heart muscle, but it too responded to medication. The patient's recovery was just as precarious and precious as the first, and I decided to keep this method of treatment in mind. There were others who were cured that way, but I also regretfully lost at least one typhoid-perforation patient with non-operative treatment. And then I wondered if I should have operated.

I never found a sure way to diagnose or treat typhoid. Tests were unreliable, often unavailable and not helpful to the treatment anyway. Our mortality rate for the 20 to 40 cases per year ran between 10 and 25%. It was discouraging that in spite of biennial immunisations both missionaries and African staff occasionally came down with the disease. I learned to fear this formidable enemy!

The abdomen is the general surgeon's field of play. And it is acknowledged to require years of training and a lifetime of experience to become somewhat familiar, but never too comfortable with its many challenges. No wonder some of the young graduates from Yaounde medical school sometimes felt lost in it when practising alone in rural hospitals. Had I not been in those situations myself? How I wished I could have referred my problems in those early days, like the patient I received from a young GP with the very brief note: "Megacolon, and for splenectomy". The colleague had taken a look, sewed up the abdomen in resignation and put the 14-year-old just-operated girl into a crowded taxi with her mother, for the one-hour bumpy ride to BBH.

I felt obliged to re-operate and found only a very distended stomach containing four litres of fluid, but no other pathology. Naso-gastric tube suction was the only treatment this patient required. I strongly suspect that a traditional doctor was the initial cause of all her troubles when he overdosed her with his atropine-like native medicine, causing her stomach to dilate to near bursting. The young girl's recovery was routine. The mother's deep concern melted away. She "oozed" quiet gratitude.

I am not sure just how much small bowel one needs in order to survive, without running into serious malnutrition. 50%? 30%? How about 20%? But when I was faced with coils and coils of black gut, resection was the only hope for at least temporary survival.

A gentle giant of a man from the picturesque mountain village of Mbesenaku had been in agony for a couple of days when I had to resect 80% of his twisted dead bowel. He recovered quickly from the surgery, but will someone remember to give him extra vitamins and high protein food for the rest of his life? Even though I told him about his need for life-long supplement, I am sure he only heard half of it in the euphoria of receiving the gift of life all over again.

I vividly remember an incident with another patient who had a similar problem, that ended as close to a "miracle" as I have come to one.

This middle-aged lady needed surgery badly. The picture of her entire small bowel in that unmistakable state of imminent necrosis, and me faced with the dilemma of resection was just too much. I examined the sick intestine from end to end, may have unwittingly untwisted its strangulated coils, and waited for the return of a healthier color of this essential organ, only to be disappointed. I closed the abdomen in resignation. One cannot live without any small bowel at all. The surgeon cannot save all.

The adult son waited at the operating theatre door. I told him the news. I had done nothing. There was no help. Oh yes,…. he should pray.

And so he did.

It took a few days, but the lady recovered. I have no explanation, just gratitude and the humble admission that I don't know a lot about abdominal surgery yet.

The operating theatre certainly had a central place in the hospital and in the minds of patients. The drama that so often occurred there justified its fame. The satisfaction of a confirmed diagnosis, the surprise of an easy cure, the drama of a saved life; no wonder many of our staff did not mind the gruelling hours it took to be part of the team that laboured there.

Very occasionally visitors were allowed to observe certain procedures in the operating theatre. Besides the usual students, visiting dignitaries and donors of funds would be invited to observe suitable routine cases. Occasionally, when I had double duty as doctor and baby-sitter while an emergency arose, my young son would have to sit on the window-sill properly gowned and masked in oversized OR attire, while daddy did emergency surgery. Our children's play was certainly enriched by these experiences.

A visitor from one of our supporting churches expressed the desire to observe the cure of a blind cataract patient. He assured me that he would be able to watch without feeling queasy. Eye surgery demands the uninterrupted gaze of the surgeon upon the operative field. But out of the corner of my eye I saw a falling shadow and stuck out my left foot to prevent the fainting visitor's head from striking the concrete floor (soccer reflex?). He was up in a few seconds and effusive in his assurance that he was perfectly fine.

When my best friend Andy, an RCAF Search and Rescue medical technician visited from Canada he won immediate favour with our OR staff because of his unceasing jokes. Cameroonians love to laugh. And if a joke fell flat because of a cross-cultural block, Andy would have another one or two to follow quickly. One day he met a worker pushing an empty wheelchair down the long verandas of BBH. Quickly, Andy caught a free ride and immediately aroused deep concern from onlookers: "Oh, Mr. Andasen, what is the matter, are you sick?"

To which Andy replied: "Oh, its nothing…, just **circumcision**". (The uncircumcised adult male is the butt of many a joke in Cameroon.). The staff laughed for days. No wonder the theatre staff said: "The sun has gone down!" when Andy left.

That remark mirrored my own feelings, as I too would have liked my friend to stay at BBH for a long time. His humor would have wonderfully balanced my altogether too serious outlook on life.

Andy had an in-exhaustible positive attitude and courage in spades. He had things "together" no matter what situation he faced. His 300-plus parachute jumps in "Search and Rescue", into all kinds of treacherous territory, from ocean to arctic, ruined his knees, but not his spirit. He admitted that he used to be afraid of dying, but not any longer since he and his wife met the Christ who remade them both. Regardless of his metal knees and a few other medical afflictions, he told me often that he would have liked nothing better than working with me in Cameroon. It was evident to my Cameroonian colleagues and me that his attitude and view of life allowed him to fit in admirably and immediately. We were certainly able to put him to work in the OR where an extra pair of skilled hands was always welcome.

A concerned dad brought his ten-year-old son who had a swelling and much pain in his lower leg. He was unable to walk and had a high fever, but his history did not include sickle cell crises (a common reason for distressing bone pain in the black race who often suffer from this congenital malady). His blood picture suggested infection. I made the diagnosis of acute osteomyelitis and suggested emergency minor surgery. Permission was granted and within two hours of arrival we were able to put him to sleep, drill his bone and confirm the diagnosis. Because of the timely intervention the pressure of pus inside his shinbone was released, preventing the lifting of the nourishing periosteum and death of a large segment of bone. Antibiotics would now have a chance to get to the endangered tissue and bring the infection under control. The boy was spared months of pain, debility and further surgery.

This scenario was all too rare. At least nine out of ten osteomyelitis cases came too late, with chronically draining sinuses and a variable length of dead bone lying encased in the prison of newly forming bone, never ceasing to produce pus. The only cure would then lie in radical surgery. The old dead bone would have to be removed through a freshly cut channel of the new bone. Plaster casts supported the new bone. Painful repeated daily or biweekly dressing changes of the wound allowed it to heal from the bottom up. Usually this took many months, but would eventually result in a cure. Chronic osteomyelitis patients were constant visitors in our outpatient dressing clinics.

That is why there were few surgical procedures that gave me greater satisfaction than catching an acute osteomyelitis in time.

Treating the many dislocations of shoulders, jaws, fingers, hips and elbows (in decreasing order of frequency) gave me almost as much pleasure, especially if there was a student to be taught how to reduce them.

When these patients came shortly after their injury it was usually a simple matter. The poor misguided souls who were left untreated by either neglect or native medicine could only wait for the orthopaedic specialist Dr. Tom Coleman who volunteered his service every winter since his retirement in 1987. Until he came, people with chronic unreduced dislocations simply continued to suffer from unrelenting pain and disability. It can be very difficult indeed to reduce a chronically dislocated major joint months after the initial injury. It seems to always require surgery.

The "biggest" surgery I ever undertook was an amputation through the hip joint for a malignant tumor in the knee area of a 20 year old man. When the gruesome task was done my assistant Gwaksi gave a sigh of relief: "I have never seen anything like it" to which I could only reply: "nor have I".

BBH enjoyed a huge advance with the arrival of the second full-time physician in 1969. Dr. Helen Marie Schmidt was our first fully qualified surgeon. We could now spell each other off on night-and Sunday call-duty. We could leave the hospital for clinic visits without first anxiously trying to anticipate emergencies in our absence, and we could actually pursue some areas of special interest to either of us. The "second opinion" was another reassuring bonus. With a dramatic increase of more and more complicated operations the emphasis started to shift away from general and internal medicine. It led me to the erroneous belief that an internist could hardly be happy to work in our situation. With but few lab tests and little time for lengthy and thorough examinations such a colleague would be extremely frustrated and depressed, I thought. It's a good thing I had a chance to later correct that idea when I worked with such a specialist during my first 6 months of volunteer service in 1986. I deeply appreciated Dr.Mike Anderson for his brilliant clinical diagnoses, his daring treatments and pure enjoyment of the work. The very day he went home to the United States I had a painful reminder of the huge gap he left in our ranks. First, I had great difficulty in dealing with a Fulani woman with malignant hypertension, giving her inappropriate medication and almost losing her. Then another patient came who would have had the immediate attention of at least two specialists in Canada. She was the daughter of a diabetic woman whom we had treated for years with difficult control. The daughter had become diabetic herself 6 years ago and she also had high blood pressure. She was now in the seventh month of her first pregnancy that was complicated by a persistent kidney infection, which was resistant to all our antibiotics. The morning of her arrival she had had two seizures, so now she also had eclampsia. Where was Mike when I needed him?

Fortunately, the lady survived, as did her premature baby, but I was distinctly uncomfortable with the management of five diagnoses in one patient, whereas an internist would probably have liked the challenge!

Bowel transit times seemed to be twice as fast in my African patients as in North American surgical patients. This had the wonderfully beneficial effect of shortened post operative bowel paralysis. It simplified management and forestalled dangerous complications. Besides, our patients did not like to go without food for any length of time, to them it was an omen of impending death.

My patients also held strong beliefs about "elimination of waste materials". Most adults ate twice a day and expected a bowel movement (B.M.) as often. One B.M. per day gave rise to complaints of constipation whereas three constituted a *"running stomach"*. Native doctors spent much energy in these areas of concern, and I could hardly build my reputation without paying considerable attention to matters of the stomach. The stomach is the seat of the African soul, not the heart, as it is in the Western world.

Certain coastal tribes have a particularly drastic custom. New-born babies have to undergo a thorough pepper enema shortly after the trauma of birth. And it is always effective. Does it not remove all the bad, abnormal-looking, dark-green stool from the baby?

Curiously, Canadian proponents of alternative medicine have been calling for periodic "colonic cleansing" as essential for superior health in the new millennium.

Perhaps they would consider the pure, natural, organically grown non-genetically modified Bakweli pepper for this purpose?

A middle-aged man complained: *"my powa done finis"*. And his complaint was not the usual one about unreasonably high expectations in the sexual realm, annoyingly common among my male patients. He had a problem with muscle strength. I lacked any sort of laboratory facility to confirm the diagnosis of a neuromuscular junction disorder, but was restricted to a thorough physical examination and observation. The patient was able to walk for only a few minutes before his overwhelming weakness forced him to stop, or he would collapse from intense muscle weakness. His facial muscles and especially his eyelids would droop. He suffered from intermittent double vision and would close one eye to resolve the confusion. A short rest invigorated him and the cycle repeated itself. I achieved a small improvement of his symptoms by giving him ephedrine, the mainstay of treatment for our asthma patients, and therefore in good supply. But not until a visitor from abroad delivered the specific drug for myasthenia gravis: "Neostigmine", did the patient improve dramatically. He left the hospital happily, but never returned for additional medications.

The idea of preventive medication seemed to be a difficult concept for people to grasp. This was especially true in chronic conditions that deteriorated only gradually and painlessly over the span of months or years, like glaucoma. Most of our glaucoma patients did not return for refills of their eye drops, since they did not see any improvement in their vision. They would sometimes show up again when it was too late to save their eyesight.

A young woman with headaches was admitted because her blood pressure registered dangerously high. I demanded immediate repetition of the blood pressure recordings when the nursing staff reported a series of grossly variable readings. Student nurses were accused of incompetence. When I took the blood pressure myself, it was normal, only to be told minutes later that it was sky-high again. I began to suspect a rare problem and ordered the cuff to be left on the patient's arm during sleep, so that a nurse could sneak up to the bed and try to get a reading without waking the patient. We made the rare diagnosis of an adrenaline-producing pheochromocytoma. Knowing that 90% of these tumours would be found in one of the two adrenal glands sitting atop the kidneys, my colleague and I decided on surgery as the patient's only hope for survival. We obtained a small supply of phentolamine from overseas, the adrenalin-blocking drug that would control the blood pressure during anaesthesia. I was to be in charge of the tricky anaesthesia, when the surgeon's handling of the tumor would cause the pressure to Yo-yo in synch with my anxiety, and my trusted surgery-colleague would do the search for the (usually) small tumour.

The day of surgery came. We had read up on the problem, as we usually did when venturing into unknown territory, we prayed with the patient, as we always did before surgery and I began the slow process of anaesthesia induction with our "E.M.O." air-over-ether machine. Then I intubated her trachea "on the run" as we could not risk paralysing a patient. We had no positive pressure anesthesia machine, which would have done little good in our primitive hospital without regular electricity. When the precious Phentolamine dripped into her veins, we were finally ready to proceed.

My colleague never found the tumour. It was definitely not in the adrenal glands. It could have been anywhere along the sympathetic chains adjacent to the spine, even in the chest, and we decided that we could not venture there on that day. We were very discouraged and disappointed.

The patient died a few weeks later.

The number of congenital anomalies I saw was inordinate and fully to be expected, since I saw so many more patients than the average North American doctor would see in a lifetime. In new-borns I saw intestinal atresia (failure to develop normal bowel), hypertrophic pyloric stenosis (an abnormally strong outlet muscle of the stomach) and imperforate anus (failure to form an opening for stool to pass) fairly often, but mal-rotation of the gut, volvulus (twisting and obstruction) of the stomach and volvulus of the caecum I saw only once each and was able to cure at operation.

We saw buphthalmos (congenital glaucoma), anencephaly (absent forebrain), exomphalus (absent abdominal wall), different types of spina bifida (spinal cord abnormality with often serious and multiple lower body dysfunctions) and fetus papyraceus (paper-like shrivelling up of one twin because of a common blood supply, when one identical twin "steals" most of the blood supply).

Sixth digits (extra fingers and toes) were very common in our hospital population. I estimate the incidence to be in the order of 1 in 30 deliveries, and have no clue as to why it was so common. The babies with extra digits were simply included in the line-up for male circumcisions (which we scheduled twice a week) and the extra digits were removed unceremoniously. We had no problem getting maternal consent for this minor procedure, but when I asked a man of 60 during an unrelated consult if I should remove his useless extra thumb he said: "I will have to ask my father". I had committed another cultural gaffe.

For some reason I had been under the impression that "von Recklinghausen's multiple neurofibromatosis" was a rare inherited anomaly of eastern Europeans. (The "Elephant-man" of circus fame suffered from this disorder of the nerve-endings in the skin). But I found many in Cameroon, nearly as many as albinos (people with total absence of skin pigments), who always suffered from premature ageing of their delicate skin and subsequent skin cancers before middle age. Nearly every village had a few albinos, and I tried to warn the mothers of these beautiful babies about the need for meticulous avoidance of sunlight.

A 2-months-old infant was brought in because of "too much crying". It had a fractured femur and my probing fingers found several other suspicious swellings over collarbone, arms and legs. Child abuse among the Nso people? No, just a very rare case of osteogenesis imperfecta (fragilitas osseans or "brittle bone disease"), and the bluish sclera were the telltale sign of this distressing congenital anomaly. Achondroplastic dwarfism (very short arms and legs with normal head and torso), absent clavicles and radii, syndactilism (fused fingers), Turner's XO and other suspected chromosomal anomalies, and hermaphrodites (indeterminate sexual development) of various etiologies kept me interested, even though I could obviously not do much for most of these.

It is well known that advanced maternal age predisposes to chromosomal disorders, and there were a number of the loveable but intellectually challenged children with Down's syndrome because many mothers continued delivering babies up to the menopause. The population did not seem to attach any stigma to this genetic disorder.

And then there was the striking difference in disease patterns compared to the western world of medicine. We saw practically no cancers of the large bowel and very little appendicitis and hypertension until the advent of western diets. There were but few strokes and no heart attacks at all. I saw only two patients with kidney stones, both of them missionaries, and one of them looked at me out of the mirror one day. Those episodes of intense and unremitting waves of pain helped me to become more compassionate with my patients. But it is indeed curious that West Africans simply do not get kidney stones, in spite of subjecting themselves to prolonged periods of dehydration. I guess it's just another area for the medical researcher to explore.

The incidence of Blount's disease, a serious deformity of children's legs with sideways angulations of up to 90 degrees (in opposite or same direction) above or below the knees was distressingly common. One Dutch Physician practising in a small remote hospital corrected 50 of these in the short span of two years in the seventies. In recent years, Dr. Tom Coleman, our venerated octogenarian orthopedic surgeon accumulated a spectacular series of these cases of obscure origin. He counted these children and early teens among his happiest patients as he corrected their grotesque deformities and often added 20 cm to their height.

Infectious disease was far more common and the cases were usually more advanced than in the West. Fortunately we were able to treat most infections with the antibiotics that were cheap and increasingly ineffective in the West. I used Penicillin, Sulpha drugs and Tetracycline "by the bucket". I do not recall seeing a Penicillin allergy in the first 10 years. Lately there have been increasing cases of drug resistance because of the uncontrolled sale of antibiotics in open markets, wrong prescriptions by unscrupulous medical personnel and self-medication by ignorant patients. The Third World is rapidly catching up to the First.

Fortunately, I witnessed only one case of rabies, though there are rabid dogs killed regularly by courageous hunters. All I could offer the patient was sedation and pain relief for the agonising spasms. It was a horrifying death to watch impotently.

We treated Tetanus as often as once or twice a month, with a better than 65% cure rate except for new-born babies who rarely survived this terrifying infection. Several of these patients remain vivid in my memory as their care taxed my clinical skills to the limit.

A young Pastor, who had been bitten by a snake in Mbembe area, trekked for four days to reach the motor road. The tourniquet that was to save his life was left on his wrist too long, and his right hand was now black with gangrene. I watched him agonise over the need to have his dominant hand amputated and agreed to wait for his decision until the next morning. In the night his tetanic spasms began with sudden force and he died in spite of our best efforts.

There was the middle aged woman with far advanced cancer of the breast who had the usual native treatment (mud compresses). Offers of surgery were refused. She died of tetanus 4 days after arrival.

But there was also the rather mild case of tetanus in a 7-year-old boy who refused to stay in bed during daylight hours. Stiffly, grinning "sardonically" (because of spastic facial muscles), he even ventured up the 500 meters to my residence. "I have come to greet you!" Up and down the corridors of the hospital he lumbered, falling frequently as he tried to move his rigid muscles, eliciting much mirth from the bystanders as they helped him back to his feet.

And then there was the 12-year-old girl who had the disease twice, and survived. She had not received the protective vaccine after her first ordeal because it was out of stock at the government hospital where she had been treated. We made sure she had the full course of tetanus immunisation following her 14-day battle with death in our hospital. No one should have to go through this disease more than once, and she had done it twice. Near the time of her discharge a 13-year-old boy was admitted with the same diagnosis and she became a source of encouragement to him. He also survived.

The Chief of Bambalang, the great Ghogomu, died of tetanus just before my arrival at BBH. I would have loved to meet this man, as I was impressed by many of his 156 children. This chief sent all of his offspring to primary school when the idea was not yet commonplace. They in turn taught their father to read and helped each other financially to attend secondary schools. Most of them exhibited their father's thirst for knowledge and wisdom in schools and colleges of Cameroon and overseas. Many of them now occupy leadership positions throughout the country and many have earned degrees in the U.S., Canada and elsewhere. There are a number of nurses, midwives, teachers, civil servants and several medical doctors among his children. He also must have been a sickle cell carrier, as I treated some of his children for this inherited disorder. (Here is yet another common "tropical disease" that cries out for more research).

Tetanus struck terror into my bones every time we made the diagnosis, mostly because it meant a commitment of 10 to 14 days of an Intensive Care type of effort by both hospital staff and family. The relatives were instructed to keep count of the number and severity of spasms by piling small stones on the bedside table, sleeping by day and keeping vigil by night. The relative "on duty" would have to alert the overworked (or sleeping) nurse in case of the dreaded spastic choking attacks that would take the fully conscious patient to the frightening edge of death, over and over. During the day the nurses would adjust their procedures according to the severity of spasms. They would strive for a quiet atmosphere for the patient amid a bustling general ward with a hundred other needs. Food and bedside care was given when the spasms were least severe.

Meanwhile I was trying to judge the timing of my visits, the amount of muscle relaxants, sedatives, and liquids. Was I over-or under-sedating the patient? Were his vital signs stable? Was he able to take enough nourishment? How long was the patient breathless during the most severe spasms? Was his pain tolerable? How was his spirit holding out?

I gleaned new modes of treatment from medical journals and visiting experts: We tried a variety of therapies: from 50 000 units anti-tetanus serum (ATS) to none at all (when we ran out of it), then 750 units intrathecally, (into the spinal canal) which seemed to make a difference if given soon after the onset of spasms; Penicillin or other antibiotics, dark quiet rooms or well lit rooms, feeding tubes or spoon feeding, Valium by mouth, Valium by suppository, Valium by IV. The outcome seemed less related to the exact mode of treatment, than to the initial presentation, the speed of onset, and the severity of spasms. We could almost predict on arrival of the patient who would, or would not "make it". Nevertheless it was always heartbreaking if a baby would survive for 12 or 14 days and then succumb unexpectedly, just as we were starting to relax and dream of victory. The single most effective drug in our hands was the "mild" muscle relaxant Valium. Some patients would need up to 100 mg every four hours to control the spasms. Though this was twenty times the dose that "normal" people would need to induce sleep, tetanus patients would be easily rousable and ideally just "comfortably asleep" with this huge dose of sedative/relaxant. Valium definitely reduced the violence of the spasms to tolerable levels.

I wish I could say that the incidence of tetanus decreased with the years, since both government and mission health centres developed excellent preventive public health programs. Yet there were still too many cases of this terrible disease, certainly in adults. The incidence of tetanus in new-borns did decrease over the years as mothers attended antenatal clinics in ever-greater numbers and were given tetanus toxoid inoculations during pregnancy. This prevented tetanus of the new-born even if the delivery happened on the road to the hospital when the cord was cut with sharp elephant grass and the cord stump rubbed with dirt and ashes (tetanus spores live in the soil).

I never recognised a single case of multiple sclerosis (which is very common in my home province of Alberta), saw only one case of "Lou Gehrig's" amyotropic lateral sclerosis and but a few Guillain Barre's syndrome patients. (This latter viral disease leads to varying degrees of paralysis that may be fatal, but more often ends with a complete recovery).

Keloids (hypertrophic scarring) plagued a lot of my patients. It is generally known to be much more common in dark skinned races, and with the very common tribal scarifications I saw many grotesque examples of disfigurement of face, neck and shoulders. Some faces were so repugnant that these patients covered their heads whenever they were in public. A twelve-year-old girl had undergone the customary simple ear piercing at birth. From this minor scar she produced a tennis ball sized round, skin covered ball of hard scar tissue hanging from the earlobe to the shoulder and weighing over 300 grams. Meticulous surgical technique and subsequent local steroid injections could help a few but not all of these unfortunate patients, as the recurrence was almost inevitable.

Polio was very rare, probably because most children had the mild gastrointestinal form of the infection early in life when they were spared the horrifying neurological complications. Only in recent years and in families that practised MORE stringent hygiene did we see clinical polio in older children once in a while. I faced the dilemma: Should I raise the price of diphtheria/pertussis/tetanus (DPT) inoculations for thousands of children from 20 cents to 30 cents by including polio in the routine immunisation schedule? We did, and so pioneered effective vaccinations before WHO and Government programs became the norm in our remote area of Cameroon.

Polio Vaccination is now routine and World Health Organisation officials have reasonable hope for complete eradication of this disease worldwide within a few years.

I graduated from medical school convinced that there was steady progress to be expected in the fight of man against microbe. I am no longer so convinced. Only one disease, smallpox, has been conquered by modern medicine. Several previously unknown diseases have since been discovered, and some of our old nemeses are making a strong comeback, notably tuberculosis.

Our children went to school in Jos, Nigeria at the time that Lassa fever was first discovered at "Evangel", a busy mission hospital where our boys usually attended for their health needs. There I met the first known Lassa fever survivor, nurse Penny Pinneo. Lassa Fever is but one of a number of frightening "new" diseases with a very high mortality rate that has the potential for disastrous epidemics. It killed at least 50% of medical personnel who contracted it. 8.)

We had a run of an unknown (viral?) disease at our Mbingo Hospital that we called "Belo Valley Fever". People would come with respiratory symptoms, low white blood counts, and frighteningly high fevers. Few of them succumbed, but we could only treat the fever, not the disease. My *turntalk*, five months pregnant with her first child, became ill with the symptoms of Belo Valley Fever. There was great concern when the mercury reached the very top of the scale (44 degrees centigrade) and burst the glass thermometers not once, but twice. The young expectant mother complained of serious loss of vision and we feared for the baby. Finally the fevers subsided after a tense and anxious week. A short course of corticosteroids improved her vision from 20/200(legally blind) to 20/70, where it remained. There was also a mild ocular muscle weakness ("lazy eye") which persisted. A healthy girl was born 4 months later. She had suffered no apparent ill effects, qualifying thereafter for university entrance.

Chuck Kunkel, the Mission Aviation Fellowship pilot who served in Cameroon returned from a flight to Zaire with jaundice. He did not feel very ill and his appetite was undiminished. That pretty well ruled out a serious hepatitis and the common dengue ("bone-breaking") fever. I ordered hepatitis precautions and rest when lab tests where inconclusive. But what could it be? I searched my tropical disease texts and sent a radio message to my patient that caused more laughter than concern: "You probably have either Chikungunya or O-nyong-nyong fever and should expect to get better without treatment." He recovered quickly. Incidentally, Chuck is presently based in Mali and flies a regularly scheduled route into Timbuktu.

I had included an old but functioning ECG machine in our original 1967 luggage, but I never met anyone with the common western diagnosis and symptoms of a myocardial infarction until 1998. That is when the 18 year old son of one of our staff members collapsed at the side of a football field with severe chest pain, while he was waiting for the match to begin. He felt faint and started coughing frothy sputum uncontrollably. Minutes later I diagnosed a myocardial infarction with cardiogenic shock.

This was the clinical picture with which I was very familiar from my years in the emergency room in Canada. Fortunately the patient responded to my treatment while I hovered over him for an anxious hour. I even had the luxury of a retired cardiology consultant on the BBH compound that day. The ECG indicated a classical anteroseptal infarct, possibly on the basis of a congenital anomaly of his coronary arteries. We will not likely ever know, as the closest cardiac catheterisation laboratory is thousands of kilometers and dollars away. A viral infection of his heart muscle may have been another possibility. According to latest reports the young man is now perfectly well and back to playing football.

It is my strong opinion that atherosclerosis is extremely rare in the North West Province of Cameroon. Hypertension too, was uncommon, but increased with the introduction of western diets with their high salt content. Severe, high blood pressure is notoriously difficult to treat in Africans, just as it is in African Americans.

It was also in 1998 that the ECG machine confirmed my "once and only" diagnosis of the rare Wolff-Parkinson-White (WPW) Syndrome in Cameroon when a young man presented with occasional fainting spells whenever he exercised. WPW syndrome is caused by an abnormal electrical short circuit in the heart muscle leading to possible cardiac standstill and sudden death. Again, the diagnosis was rare and interesting, but I could do little for the patient, as the delicate cardiac surgery is only available in the most sophisticated medical centres of the developed world such as the Montreal Cardiac Institute.

One evening we were surprised by the unannounced arrival of a German couple of volunteer physicians. They had found their way upland in torrential rains on dark and dangerous roads. With increasing anxiety they concluded that they had reached the very edge of civilisation. Their concerns dissipated when I greeted them in their mother tongue with an offer of freshly baked bread. The cool bright Banso morning did the rest. The surgeon/anaesthetist team gave welcome relief and a number of helpful suggestions in their few weeks of exemplary service.

A young woman named Magdalene came to us during this time. She was seriously ill with a rare problem. The diagnosis was easy enough, she had "flesh eating disease"(necrotising fasciitis), a rapidly progressive infection that became rather well known through Quebec Premier Lucien Bouchard's case which caused him to lose a leg. But this young woman's treatment taxed us to the limit. The surgeon was confident of saving her limb when she arrived, but within hours it turned into a fight for her life, not only her limb. Amputation above the knee became necessary when the rapid progress of the necrosis allowed us to actually look directly into her knee joint. The small family watched her deterioration with increasing alarm. The young husband fled the scene. What good would she be, now that she could never again tend her crops?

Magdalene lost alarming amounts of weight. She developed large bedsores over hips and backbone. Then her sister arrived with the news that the younger of her two children had died in the village. The toddler had fallen ill, had been taken to a small health post and succumbed to her illness that night. The news drained our patient of all remaining hope and courage. Then Magdalene's mother suddenly disappeared and there was no one left to provide food for her. The church heard of her plight and women began to bring meals and pray with her. The chaplain visited regularly, and I began to drop an egg into my pocket at breakfast time to leave at her bedside during morning rounds. Slowly the 35-kg bundle of misery became interested in living again. She allowed us to turn her without complaining.

I was able to close one bedsore surgically and another one closed spontaneously. Her whispered "thank-you" gave us more hope. The men in the physiotherapy department tried their best to get her out of bed. She learned to balance herself with the help of aluminum crutches and took her first few steps. The hospital bill had now risen to $800 and only a very small amount of it had been paid. It was then that I remembered the gift I had received from a young unemployed Canadian lady of Magdalene's age. It would cover the cost of a prosthesis, once she was ready for it. This was good news indeed, even though the hospital bill would never be paid.

Magdalene left for her village and I had nearly forgotten her when the doorbell rang at my home one morning, several months later. A very pretty lady held out the gift of a *man fowl* while her round face radiated joy. Only when I glanced down along her crutches and saw the single foot peeking out from her long wrap-around skirt did I realise who this was. Magdalene was on her way to Mbingo where she would get her prosthesis. With a huge smile she beamed at me: *I don come fo greet, dis one na yu dash.* (She only came to greet me and to bring a small gift).

The only time I have been tempted to actually sit down and attempt a contribution to a Canadian medical journal was when I repeatedly saw a rupture of the patellar tendon in men. This was so common in Banso that I saw and repaired 7 tendons in a 6-month period of 1986. And once I actually saw it happen before my eyes on the soccer field. That particular patient had very little time for pensive reflection. He was on the OR table within the hour.

Two other patients stand out in my mind.

A rather rotund, respected Civil Servant and fellow Baptist whom we'll call Mr. Donatus stumbled over a market crate and sustained this particular injury to his knee. He found himself unable to climb stairs or lift his lower leg, so he came to the hospital were we repaired his tendon in the usual fashion. A few years later I met him walking with a cane and suspected the failure of my repair (with some appropriate embarrassment). No, he had ruptured the tendon in the other knee, and the diagnosis had been missed elsewhere.

My friend was reluctant to undergo the repair on his second knee. He was retired, and his elaborately carved cane actually served as a bit of a status symbol. He preferred to live with his disability.

As I recounted this and other stories to my colleagues at the Royal Alexandra Emergency department, they collectively could not recall ever having seen this type of injury in their practise. I consider this highly significant as my colleagues represented over one hundred years of experience in the busiest emergency department of the country at the time.

One day my colleague Claude called me excitedly. Had I not claimed this problem was unique to West Africa? Well, he had just seen a patient with the injury I had told him about. Would I like to see his patient?

We turned the corner of the emergency hallway, and there was his patient. True, he had torn the tendon below the kneecap. And—he was a black Jamaican.

I am postulating a genetic weakness of the infrapatellar portion of the quadriceps femoris tendon in West African (Bantu) males. Another interesting phenomenon ready for some in-depth research.

A twelve-year-old boy arrived with a serious infection of his right arm. It was grossly swollen and when touching it, I could feel air bubbles under the skin. The infection and swelling reached to his shoulder, gave rise to high fevers and general toxicity. I suspected a case of dreaded gas gangrene and the father did not hesitate even a moment when I suggested immediate amputation at the shoulder as the only hope for the child's survival. Even though I knew that there are other gas forming bacteria besides "Clostridium perfringens" I was definitely in a panic. This kid was gone if we didn't act NOW. High doses of intravenous Penicillin were started and we prepared for the mutilating surgery. The arm was removed at the shoulder joint. But, horrors, the gas bubbles could be felt beyond my line of incision. Then I had a most unscientific idea. Wasn't the bacterium that caused gas gangrene one that flourishes in poorly oxygenated tissues? What if I overwhelmed the area with lots of oxygen? While dreaming about hyperbaric oxygen chambers, and praying, I cautiously injected small amounts of hydrogen peroxide into the muscles with a syringe. The tissues did not seem to like it much, bubbling and hissing and getting hot to the touch, but I got away with it. The swelling increased alarmingly for a couple of days, before the boy became afebrile and eventually healed his stump. I would not recommend this "treatment" ever, but I was desperately trying to save this boy's life, and God granted it in spite of my unconventional and dangerous treatment.

*   *   *

Veterinary medicine must be very similar to the human kind in the public's perception, because people kept coming to me with their animal's problems. I was asked to deliver one of the Chief's sheep that suffered obstructed labor. Another time a Peace Corps Volunteer begged me to help his cat with a similar problem, but I was really less well equipped to handle these emergencies than a good farmer would be. People asked me to neuter their cats when "caterwauling" disturbed their nights. I accepted these surgical challenges with great reluctance and the mortality rates confirmed my incompetence.

What finally sealed my determination to stop interfering with animal health was my final encounter with the Matron's cat.

Eleanor was leaving on furlough. Her cat had been her treasured companion and mouse catcher par excellence. Eleanor had a serious phobia for mice. But now the time had come to part with the affectionate feline. No home would be good enough for her. It was decided that she would be best off in cat-heaven.

Being the only missionary male on station and used to providing leadership in a host of spheres, unrelated to my training, I was approached to do the foul deed after the Matron's departure to the U.S. My anxiety level rose when I reviewed my options and arsenal. The practise of euthanasia is abhorrent to me, whether of man or mouse.

Twice I had personally suffered carbon monoxide poisoning and it seemed a rather swift and humane "way to go", so I took on the job out of misplaced feelings of pity. I should have known better. Hardly had Eleanor's green VW left the station when I spotted the familiar black and white object of my foul plans sunning and preening herself on the Matron's doorstep. I quickly found a sack and, wonder of wonders, the animal seemed to have a death wish, perhaps caused by her mistress' sudden departure? The cat practically walked into my open potato sack. I tied it, covered it with plastic and let the Land Rover exhaust do the unthinkable. The cat succumbed quickly and quietly. Now for the burial. As I slunk by the rain barrel at the corner of the house, I had a sudden inspiration. Why not make sure? I had heard of "a cat's nine lives", and with my inexperience in matters veterinary, I could not be sure enough, could I? So I added death by drowning. Then, considering the number of hungry roving dogs in the village, I buried her as deeply as I could. I was quite relieved to have finished with the unpleasant task.

Who could imagine my horror the next morning when the black and white cat was sitting on Eleanor's doorstep! Three out of nine lives?

I had killed the wrong cat!

My apology to the nuns teaching at the nearby college was accepted in a truly forgiving spirit. They accepted the loss of their beloved black and white tomcat with understanding. But I was cured of my meddling in unethical cross-disciplinary practise for good.

*   *   *

My brother, an architect and builder, worked in Nigeria only 160 km from BBH by road, perhaps 80 km "as the crow flies". But communication and visits were near impossible. Letters could either be sent by hand-mail with traders, friends or thieves, or via Douala-Paris-London-Lagos, a journey of 14 000 km since Airlines do not fly as crows would. The price was variable for hand-carried mail, as was the success of communication. A 50% loss of letters had to be assumed. Only since 1998 has e-mail via satellite finally eased the harsh isolation.

My brother was turning sixty and I wanted to celebrate this milestone with him. He had also expressed the desire to borrow my old motorcycle while I returned to Canada. Nigerian Visitor's visas were not granted to Canadians since our Foreign Minister's firm stand in the Commonwealth against human rights abuses in Nigeria. My brother, however, obtained a hand-written note from the local Chief of Immigration requesting officers along the route to facilitate my entry. As members of the Commonwealth, Canadians and Cameroonians should not have needed any visas to enter Nigeria, but *Wawa* came into play again, as usual. I was also ignorant of the need for exportation papers for my motorcycle and had to rely on divine intervention on that count.

I selected a day and sent a special runner to announce my coming. It would be the day of Mbem clinic, which would get me halfway to my destination, saving my energy for the more difficult second day. I had made that journey 3 times before, and had won an argument with an experienced world traveller, that this is in fact the worst road in the world. I have since had assurance from a travelling Mambilla public health nurse that there is one road on the plateau even worse than this, but I have no desire to pursue this argument any further.

In traditional West Africa languages define people groups or tribes. These range in size from a few hundred people to several million. Cameroon has over 250 distinct people groups. This is inconvenient for modern government. It is a difficult task to create a "national identity" and "national pride" when different tribes within colonial borders of modern nation-states have very little in common and much more that should tear them asunder. If language is burdened with the added duty of serving as the glue for national awareness Cameroon is put into a double bind. It is officially bilingual, English and French, similar to Canada, but with a reverse ratio in population numbers. Politically, bilingualism could be an asset, but more often it is not as it costs enormous amounts of money. Furthermore there is a lot of cultural confusion and bureaucratic bungling is multiplied because the worst of both systems seems to prevail. Nor does it help to diffuse tribalism, which is admitted to be a major hindrance to nationalistic idealism.

The Cameroon-Nigerian border cuts right through several tribal lands. This does not inconvenience the locals much. There are advantages to living near a border: greater opportunity for trade, transport and smuggling, wider choices of goods and services from either side of the border. This contrasts with the troubles of bad roads and lack of infrastructure near borders. And there is the constant hassle with border authorities, who rely on bribes to supplement their income.

The Brits held a plebiscite in the last days before they departed from their Protectorate of Cameroon in 1960. The borders were redrawn, so that the Mambilla plateau became part of Nigeria. As a result our mission work in Cameroon was divided into a large Cameroonian and a smaller Nigerian field.

I arrived at Mbem Health Centre in less than the customary 3 hours for the 75 km from BBH. My powerful, especially low-geared Honda 250 XL delivered me without any spills. The clinic team would follow with my cargo and I was relatively fresh after only routine hospital work that morning. So far, so good.

Three student-interns from the United States arrived a bit later with the clinic team. They gushed about the spectacular scenery and moaned over the horrendous road. The old Land Rover had gained their admiration. "It was like driving up a staircase strewn with 2 to 12 inch marbles," they said. But the mountaintop view from Rom-rock had made it all worthwhile.

We held teaching rounds on the few patients in the Health Centre and had a lovely supper of pounded yam, njama-njama and beef prepared by faithful, ageless Chansak, former houseboy of pioneer missionary Paul Gebauer.

Dr. Gebauer had started Mbem mission station in 1936.

That night we slept in the idyllic brick rest house under giant mango trees. Distant drums and crickets under my window were the last thing I heard.

I awoke at 4:30, and my restless anticipation would not allow me to fall back to sleep, so I began to pack my spare parts, tools, petrol and helmets.

We started the three scheduled surgeries at 6:45, interrupted by a leisurely breakfast with the three American interns.

A child had died in the night, probably from severe electrolyte imbalance. The standard re-hydration scheme had failed.

I continued my surgery until the Chief of Post assured me that he would be able to harness the superior knowledge of the "American Consultants"(student interns) and I assessed the situation as being well in hand. There were unusually few patients that day, and by ten a.m. I was on my way. Ahead lay 86 km, one border, one major river and a very challenging track. I had the Nigerian Immigration Official's letter, which now had to prove its worth. There were vague memories of a "road" I had travelled when 20 years younger. I had a little Cameroonian money, and a wonderfully reliable 12 year old motorcycle.

At least I had started early. The first five or six steep ravines where almost fun. I took pictures of the deep-green slopes, bright blue sky, Fulani cattle, neat rows of freshly worked farms and clear mountain streams. I would not dare to replenish my drinking water from them!

The Cameroon border post of Yang near Sabonkaraji is located on the edge of a steep descent into Mbaw plain. The early rains had wiped away the haze of the harmattan. I felt compelled again and again to gaze into the vast plain with Sabongari 16 km in the distance, more than 1000 meters below me. And far in the distance I could make out the shimmering waters of a lake.

The Cameroon Immigration Official only needed to see the "BBH" inscription on my bike. His face lit up. There was no need to show any papers or give reasons for my travel. His son's life "had just been saved" at BBH. Actually, 76 year old Dr. Coleman had done one of his skilful osteomyelitis surgeries on him. The second official, an armed francophone Gendarme seemed to grasp quickly that there was no bribe forthcoming on this day in this lonely outpost and I was off in a cloud of goodwill.

Now things became distinctly difficult. No road machinery had graced these roads for 40 years, if ever. Probably no shovel even, had been exerted on these rarely travelled tracks. Passing *moto-boy* had filled some of the deep ruts with rounded rocks that abounded in every size. It may have prevented Land Rovers from hanging up on their axles, but it did not make my travel any easier as the rocks pummelled and tricked my tires into an unpredictable dance of man and machine. Some concrete bridge slabs had approaches with half-meter high steps, others had been destroyed by the torrents of many a rainy season. The worst washouts had occurred near the bottom of long steep inclines, often in the middle of the road. They appeared deep enough to bury a *guynaco's* horse standing up, should it fall in.

My muscles began to tremble with exhaustion from wrestling my 140-kg bike up the incredible inclines, even under engine power. I fell. A broken mirror, scraped knees and a sunburned neck were not too high a price to pay to be able to see my brother. I fell again. The carburettor flooded when the bike landed upside down, making it hard to restart the engine. Repeated jumps on the kick-starter exhausted me. The mountain air was thin at 1800 meters. It was hot, I was 63 years old, the bike was overloaded and top-heavy. I sat down between the many boulders projecting into the path in order to catch my breath and pray. I knew of several other people praying for me on both sides of the border.

This time the bike started. Soon I reached Lip, the Nigerian border post. The office was closed. No one "on seat" in the padlocked mud hut with the grass roof. A widely grinning Mambilla man greeted me. He seemed to have more than 32 perfect teeth. Augustine had been sent by my brother to escort me the rest of the way on his 125cc Yamaha. I was to have no further worries. He told me to let him handle all the officials and I would be fine. We left a short note to the Nigerian Immigration Officer on a scrap of paper stuck in the cracks of the "office"-door and were off.

The roads were now a bit less steep but still very rocky. No road maintenance here, either. But if Augustine made it with his little Yamaha, paddling up the hills with his long legs, then, surely my trusted Honda, Lord of the four-stroke dirt bikes, would too.

I followed, gingerly, as Augustine showed off his skills, while I inhaled his dust and two-stroke exhaust fumes. He explained that he had to lead for the next 30 km, past the checkpoints of police and army personnel. I was as surprised by their casual demeanor as they were by the arrival of a white man coming from the direction of a hostile border. (Cameroon and Nigeria are involved in periodic bloody conflicts over oil-rich coastal regions). The soldiers were well armed but dressed with only the mildest suggestion of a piece or two of uniform.

Mbamnga village came into view. A very young-appearing official dressed in a single piece of cotton print asked us to wait. He hurried away and reappeared 15 minutes later in full khaki uniform. I handed him the letter from his superior that was to expedite my passing. The letter did not appear to put him into a favourable mood. He made a long speech about the dangers to himself and me, should I venture further into Nigeria than Gembu. Eventually he began to copy my passport information onto a tiny bit of paper that looked as if it was salvaged from the edge of newsprint, just large enough to include my birthplace on it: Marienwerder. That, in turn, reminded him vividly of a place in Nigeria, "had I been there?" No I hadn't. Augustine brought me a bottle of warm pop. He did not offer the customary bribe of 20 Naira and I was wise not to interfere. The largest Nigerian banknote was 50 Naira. Forgery is not a problem of late, as 50 Naira are worth less than 2 $ US at latest market reports.

Finally, I guessed that we could probably proceed. I tied my knapsack onto the handlebar, bending the throttle cable out of the way in the process. Once more, one tired jump on the kick-starter brought the engine to life and my spirits rose in anticipation of better things ahead. Augustine hurried on, up the steep road out of the Village Square. I tried to follow, but the bike seemed to have it's own agenda. I had interfered with the throttle cable in the effort of lightening my load and the bike surprised me with some very strange antics. It got sideways, this way and that, like a prancing pony, rearing up and dumping me by the side of the road under the shade of a lovely trumpet lily bush. This was my fifth fall of the day, but the first with an appreciative number of spectators. The young immigration officer came running, along with a lot of Nigerian children of all sizes. He admonished me earnestly to go more slowly on these bad roads. I promised that I would, rearranged my pack away from the throttle cable and got going again, just as Augustine returned looking for me.

We stopped briefly to pay more bribes further on, but the road definitely improved. Soon I began to recognise the scenery around our former Warwar Mission Hospital, which had been taken over by an optimistic Nigerian government, and we descended to the bank of the Donga River. This place I remembered vividly as I had driven our VW Kuebelwagen off the grounded ferry into the shallow water and got stuck in this very place 25 years earlier.

A canoe for each of the motorcycles took us across, and minutes later I was able to greet our missionary friends working in Pastoral Education in this remote corner of Nigeria. They offered me a shower but I was happy to just replenish my drinking water from their kerosene refrigerator. Another 20 minutes and I could greet my brother, fellow labourer and Africa-lover in his home.

I think the dark urine I passed that evening included the end products of broken down muscle fibres. I decided to drink more and ignore the off-colour urine.

On the 6 hour 86 km trip I had met only two vehicles braving the road: 2-ton Steyer-Puch Austrian army surplus trucks with 6 wheel drive and 50 cm ground clearance. But they too had had several breakdowns on the "road".

We celebrated my brother's 60th birthday and talked of our children and grandchildren in Canada. I inspected his various building projects and water supply schemes and visited a few officials in the company of my respected brother. The Chief of Police assured me that I was perfectly safe from highway robbers, as he "had given orders to shoot them all, ha ha ha ha". I left my bike in Nigeria for my brother's use and arranged for

Augustine to ferry me back to Sabongari. But Augustine revealed that he had just sold his motorcycle the night before. We then met Titus, a young Cameroonian with a 125cc Yamaha whose "International Shipping Company" (consisting of one ancient Land Rover) had succumbed to the economic crisis and who was now reduced to the occasional motorcycle taxi service to and from his homeland. He had just returned from Sabongari the day before. The small motorcycle was surprisingly comfortable and in good mechanical shape. I decided to risk it. Titus told me about his young family and his struggle to make a living while we bounced along at a reasonable clip and I became more confident by the hour that I would in fact make it home. Titus branched off the road at Mbamnga where I had met the conscientious Nigerian Immigration Officer. I elected to trust my driver's better judgement, but later heard that this caused considerable concern to the official who seemed to have unfinished business with me. So I sent him a letter of contrition with a small gift when I found a suitable courier a week later. My "taxi" took a detour that involved only about 3 km of a very steep downhill scamper for me while my driver manoeuvred down some more incredible "roads" that I would be rather loathe to ascend. At Sabongari I spotted a "clandestine" *come out, make I enter* Corolla which was in the process of being loaded. I was the 9th occupant of the little car. The *moto boy* (apprentice-taxi-driver-mechanic and loadmaster) was good enough to sit on the roof among the considerable cargo. From that vantage he reported the 2 tire punctures and any other newsworthy items on our trip.

I arrived home in excellent spirits to the immense relief of my dear spouse. She told me the reason for my safe trip. Two sweet little girls, Verna and Alma, (aged 5 and 7,) had come to our house to pray with my wife for "Pa's" safety on his dangerous trip to Nigeria. And we know that children's angels have a very direct access to our Father in heaven (Jesus said so himself). As for me, I am definitely looking forward to meeting my own guardian angel someday soon. Would it be appropriate to thank him personally? I shall ask when I get there.

We had less than 10 unscheduled stops over the 60 km to Banso and I soon started to lecture my captive taxi audience on the hottest topic of the day: "The coming of AIDS".

The New Enemy

At the end of my formal missionary career in 1980 I had turned my work over to 3 doctors and one administrator, none of them Africans. At that point I had not yet achieved my long-term goal of working myself out of a job. We had trained nurses and midwives, we had participated in the training of African doctors, but I had never worked with an African as an equal with similar qualifications. Regret and disappointment were inevitable. Could I perhaps return in future years to see the goal achieved by those who followed me? Family needs necessitated our stay in Canada for the next few years.

My sabbatical leave from the Royal Alexandra Emergency department in 1986 enabled me, together with my wife and my youngest son Russel, to return to Cameroon for our first 6 months of volunteering. Finally I had the chance to work with our first African graduate Dr. Gad Fokum. We enjoyed mutual respect and unity of purpose. Eight years later I returned to BBH to work as a retired volunteer. It was most gratifying to see my long-term objective realised during my absence. My work was still appreciated, but I was not irreplaceable.

Years ago we had started weekly academic rounds alternating between the two hospitals in the Banso area. We enjoyed cordial co-operation with the Shishong Catholic Mission hospital 5 km away. These clinical teaching sessions had continued through the years of my absence. Now I joined them again with renewed enthusiasm.

During one of these clinical rounds with fellow doctors and medical students I looked around the room. There were thirteen of us, graduates and students from Moscow, Kigali, Addis-Ababa, Kinshasa, Berlin, Sofia, Edmonton and Yaounde. And suddenly I realised with deep gratitude, that on this particular day, mine was the only white face in the crowd. Volunteers and specialists from the West were still welcome to work alongside our African colleagues, but we could see the closure of a chapter in our history.

However, a new chapter was now being written in ever-darker print. The scourge of AIDS was upon us.

In 1986 I was asked to address the hospital staff during their "in-service education" session. They wanted me to speak about "AIDS in Africa". I delegated the majority of the task to a senior nurse in order to encourage his involvement. "Time" magazine claimed that sub-Saharan Africa would soon be swept up in this modern plague, though we had not yet recognised nor tested for HIV infection in our hospitals until then. Our two interns from the National Medical School told us about the most recent surveys in two of the nation's large cities: 4 of 100 prostitutes in one of the two cities had been found to be HIV positive. There were no cases of clinical AIDS as yet.

Eight years later AIDS was the leading cause of death in our hospitals. It affected mostly women in their twenties and men in their thirties, the very age groups who were to provide leadership, productivity and economic stability. 3 to 5% of healthy blood donors were already HIV positive. The numbers of AIDS patients were nearly doubling annually. Cameroon's political and economic crises were serious but paled in comparison to the crisis of a universally fatal sexually transmitted disease (STD).

Perhaps I could see the threat to 30 years of gradual but sure progress more clearly than others could because of my prolonged absence. I had seen the arrival of clean public water, 24 hour electricity, telephone, fax and e-mail, better roads and public transport, better public health and infrastructure, enormous growth in educational facilities, better housing for many, and the growth of a true middle class. There were many Cameroonians for whom this advance was too slow and painful, especially in the political realm, but for an outsider it was nothing short of miraculous. And now it was all going to be jeopardised!

Since we saw HIV patients from 8 different tribes regularly, and more from all corners of the country we were now clearly facing a major health disaster. The time spent in pre-test counselling and the shortage and expense of testing supplies restricted us considerably. Many hospital employees stopped donating blood for fear of a possible test result that meant a death sentence. Many patients also refused the test. One highly educated chief told me: "some of us would rather not know what we are dying from". Four years later he buried his oldest son.

Cameroon has great music. Tone deafness is practically non-existent. Even children under two have an extraordinary sense of rhythm. Drumming and dancing are taken to great artistic heights in every village. People love to sing. My own love of music came in handy when I was asked to participate in the worship time of Protestant students in a Catholic college near my home in Banso. I learned and taught many songs accompanied by my Autoharp. Angela, the song-leader of the group met me again years later when she worked in the vicinity. She was still singing, even though life had not been easy for her. While in college she had "fallen in love" with the son of a school principal who belonged to another tribe. This young man had recently been found to be HIV positive when he offered his blood for donation. Their relationship had led to marriage in spite of contrary pleading by family and friends who feared for the future of the young couple. A healthy daughter was born, but soon the strain of living under the threat of a deadly disease proved too much to endure and the couple separated, with the child becoming a pawn in the struggle for custody. Traditional and modern rights clashed. Tribal differences now became an issue. Finally, the husband became ill after more than seven years of a healthy HIV-positive status. He was found to have pulmonary tuberculosis and was admitted to hospital. Fortunately he responded to my four-drug treatment and was able to go home. But the estrangement from his wife continued in spite of several attempts at reconciliation. Then the patient came down with severe headaches and was readmitted. As the illness progressed and gave rise to increasing anxiety, the couple drew closer and actually came to a full reconciliation. The husband's parents did not appreciate this. The father had retired from teaching and had become a native doctor. He had determined by witchcraft that his son was being poisoned. He forbade the young wife to bring food to her sick husband. All counselling efforts were futile. The grandparents remained intransigent and kept their young grandchild. Meanwhile the patient's headaches became intolerable. The second spinal tap finally yielded the elusive diagnosis: a rare fungal meningitis for which no appropriate treatment could be found. The drugs were ordered, but did not reach the hospital before the young man died. The grandparents escaped to their village with the grandchild after stripping their daughter-in-law's home of all furniture. An elaborate set of pagan rituals preceded the "Christian burial" after a full night of dancing at the customary die cry. While civil law may clearly identify the wife as the rightful custodian of her daughter, no social worker or policeman in his right mind would dare to enter the remote village to apprehend the child. The grandfather's "powerful medicine" will protect it against any such attempts.

Amazingly, both mother and child have remained HIV negative.

A 25 year old woman with end-stage AIDS developed a stress ulcer in her stomach and bled down to dangerously low levels. We were usually unable to find more than a pint or two of blood in such situations. But since my own blood matched hers and was at its.usual 110% level due to the high altitude, she could have some of mine. It was unsuitable for anyone in Canada because of my long residence in the tropics, so she got my 500 cc and had a temporary recovery. Her ulcer stopped bleeding and she went home.

It is true, of course, that more than 50% of AIDS victims do not contract the disease through any fault of their own. Babies born to HIV positive mothers, faithful spouses, unwitting recipients of falsely negative blood transfusions plus the small number of health workers who contract the disease on the job cannot be blamed for being infected. It is difficult for North Americans to keep this in perspective. The epidemic in North America started among homosexuals. In Africa it is almost exclusively transmitted heterosexually and from mother to baby. It is difficult to impress North Americans with the magnitude of the pandemic now. People reason from their own narrow perspective that the disease is likely self-inflicted. They do not believe that intravenous drug use and homosexuality is exceedingly rare in Cameroon. (I finally heard of a single practising homosexual pedophile after 30 years of medical practise, in which people have been very open with me about their very personal and sexual histories.)

In our hospitals it is now commonplace to have 3 or 4 AIDS deaths on a weekend, or to have 7 of 8 HIV tests reported positive in a single day. Chaplains and nurses trained in counselling show signs of weariness—often spending hours with distraught and despairing or sometimes even hostile patients. Every case a tragedy!

One anxious 30 year old student implored me to hurry his treatment, as he needed to leave for an overseas scholarship to earn a PhD. All was set for his journey, if not for this annoying delay caused by his illness. His AIDS was terminal. He did leave the hospital quickly—feet first, straight to the morgue.

A lovely young couple came from a far away province. They were expecting their first child. The strapping husband, a teacher, fell ill with a nasty cough. He had to be treated for tuberculosis. His immune system showed signs of strain. His weight loss became alarming. Three HIV tests were negative, but I am convinced that he was a falsely negative HIV/AIDS patient. He requested discharge while in a desperate state.

A mother of six, wife of a highly placed civil servant brought her youngest child with a "failure to thrive" diagnosis. She readily agreed to the HIV test when all other investigation was inconclusive. The test was positive, of course, and there will be 5 orphans in that family, before long.

A chief's wife had undergone abdominal surgery at another hospital and came to us with a massive wound sepsis. The patient's fever did not respond to my choice of antibiotics. The infection spread alarmingly and developed into gas gangrene. The patient showed signs of immuno-suppression and died from overwhelming infection. I found out later that the husband was the second chief who had tested positive for HIV. This woman was the first of about 50 of his wives, who will likely die of AIDS in the next few months or years.

A University graduate with an equally educated husband presented with huge ugly purple swellings in both thighs while in the 5th month of her first pregnancy. She did not seem to grasp the horror of her prognosis, and I could not bring myself to paint the picture for her. She faced a painful confrontation with her husband, a likely C-section, the difficulty of securing very expensive drugs for her Kaposi's sarcoma, and a 30% likelihood of her baby dying from AIDS in a year or two.

A mother of two presented with the minor problem of a Bell's palsy. She was in wide-eyed shock when hearing of her positive test: "but I have always been faithful to the only man I ever knew, why do I have to die?"

A dying medical doctor insisted on absolute secrecy before an equally insistent large family who wanted to know the diagnosis but finally respected his wish to be allowed to die quietly in our hospital.

An angry high-school student shouted and threatened: "I did not ask for this disease, I was only looking for some **fun**. Now I am not going to die alone, I will take as many girls with me as I can".

Confusion and misinformation often led to violent action of a frightened populace. A military officer died in our hospital of AIDS. His relatives not only confiscated all family belongings but also accused the widow and her brother of witchcraft as the cause of his death. They beat the surviving wife mercilessly. At the point of death she begged for water. They mocked her: "ask the choir members of your church to bring you water". Shortly after she died they caught her brother, poured kerosene over him and set him on fire. He died two days later.

A market woman sold *"alaska"* (homemade popsicles) in a coastal town. She was said to be HIV positive. A youth accused her of mixing her infected blood into the popsicles. An enraged mob beat her to death. No matter that it is considered impossible to infect people with the virus in the alleged manner!

Once patients showed the obvious signs of immuno-suppression, their life could be measured in only weeks or months. Our only available drugs were inexpensive antibiotics and anti-fungals that might buy a patient a few comfortable months. If a patient presented with the rarer fungal meningitis they could be gone in days.

The newer protease inhibitor drugs that help so many North American AIDS victims to survive 10 years or more are simply not affordable for millions of Africans. Few people realise that more than $16 000 a year are required from Canadian Health Insurance or Provincial Government sources to supply the drugs for a single patient. Most African countries have an annual per capita health budget of $20 or less.

A medical student from overseas heard about the challenge of Third World Medicine and believed it would enrich his clinical experience if he could spend a couple of months at one of our hospitals.

His application was approved.

Knowing about AIDS in Africa he was trying his best to protect himself against the possibility of picking up a lethal infection while learning about rare clinical conditions and helping to alleviate suffering.

He was able to obtain the necessary 3-day, 3 drug emergency starter-medications recommended for exposed medical personnel. This was to be taken within 20 minutes of an "incident" such as an accidental needle puncture or a break in the skin during surgery or delivery of a patient who might be HIV positive. (In January 1997 a full 10% of ante-natal patients at BBH were HIV positive, 26% if unmarried!)

The medical student was apparently well-to-do, enough to afford rather expensive evacuation insurance. A Lear Jet would be dispatched to

Douala to whisk him home in time for another 6 months of the best currently available anti HIV therapy, should it become necessary.

The 500-km inland transport to the airport, the problem with sporadic e-mail and phone connections would have to be overcome once the student was on site.

All went well. The student had a good experience and went back to the "real world" without upsetting our staff and routine. Unlike the next group of young volunteer doctors: they greatly disturbed our staff by wearing gloves and masks whenever going near any of our patients. This was completely counter to our efforts of teaching our staff that AIDS is not very contagious at all. For those who work directly with body fluids of HIV positive patients the annual risk of infection is only about one percent. In 25 years of working in this setting one has a 75% chance of survival.

When it comes to tuberculosis, however, there is a very real danger to North Americans coming to work in our hospitals now. For some reason public health experts in Canada and the U.S. still refuse to routinely provide the partial protection of BCG vaccinations for the general public, and medical students in particular. During the last two years three of our volunteer medical students and one of our North American physicians became Mantoux positive and had to take an anti-tuberculosis drug for 6 months. With a good number of our AIDS patients presenting with pulmonary tuberculosis that is resistant to the 4 best drugs available, this has the potential for disaster and tragedy.

WHO experts are very worried about the 20 to 60 percent of AIDS patients in Africa who also have tuberculosis. And AIDS patients are particularly susceptible to develop resistance to all known drugs for tuberculosis, this ancient scourge of mankind that rears its ugly head again. 9.) 10.)

AIDS is real. The old women in the village know. They see their sons and daughters wasting away and dying in frightening numbers. They are left with growing numbers of orphans to feed and educate. They have even coined a local name: "You are looking so thin, could you possibly have *whame*?" *Whame* is "eight" in the Nso language, and that sounds close enough to "AIDS". I soon got the nickname *Pa Whame* (father AIDS) because of my well-known efforts in AIDS education.

Six BBH employees have died of AIDS as have three of my football team buddies in Banso.

Three of our sons' former playmates died in '98, among them the daughter of our "garden mammy" who used to play on our veranda twenty-five years ago. Her older sister, mother of ten children, agreed to take in the two orphans, six and two years old. But she had already given a home to six other AIDS orphans from a brother in law and wife who also died recently.

Many years ago, my wife and I were present at the cross-tribal wedding of Nurse Mary and her teacher-husband John. Their marriage proved to be childless year after year. This was a strain on their marriage and led to a rather morose countenance on the wife's part. One day she became seriously ill and had to be hospitalised with fevers of 42 degrees Celsius. I suspected typhoid fever but had no laboratory confirmation. She begged for surgery since her abdominal pain was considerable. I agreed reluctantly, knowing that the surgery would certainly worsen her prognosis if it were in fact typhoid fever. At laparotomy we saw the typical Peyer's patches on the ileum but no perforations. So we confirmed the diagnosis, but now my patient became very ill indeed. She went into the dreaded complication of heart involvement with failure. The devoted husband sobbed by her bedside, while the people in town spread the news that she had died. Christians everywhere prayed. My colleague suggested "the laying on of hands" according to Holy Scripture. Following this prayer we reviewed our treatment and I added several medications that might possibly help the patient.

By morning her fever was gone and never rose again. Within ten days she was back at work.

She later delivered 2 healthy children.

Her husband switched occupations and the family moved away. They became wealthy.

About 20 years later Mary was surprised to see me back in Cameroon, when she accompanied her husband who came for consultation. The joy of the reunion turned into horror when I saw the "shingles" rash on her husband's torso. I had seen this common first sign of immuno-suppression in case after case since returning to Cameroon.

I do not even know who completed the counselling, or how my friends coped with the terrible news. It seemed as if they went through the usual stage of denial because the husband improved for a few months and greeted me with a triumphant smile the next time I ran into him. I was obviously wrong in my diagnosis!

But less than a year later he was admitted with full-blown AIDS. We battled valiantly against five different medical problems and the patient was able to go home. About a week later there was a huge die cry for him. I could not even attend my friend's funeral because of pressing hospital duties. Another battle that could not be won. With AIDS there are no winners.

A 1998 quotation of an adoption official in the central Nigerian city of Jos claimed 284 new AIDS orphans in Nigeria per day. By that time the official estimate of AIDS related deaths for Nigeria was 500 000. In the past five months of reading a daily Canadian Newspaper I have not seen a single article about AIDS in West Africa. It is not newsworthy. It seems that only rare, obscure or controversial cases of AIDS make it into the news, such as the few Nairobi prostitutes who have remained healthy for 20 years in spite of their positive HIV status. Meanwhile, millions more get infected with a preventable disease. World Health Organisation officials are quietly saying: "we may have to write off sub-Saharan Africa". The small country of Uganda had one million AIDS orphans by 1999. In Zimbabwe AIDS patients occupied 70% of hospital beds in 1996. The life expectancy at birth has dropped from 64 to 39 years in the same country. In a Haiti hospital AIDS patients are not even admitted, because "nothing can be done for them, anyway".

At the time I left BBH there were days when 30 to 50% of men's or women's ward beds were occupied by AIDS patients. One of our supervised clinics is located on the Trans-African Highway. Twenty per cent of 1999 blood donors at that clinic were found to be HIV positive. I found denial of the AIDS problem more prevalent among the educated elite of the Capital Yaounde than among illiterate grandmothers in the villages. Foreign Aid has begun to trickle in, primarily for prevention. But the message is often culturally inappropriate. There was only a single AIDS prevention advertisement on Cameroon TV by 1998. It was several years old and very misleading at that. Grassroots preventive work is very slow to get off the ground. Knowing about the problem and warning one's children is inadequate in the face of this devastating epidemic.

For unknown reasons AIDS reached Cameroon and Nigeria about 5 years after it struck the East African countries around Lake Victoria. This could be interpreted as a period of grace for Cameroon. There was ample time to learn from the experience of preventive health efforts in other countries. That opportunity has been largely wasted. The temptation to prophesy inevitable doom is hard to resist.

I channelled my personal concern and despair into action.

In five months of 1997-98 I visited 132 primary schools of our division on my off-days and spoke to over 10 000 children in grades five to seven.

I spoke about the reasons for the widespread denial of the problem:

1. The long incubation period of 8 months to 8 years, and the difficulty of linking past behaviour to present fatal illness.

2. The great variation of disease presentation and the resultant confusion in the layperson's mind. (I have seen AIDS present itself in at least 27 different ways).

3. The natural shame, fear and anger people feel when confronted with an incurable calamity of obscure origin.

I talked to the children about my daily experience with AIDS patients, encouraging them to examine their beliefs and the behaviour of their seniors, to determine to change and choose LIFE.

The Delegate for Public Education had given me authorisation to enter any government school and ask for permission to address the students. I also had full co-operation from the Delegate for Public Health of the NorthWest Province. (The correspondence can be found in the appendix)

The largely non-existent mail and telephone service made appointments at primary schools practically impossible, so I simply rode up on my Honda attracting everyone's attention and presented the delegate's authorisation to the principal. He would usually interrupt the teaching of classes 5 to 7 and I talked to students and teachers with as much passion, conviction and skill as I could muster. Many children had already heard of the disease, or had seen relatives dying from AIDS.

These children needed more than "information" or condoms. They needed motivation to seriously examine their beliefs, to challenge their elders and to determine to join the "True love waits" movement. The success stories of Senegal, Uganda and Malaysia in their preventive education efforts prove that only intensive repeated motivation of young children is effective in changing traditional cultural sexual practises.

I answered the many questions and left free literature with teachers who promised to continue with preventive efforts. Then I roared off to the next school. I got to know the roads of an entire division of 250 000 people, met universal co-operation and a ground swell of goodwill. Here again I often needed to adapt. A group of students were making mud bricks to repair their schoolhouse which had suffered in a windstorm. So I addressed them while they rested sitting by the clay-pit with muddy hands. At another village a parent-teacher meeting had been convened as I arrived on the scene. I was given permission to talk to concerned parents. Three other schools met for a volleyball tournament—I followed the crowd, and at half-time children and adults gathered to listen under a giant cola-nut tree while I climbed a rickety table for attention. I also re-visited a few secondary schools to give them an update on our earlier hospital-team visits. The audience appeared much more serious and attentive this time around.

Through sexual behaviour surveys in secondary schools we shall be able to monitor the results of our efforts. Drama, video and film presentation in schools, clubs, societies and institutions have also been tried. It is reasonable to ask if these efforts are effective.

Alain was the captain of the 1st division soccer club I was asked to address during one of their practise sessions. Most of the players were from the francophone provinces but could understand my *pidgin* adequately. I spoke passionately and tried to impress them with the seriousness of their vulnerability. During question time one of the players wanted to know if double condoms might be a good idea. I felt that my talk had failed and was rather disappointed that I did not seem to have made an impact. A year later Alain had a knee problem and I promised to take him to the best consultant available. During the six hours we shared the seat of my Honda, he told me how my talk during the previous year had shaken him. He had immediately asked to be tested for HIV, not once but twice, and had encouraged his young wife to do the same. He was thrilled to be told he was still negative. And he had resolved to keep it that way.

Parents stopped me on the road to tell me about their children's reaction to my school visit and AIDS lecture.

After I was interviewed on Radio Cameroon we received hundreds of telephone calls from concerned listeners in the following week. Awareness is rising. People are beginning to ask the right questions.

What then are the main cultural reasons for the explosive spread of AIDS in Cameroon? My wife and I have gained some insight into the beliefs and practises of a few tribes in the Northwest Province. But what we heard and saw made us expand our efforts to teach about "Christian sexual behaviour", "Christian love marriage" and "How to teach your children about sex".

We became convinced that there will be an enormous death toll that will be without equal in the history of the Cameroon we love.

I have already written at length about the strong taboo that forbids sexual relations between married people after the birth of a child. This custom was largely to blame for polygamy, prostitution and the spread of STDs. Chief's wives, of course, also follow this taboo. At one time a chief complained to me that he had reigned for 15 years and had fathered only 56 children so far. A couple of years later he asked me to treat him and 8 of his wives for gonorrhea. He accused one of his very young wives of having been indiscreet. It is easy to see how AIDS would, at a later date, have devastated this particular chief's compound.

The "garden concept" of marriage in African society is another cultural error in thinking that leads to trouble: The man is the gardener who plants his seed in the woman, the garden, who contributes nothing to the child, except nurture. What good is a garden left un-planted? A widow will look for a married friend to "help her not to lie waste". A wife who has an infertile husband will accept a surrogate "sperm-donor" to produce children. A family will put great pressure on their highly educated daughter to have a child, even if she cannot find a suitable husband.

What good is a garden that produces no fruit? It can never be the gardener's fault! Better to find another garden. It is the gardener who decides how many gardens he can afford to own. The garden is entirely passive. The worst joke is a gardener without a garden. If you don't use it, you may in fact lose it! There is a widely held belief, that abstinence leads to illness. Many a young man has come for consultation, poorly disguising his fear of infertility or sexual dysfunction. Literally hundreds of educated young men drift from clinic to clinic in search of elusive cures for imagined STDs. They may or may not have had such a disease once, but they can never quite accept the assurance that they are free of disease. And the next doctor's injudicious prescription of yet another antibiotic just reinforces the vicious circle of symptoms leading to fear, leading to symptoms, leading to fear....

Many Cameroonians place an unreasonably high value on formal education. They have seen their parents or grandparents come out of the stone age and with a few years of education land great jobs, become wealthy and well respected over the span of two or three decades. Their children will not believe that formal education cannot guarantee the same for them. But the grim reality of modern life disappoints them. 84% of youths in Cameroon are unemployed. University graduates sell newspapers and drive taxis if they are lucky. Long educational programs have shifted the age of marriage upward. This puts added strain on sexual continence before marriage.

Once married, ambitious scholars may abandon wife and family for long years of overseas education, hoping for ever higher status for themselves and their children. Years of separation strain marriages severely.

In addition, people married in traditional unions will bow to family pressure and agree to long periods of separation. The young wife will return to her compound in the home village for many months after the birth of her baby. Or she may be forced by her relatives to return to her native compound with her children if the bride-price is deemed inadequate retro-actively by a meeting of the wife's clan, even years after the initial union.

In areas where a high traditional bride price made marriage unlikely before age 30 or even 40 for males, girls would often be given in marriage at age 15 to men of means, who might easily be 3 times their age. This is certainly not conducive to a marriage "between equals". The migration to the cities of large numbers of job-seeking Youths, and the arrival of western movies and videos has shattered traditional patterns of dress, modesty and morals.

Another cultural reason why AIDS is making such a large impact is the fact that Central Africa is a "hand to mouth" society, i.e. long-range planning, foresight and prevention have a low social priority. Few can imagine how a disease can remain undetected in one's body for years without giving any discomfort. The long incubation period is simply incomprehensible to most victims.

Even though we knew little about the culture of the Fulani tribes, my wife and I agreed to speak to separate groups of men and women about the threat of AIDS. We had begun to treat the first few Fulani AIDS patients. I spoke to about 60 men while my wife addressed 40 illiterate women. We both had excellent interpreters and were struck by the perceptive intelligence of our audience. Instead of suggesting behaviour change to them, I asked for their ideas. They immediately had concrete suggestions about curbing the revelry at their weeklong religious festivals. They realised the dangers to their ways of life from the ease of divorce and remarriage, and they realised the nearly defenceless role of their women in the epidemic.

Peace Corps Volunteers have confirmed to me the custom of Fulani compound-heads offering the "services" of a young Fulani girl for overnight visitors to enjoy. Some Peace Corps Volunteers have reported their HIV-positive status to their Cameroonian friends after their return to the US.

There were a couple of particularly ominous cultural practices among two tribes in Cameroon who will almost certainly suffer the highest rates of death.

An educated native historian wrote about a custom among one tribe I know particularly well. It was expected and permissible for a girl who was about to be married to be "visiting" all her former male friends in the 2 weeks before finally joining her new husband. Presumably this was to assure a pregnancy as soon as possible. But in the days of rampant STDs it would, more likely, have the opposite effect, now that there are at least 26 STDs. Several of them often lead "only" to infertility, but one is universally fatal.

It was reliably reported on national radio and confirmed by members of another grassland tribe that on "country Sunday" it was customary for both married and unmarried folk to feel unrestrained by the socio-sexual mores of everyday living. I know of a rapidly growing number of AIDS patients living in that village, and the chief has tested positive. He has many wives.

My wife and I judge these practises to be extremely destructive to the marriage relationship and healthy sexual expression—but even if one would find my personal opinion not to their taste, there is no denying that such practices now had the added, lethal dimension of literally taking your life into your own hands.

AIDS is devastating sub-Saharan Africa. No other disease can rival its impact. There are only about 3 main weapons available to us at present. And they are not terribly effective:

1. Education is our most potent weapon. Yet, when given without passion and in ignorance of the various cultural forces; when it is a sterile presentation of facts and information without compassionate caring; when it is **late** or **wrong** or **misleading**, education will not be effective.

2. Testing. What is wrong with the attitude that says, "I would rather not be tested since I cannot be helped anyway if I am positive?" Ignorance spreads the disease further. Most people are unaware that they are positive. Time magazine quoted 90 to 95% of world-wide HIV carriers unaware of their infection. 11.)

The healthy HIV positive person represents the greatest danger in the spread of AIDS. Unknowingly he or she infects others, and health personnel may drop their vigilance in handling these patients' body fluids.

There is also a problem with several newly emerging strains. They are not yet detectable with standard tests. This obviously adds to our dilemma. HIV type O appeared in Cameroon a few years ago. Researchers in Yaounde developed a test, which is now available in our hospital laboratories. Later type M appeared, and in 1998 the first type N was found in a Cameroonian woman living in the U.S. Tests for M and N strains were not yet available in Cameroon at the time of this writing.

Testing helps in the overall picture of control. Couples wishing to get married should be encouraged to have the test. Pregnant mothers should be tested. If positive, their infants could improve their chance for survival threefold by treatment that may be relatively inexpensive. In Alberta, Canada the Public Health Authority has quietly and without new legislation implemented compulsory HIV testing of all pregnant women. I agree with this measure.

Health personnel in Cameroon need to be tested so they can, if positive, at least take anti-tuberculosis prophylaxis, even if expensive protease inhibitors are out of reach.

3. Counselling is a major weapon against despair. It is imperative before all testing. (Random research pilot projects without counselling may be ethically permissible).

Expert counselling is a unique opportunity for the Christian church to show it's best in compassion, in ongoing care of widows, orphans and a sick nation as it suffers the loss of its productive generation.

AIDS will not completely destroy Africa's millions. But it may take a very large number of deaths before some people will realise how seriously they need to change beliefs and behaviour. Change they will, eventually.

A seventeen-year old youth in Uganda told my friend that he was the sole adult survivor of his family, responsible for eleven younger siblings. "What do I have to do, not to catch this AIDS" was his concerned plea. He was highly motivated to remain alive. And others will be likewise motivated when they see family and friends dying in large numbers.

If the enormous economic and social costs of losing most of an entire generation can be reduced by timely education and the best we have to offer in motivation, is it not urgent to do the utmost possible?

In sexual behaviour surveys of 2 000 secondary school students in our division we found a surprising consistency whether we went to remote or urban areas: 9% of ten-year-olds had experimented with sex. 40% of fifteen-year-olds were sexually active. 40% of seventeen to twenty-year olds had had more than one partner. (These results are really not all that different from statistics in North America. Student health services in a prominent U.S. University recently published the results of their STD survey.

The incidence of the sexually transmitted Human Papilloma Virus rose from 20% of incoming students to 80% of students in their final year).

Our survey results induced me to direct my preventive focus towards primary rather than secondary schools. I heard reports from Uganda and Malaysia, that intensive education of 5 to 15-year-olds has begun to reduce significantly the percentage of HIV carriers in high-risk groups. Uganda reported a 35% drop of HIV rates between 1992 and 1996 among nineteen to twenty-three year old females. The overall incidence of HIV infection among the adult population of Uganda has fallen from 15% to 9.7% by 1999 12.) and from 14% in 1990 to 8.3% in 2000 13.)

My wife began to develop a course for parents: "How and why to teach Children about Sex". Among other culturally revolutionary ideas she proposed, she also encouraged parents to use correct anatomical terms when speaking to their children. This had some unexpected results:

Jude, age 7, accompanied his mother when she took the family car for repairs. He listened to the long litany of his mother's complaints to the mechanic, which ended with the description of a problem in the exhaust system, when Jude broke in with: "Yea, and this time it's the penis."

Meanwhile, Botswana reported the highest incidence of HIV positive adults at 35% during the World AIDS conference in Durban in August 2000. A fifteen-year-old girl living in Botswana today has a fifty-percent chance of dying from AIDS before the age of 50.

Yet the answer to this enormous problem is not unknown. WHO officials announced in South Africa: "We know what needs to be done". Education campaigns that concentrate on behaviour change such as those carried out in Uganda, Malaysia and Senegal have proven largely effective in either reversing the trend or even preventing the epidemic before it starts.

No Bi Man Fit Try

So here I was, back in Cameroon, in the spring of 1999—this last time, to battle just one enemy. Schools were on spring break for the first full week after my arrival. I had ample time to prepare my reliable motorcycle, stockpile 5000 New Testaments, arrange my living quarters in the Provincial Capital, hire a part time housekeeper and meet the Provincial Delegates of Health and Education as well as several school inspectors in their offices. By week's end I had a plan, a message, a vision and the means to realize it. The "fire in my belly" was fanned by heartrending stories about AIDS tragedies in many Cameroonian families. Doctors and chaplains, football buddies and market traders all had stories to tell me. A usually jovial government official welcomed my offer of help with unusual gravity and a sense of newfound urgency. He had just lost two family members to AIDS. New statistics and personal stories filtered down to me from all kinds of sources. A Jesuit priest/doctor working in Uganda and Kenya reported 700 of 900 incoming University students HIV positive in 1998. That would shock the cynical high school seniors I was going to address! Three wives of last year's AIDS victims had remained negative. That would flesh out my statistical analyses.

Geoff Mitchell, a British volunteer working in primary health care, told me about the distribution of "True Love Waits" promise cards to schoolchildren in Uganda. Interested children had signed and carefully kept these until their wedding day, when the bride and groom would offer them to each other, as a poignant and lifesaving demonstration of their commitment to abstinence before marriage. I hurriedly had 15,000 commitment cards printed.

My 1998 twenty-minute radio interview on "Baptist Voice" had been multiplied and sold like hot cakes at bible conferences and village markets. I was asked whether I would be willing to consider similar interviews for National Radio and Television this time—which I gratefully accepted.

I saw my work unfolding before me. Armed with letters of authorization, free literature for primary school teachers, large posters for principals and New Testaments for primary school graduates I would get up early every school day, reach the farthest school in a targeted rural area before morning assembly and visit as many schools as possible on any given day. I prayed for wisdom and sensitivity, open doors and opportunities, and a passion for the lives of the children and youth I would face by the tens and hundreds and thousands. I sensed an overwhelming feeling of God's affirmation, as people prayed for me. A ground swell of goodwill from teachers and parents met me, and thousands of curious eager young faces gave me their undivided attention day after day. I spoke to as few as 16 dirt-poor children in class 5-7 in a remote mud block schoolhouse while the rain rattled off the leaking tin roof. I also had crowds of 2000 sophisticated high school students loosely gathered under the flag in the brilliant morning sun, questioning my sources, probing my motives, venting their fears.

One principal of a secondary school agreed to let me speak to about 1000 of his 3650 students at 7:30 on a Monday morning. When I arrived on my motorbike at 7:20, I was met by hundreds of students streaming away from the school. None of the 210 tutors was in sight. Students told me: "all classes and examinations are canceled due to a female teacher's death from AIDS on the weekend". (Her husband, a parliamentarian, had died the previous year.) Students and teachers were on the way to the hospital mortuary to witness the transfer of the corpse to the family compound. I assessed the situation and seized the opportunity. Climbing a mound of red earth I was able to attract the attention of an estimated thousand students who were milling about in the schoolyard. I got unexpected help from a few student leaders who shouted for order. A teacher appeared half way through my 25-minute presentation. He was caught up in the urgency of the timely message and helped in the distribution of my follow-up material. Then he became enthused about the other students still in need of hearing the same message. He rang the school bell (a rusty truck wheel suspended from a tree in the yard) and managed to round up another 500 older students who were in the process of leaving the school for the mortuary. They got a slightly different version of my challenge to "choose life".

Altogether I traveled 5000 km on (mostly) dirt roads, reaching 174 primary schools in 2 of the 7 Northwest Province divisions. I also spoke in another 36 secondary schools and colleges to a total of over 40 000 students. Muslim, Baptist, Presbyterian, Government and Private schools welcomed me. Only one principal denied my request for permission to speak to his students.

My message had to be culturally sensitive, urgent, compassionate, Christian and personal. I was repeatedly assured that I was communicating effectively.

The results of my work will be measurable in two main ways: Repeated sexual behavior surveys among high school students can be compared to our baseline statistics from 1995, and the emergence and support of similar grassroots activities in other divisions.

My eleven weeks in Cameroon ended with several significant events:

1. My wife and her 87-year-old father joined me, documenting and reinforcing my efforts on film. There was marked improvement in my physical well being.

2. I was part of several interviews and video productions which will facilitate nationwide awareness as well as help in training suitable coworkers in AIDS prevention.

3. The fiftieth anniversary of Banso Baptist Hospital and its expansive ministry to the nation was celebrated with appropriate gratitude to God.

Finally,

The second of four traditional chiefs in the Northwest Province, all known AIDS carriers, died suddenly, leaving 80 wives and a tribe of about 25 000 to mourn his passing with week-long ceremonies. The selected son was seized forcefully and placed on the throne. There followed multiple animal sacrifices to the ancestors, colorful dances and multiple gun salutes. My AIDS prevention visits included the village schools of this particular tribe during this time. I thought about the new chief. Had he known of his father's illness? Was he aware of his own mortal danger, now that he had to inherit most of his father's wives? Who would warn him? Was it my job? I barely knew the deceased chief and had no idea who the new one was, (though it later turned out that he had consulted me with an untreated testicular torsion some years before.)

I pondered the problem. It was already four weeks into the new chief's reign. I knew little about the particular customs of his tribe, though we had seen many AIDS cases from the area, and knew of some customs, which would make this tribe particularly vulnerable to the rapid spread of the epidemic. Cautiously I asked the advice of two or three friends. Everyone urged me to act without delay. I prayed for wisdom and opportunity and was able to visit the palace a few days before my return to Canada.

The new chief was a tall young man in his twenties. He had quickly learned the royal demeanor expected of his status. The measured gait of his bare camwood-and-oil covered legs was accompanied by the tinkling of tiny bells on the walking spear that struck the floor with each of his deliberate steps as he proceeded to his carved throne, surrounded by a profusion of traditional carvings and native cloth. He readily agreed to a private conversation once my need for food and drink was met by one of the few young wives who walked in a hunched-over posture every time they traversed the large room. Only one trusted elderly *nchinda* (manservant) remained hovering in the corner.

I came straight to the point of my visit. Had he known the cause of his father's death? Was it appropriate for me to reveal it to him? Did he understand the danger he was in?

And now it became very clear that God had already prepared this man for an extraordinary task. Only months before he had personally cared for his brother who had died a slow and agonizing death from AIDS in his very arms. Many a time they had cried together, enduring the isolation and dread of death. The memory of the deceased prince's agony was still mirrored on his brother's face. The chief buried his head in his hands and sat still for a long time.

And then came his questions: "how long did my father know about his AIDS status? Should the royal household or at least the senior advisors know these facts? What was the appropriate action now? And why, why? have you not come sooner? You have made a mistake!", he said. Only days ago had he heard rumors from a hospital employee and had sent four of his young wives for HIV tests. They had returned "negative", but could he trust the results?

I sent up a flare prayer for wisdom. Certainly, he needed much wisdom. Certainly he needed to be tested urgently. Certainly he needed counsel. As we turned to leave the room, I saw the chief as the prisoner of a powerful tradition which would kill him, should he prove unwilling or unable to fulfill its expectations. Even now he was on his way to make required animal sacrifices, while serious elders and armed sentries and trumpeters using intricately carved elephant tusks accompanied him. He beckoned me hurriedly as I walked backwards out of the courtyard in the appropriate show of respect: could I return some night and take him to the hospital laboratory under cover of darkness? I made a promise, and left with heavy heart. What if he was already positive? I would have 3 hours with him in my borrowed car. How would I counsel him? This took more wisdom than I could muster. How could I answer all his questions? God would have to equip me for the task, for I knew of my inadequate counseling skills.

A heavy thundershower accompanied my next visit to the palace as darkness fell. I waited in the audience room with food and drink again provided by a "wintoh"(slave-wife).

The chief tucked a short homemade shotgun pistol into his belt as we got ready to leave. (Whom was that intended for?)

We entered the 4 wheel drive Tercel in pouring rain and left the village on rocky paths and increasingly slick mud roads towards the hospital, a good hour away. My passenger began to share his fears and feelings as he recounted his childhood, his life in the big city, the care of his dying brother and the momentous events of the last month. He told me how he was cunningly and forcefully brought to the palace by the elders to become the new chief. In spite of the secret rituals and revolutionary new tasks before him which clashed with his nominal Christian upbringing, I sensed that the man had found some solace in the fact that he was following a higher calling on his life. He was willing to serve his people as their spiritual leader. I tried to impress him with the fact that he might be placed into a unique position by God in order to make some drastic changes in the traditional lifestyle—now that AIDS was devastating his people. It seemed to me that a complete review of customs and culture was in order. I encouraged him to educate himself thoroughly and to enact legislation that would help his people to survive.

His HIV test was negative. My patient was very visibly relieved. He now talked even more freely about his hopes and plans for the future as leader of his people. On the midnight trip home we came across a car completely blocking the narrow road and the chief warned me urgently not to open the car window, as these people could be highway robbers. Now I remembered his gun.

The roadblock proved accidental.

We talked freely about his sexual behavior, the learning and teaching that had to occur in his household, the need for further confirmatory testing and some of the decisions he would be facing in future. I tried to impress him with the limitations of tests and the risks he faced whenever he would add new young wives to his household (which he would traditionally be expected to do).

When we finally reached the palace after midnight, he was in a jovial mood and proceeded to show me the inner repository of the tribe's carved idols. We had to step over a number of sleeping guards and half-brothers. Many of the life-sized polished and adorned "gods of the tribe" would fetch quite a price in western museums, but were only interesting artifacts to an ignoramus like me. Nevertheless I could appreciate their artistic excellence. The chief showed his gratitude by presenting me with a beautifully carved sitting stool.

At latest report seven qualified AIDS educators have begun to carry on with the educational efforts in the two anglophone provinces of Cameroon. In only six months they had spoken to over 250 000 children with the full approval and concurrence of the provincial authorities.

I praise God as I see what continues to happen when his creatures are in tune with Him. You can't argue that "man no be God". But with God's help, "nobi man fit try" (let's give it our best shot) becomes more than just a wish for success, but a guarantee of changed lives.

Appendix

Open letter to Public Health Authorities in the Northwest Province of Cameroon and the Cameroon Baptist Convention Health Board Director Prof. Pius Tih, Ph.D.

Aids epidemic demands urgent action
Personal Observations and Proposals
by Dieter Lemke MD
April 1998

AIDS prevalence in the NW Province

Official claims that 6-7.5 % of the population is infected with HIV seem to correlate with our own findings. 10% of healthy antenatal patients and 26% of unmarried antenatal patients seen in Jan.97 at Banso Baptist Hospital (BBH) maternity were positive. 4.5 % of 1100 healthy blood donors screened at the BBH lab in 1997 rose to over 6% of 300 donors this year to date.

Annual cases of clinical AIDS seen at the hospital in the last four years show a steady rise from 290 to 350, 459,and 790 in 1997 to a projected 900 in 1998. The cumulative figures are over 3000 by now. This correlates well with reported estimates of NW Province cases of 73 000 HIV infected persons.

We observe no particular preponderance of cases, nor any particular sparing of populations, compared to reports from other countries. AIDS affects all classes of people, from professionals to unsophisticated rural people. The major incidence is among young females and slightly older males, though babies and old men are not exempt. The case of a 13-year-old boy with end stage disease would be the most unusual presentation so far. Our most remote health centre with 900 inpatients per year had 49 AIDS cases last year.

Some cultural factors aiding the spread of AIDS in Cameroon

1. Traditional beliefs:

a) Low expectation of fidelity between spouses.
    There is lack of intimacy, sharing and communication between married couples.
    The old "owner of the garden" relationship of husband and wife continues to persist. The lack of privacy in crowded homes is often so acute, that couples need to share their beds with several children. Multiple relatives usually live under one roof. All these factors lead to rather un-satisfying marital relationships.
b) Customs of sexual indiscretion prior to marriage. (Often there is open encouragement to "find pekin anyhow.")
c) "Trial marriage" as proof of fertility.
d) Ease of divorce for trivial reasons and in cases of infertility.
e) "Substitute sperm donors" for infertile husbands.
f) Prolonged abstinence following childbirth.
    Prolonged separation of spouses for incomplete payments of bride price or "misunderstandings."
g) Elderly polygamists marrying young females.
i) Coercion into prostitution after failed first pregnancy.

These are just a sample of the many tribal customs that often lead directly to infidelity and AIDS.

2. Newer cultural developments:
Television and the Young

The widespread introduction of more liberal cultural practices from the Western World with their differing sexual mores via TV and Videos has a negative influence on the Young. This is not yet recognised as a disruptive force in the moral fibre of the country.

Lack of Law enforcement against the spread of pornography.

Alcohol is freely available to Youth.

High unemployment and migration to urban slums by job-seeking Youths are other factors. The high value attached to "further education" at any price often leads to postponement of marriage to an unreasonable age.

Fortunately, Cameroon has not had to contend with the truly devastating effects of war, mass migration, refugees, mass rapes etc., that have accelerated the spread of AIDS elsewhere.

Strategies for health care providers

Even though denial and ignorance often seem worse in sophisticated circles of Yaounde residents than among simple village mammies of Kumbo town who lament the dying of their Youth, the emphasis in **our** efforts has shifted from giving **information** towards attempts to elicit **behaviour-change**.

In line with reports from Malaysia and Uganda where heavy emphasis is placed on education of the very young (5-15 year olds) we have tried to put our emphasis on primary school visits, not forgetting our previous commitment to **counselling, testing** and **teaching** wherever opportunity arises.

Proposals for urgent action

1. Do not produce **new** material for distribution, as excellent posters, booklets, videos and teaching aids are available from many sources.
2. Someone in authority needs to visit Uganda (an invitation has been received from their Ministry of Health) to see firsthand both

the devastation and the efforts to cope with the epidemic, and to review their methods, statistics and successes.

3. Recruit highly motivated educators from all walks of life who have some ongoing personal knowledge of the problem and good communication skills as well as a passion for people.

4. Continue to search for AIDS victims who are willing to join the public education campaign. Help them to form Care groups.
(AIDS victims would be far more effective than health workers in getting people's attention and changing their beliefs and behaviour)

5. Continue testing on a wider scale, making tests available wherever counsellors are present.

6. Provide refresher courses for counsellors regularly (annually?) so they do not stagnate.

7. Establish primary school visits in all of our areas of influence until at least biennial visits can be achieved for classes 5-7. Leave educational material for teachers after each visit. Provide funds for travel, keep teams small, review and update methods, use simple communication, seek co-operation and authorisation from authorities.

8. Seek for ways to educate mothers in sex education of 5-10 year olds.

9. Keep accurate statistics in all our institutions to document the worsening crisis.

10. Do sexual behaviour surveys every 2 years in secondary schools open to us to **monitor behaviour change.** Use our original form to validate such change.

Keep in mind the goal of **CHANGE IN BELIEF AND BEHAVIOUR** rather than simply giving information.

Why wait till 40% of our population is infected (as projected by reputable organisations in as short a time as 10 years) before we shall be motivated to **do something** that may work?

I have personally observed the situation in Cameroon over three decades:

1967-80 pre-AIDS medical practise in Cameroon
1986 Present when first HIV cases were reported in Cameroon. Beginning of AIDS information in CBC hospitals.
1994-99 Volunteer service for 39 months, intermittently, in Cameroon Baptist Convention Hospitals and Health centres. AIDS Team prevention in all Bui division secondary schools (except catholic schools) followed by sexual behaviour surveys. Primary school visits (Presbyterian, Baptist, Anglo-Arabic and Government) to over 300 schools in Donga-Mantung, Bui, Mezam and Ngoketunja divisions in the last 3 years, as well as visits to a number of churches, political rallies, female organisations, clubs and ethnic groups.

My wife joined me in these efforts with marriage enrichment and communication seminars, as well as giving a course in child sex education for parents.

I am alarmed at the pervading denial and **passive fatalism among the population and even among members of the health care sector.** I plead for urgent and drastic action that unashamedly addresses issues of moral behaviour and family life as well as "health education".

D.Lemke MD

Notes

1. Laurie Garrett: "The Coming Plague". Penguin Books 1994, p. 440

2. Ajayi/Espie: "A thousand years of West African History". Ibadan University Press 1965, p. 312

3. Edward Bean Underhill LL.D. London: "Alfred Saker, Missionary to Africa". The Carey Kingsgate Press. **1884**

4. Paul Gebauer: "Art of Cameroon". Portland Art Association 1979

5. Laurie Garrett: "The Coming Plague". Penguin Books 1994, p. 439

6. Dieter Lemke: "Ten Common Health Hazards in the North West Province". North West Health Mirror, Cameroon. Vol. 3, May 1982

7. Takougang/Krieger: "African State and Society in the 1990s". 1998. page 126

8. Laurie Garrett: "The Coming Plague". Penguin Books 1994, chapter 4

9. Frank Ryan: "The Forgotten Plague". Little, Brown and Co. 1992, chapter 22

10. Laurie Garrett: "The Coming Plague". Penguin Books 1994 pages 515-527

11. "Time" magazine, Dec.6 1999, page 20

12. "Newsweek" magazine, Jan. 17. 2000 page 37

13. "The Washington Post", July 4,5,6. 2000: "Death watch, the global response to AIDS in Africa".